Sermons from the National Cathedral

Praise for *Sermons from the National Cathedral*

"These sermons preached by Samuel Lloyd from the Canterbury pulpit of the National Cathedral encourage in us all a love for the Gospels and help us to find Jesus in a multitude of different situations in daily life. The illustrations that Sam uses to preach profound and challenging truths are endlessly imaginative and drawn from his great love of literature, and also quarried from his own journey of faith. This book will be helpful alike to those who read it and to those of us who, like Lloyd, preach the word of God to others." —**The Very Rev. Dr. Robert Willis**, DL, dean of Canterbury

"It was my pleasure to hear many of these sermons as a member of the congregation of the National Cathedral. Samuel Lloyd offers thoughtful soundings of generous spirited Christianity to help navigate life's journey. He is clearly one of the most outstanding preachers in the country!" —**John H. Dalton**, former secretary of the navy

"The Very Reverend Samuel Lloyd III is a stunningly gifted teacher and preacher. Powerful, relevant, and immensely thought-provoking, *Sermons from the National Cathedral* reminds us that the basic tenets of faith, love, acceptance, compassion, respect, and forgiveness have always been, and will continue to be, the means by which mankind can face even its darkest challenges. *Sermons from the National Cathedral* inspires, illuminates, and leads the reader to a life of higher purpose and to a mission of more devoted spiritual understanding." —**Sharon Percy Rockefeller**, president and chief executive officer, WETA TV/FM

Sermons from the National Cathedral

Soundings for the Journey

Samuel T. Lloyd III

ROWMAN & LITTLEFIELD
Lanham • Boulder • New York • London

Published by Rowman & Littlefield
A wholly owned subsidiary of The Rowman & Littlefield Publishing Group, Inc.
4501 Forbes Boulevard, Suite 200, Lanham, Maryland 20706
www.rowman.com

10 Thornbury Road, Plymouth PL6 7PP, United Kingdom

British Library Cataloguing in Publication Information Available

Library of Congress Cataloging-in-Publication Data Available

The hardback edition of this book was previously cataloged by the Library of Congress
as follows:

ISBN 978-1-4422-2284-7 (cloth : alk. paper)—ISBN 978-1-4422-2285-4 (electronic)—
ISBN 978-0-8108-9618-5 (paperback : alk. paper)

♾™ The paper used in this publication meets the minimum requirements of
American National Standard for Information Sciences—Permanence of Paper
for Printed Library Materials, ANSI/NISO Z39.48-1992.

Printed in the United States of America

For Marguerite

Contents

Foreword   xi

Jon Meacham

Preface: Sam Lloyd, Dean and Preacher   xv

John Shenefield

Introduction: Sermons from the National Cathedral: xix
Soundings for the Journey

Samuel T. Lloyd III

Book One: Reflections on Faith

A God We Can Trust   3

Follow Me   9

The Calling of Holiness   15

Costly Discipleship   21

Will You Dance?   25

Commanded to Love   31

When God Throws a Brick   37

Following an Elusive Lord   43

Haggling Prayer   49

Does God Care?   55

The Silence of God   61

God, Science, and the Life of Faith   67

The Night Visitor   73
The Miracle of Forgiveness   79
Holy Laughter   83
Trusting against the Evidence   89
Grace   93

Book Two: Events and Issues

Cathedral Life
Installation Sermon: A Voice, a Place, a People   103
An Unfinished Cathedral   109

Presidential Inauguration
A New Community   119

Anniversary of 9/11
Doubts and Loves: A Sermon on the Tenth Anniversary of 9/11   127

Place of Reconciliation
On the Far Side of Revenge   135

Religious Diversity
The Spirit of Understanding   143
A Big Enough House   149

Race and Poverty
In Thanksgiving for the Life of Dorothy Height   157
An Extremist for Love: The Legacy of Martin Luther King Jr.   161
Black and White on the Road to Emmaus   167
Mind the Gap   173

Earth Day
To Save This Fragile Earth   181

Independence Day
A Humble Patriotism   189

Thanksgiving

A Thankful Heart   197

Giving Thanks in All Things   203

Book Three: Church Year

Advent

Waiting   213

Making Room for God   219

Mary Said Yes   225

Christmas

God Comes In   233

The Birth of the Messiah   237

The Plunge   241

Epiphany

The Magi and Us   247

Beloved   251

Lent

The Truth of Ash Wednesday   259

The Joy of Ash Wednesday   263

Going for Broke   267

Palm Sunday

Love So Amazing   275

Strange Fruit   281

Good Friday

What a Way to Run a Universe   289

Staring Into the Dark   293

Easter

Death Be Not Proud   299

Nevertheless   305

Ascension

Christ Has Gone Up   313

Pentecost

The Spirit of Life   319

Ordinary Time

The Trinity and the Nearness of God   325

Who Do You Say That I Am?   331

All Saints

The Real Thing   339

The Communion of Saints   343

Notes   347

About the Author   361

Foreword

Jon Meacham

It was an early autumn Sunday—the date was September 29, 1907, the Feast of St. Michael and All Angels—when Theodore Roosevelt arrived early for the laying of the foundation stone of the new Church of St. Peter and St. Paul, the grand gothic church that was to become known as Washington National Cathedral.

In his address to a gathering that included the Bishop of London, Roosevelt challenged his listeners to put the gospel into action, saying that "the real field for rivalry among and between the creeds comes in the rivalry of the endeavor to see which can render the best service to mankind." As president, TR relished his claim on the attention of his vast flock. "I am charged with being a preacher," Roosevelt once said. "Well, I suppose I am. I have such a bully pulpit."

And so, in the fullness of time, would those men and, ultimately, women who came to preach in the Canterbury pulpit inside the finished Cathedral. This noble pulpit, a splendid work of art, sits in the heart of a church that looms over the world of earthly power, a standing reminder that for all the getting and spending that unfolds in Washington, there is, for believers, a larger final reality that dwarfs all others: that of the unfolding work of the risen Christian Messiah, Jesus Christ.

This collection of the sermons of the Very Reverend Samuel T. Lloyd III, the ninth dean of the National Cathedral, shows us how seriously Lloyd took his own hour of responsibility for the care of the souls of the Cathedral and for the legacy of the Canterbury pulpit—and how well he did when he was called to speak from it to all of us.

Carved from stone that came from Canterbury Cathedral, the spiritual home of the Anglican Communion, the pulpit is ten feet high. Its panels depict scenes from the story of the English Bible, and includes an image of the barons and King John with Magna Carta, the document that began the long, often-anguished shift of power from the rulers to the ruled. A preacher at the Cathedral has to climb up thirteen steps to the center of the pulpit. From that vantage point, one's eyes take in the rose window on the west wall and the flags of the fifty states of the Union hanging in parallel rows high atop the nave.

It is a sacred space within a sacred space. All pulpits are, but because of the place providence put it, the Canterbury pulpit is an especially important one. For it is here, from this rock, that preachers are given the peculiar opportunity to address not only those in the pews but those in power. (And the two categories are not always mutually exclusive.)

It was here that Martin Luther King Jr. preached his last Sunday sermon before dying a martyr's death in Memphis. "We are tied together in the single garment of destiny, caught in an inescapable network of mutuality," King preached on March 31, 1968, a cloudy Sunday morning in Washington. "And whatever affects one directly affects all indirectly. For some strange reason, I can never be what I ought to be until you are what you ought to be. And you can never be what you ought to be until I am what I ought to be. This is the way God's universe is made; this is the way it is structured."

In his sonorous words, words that floated out across a thoroughly full Cathedral, King used the Canterbury pulpit to its fullest, speaking of the great gulf between the kingdom of this world and God's kingdom. There was—and is—perhaps no better or more fitting place than the pulpit of National Cathedral to plumb the depths of the mysterious connection between the temporal and the eternal, between the brokenness of politics and the promise of the coming of the kingdom.

To King there was no distinction between the words of Jefferson's Declaration of Independence and the laws of the Lord. "We're going to win our freedom because both the sacred heritage of our nation and the eternal will of the Almighty God are embodied in our echoing demands," he said. Finally, citing the Revelation of St. John the Divine, King evoked "a new Jerusalem . . . a new day of justice and brotherhood and peace. And that day the morning stars will sing together, and the sons of God will shout for joy."

King was a prophet and a martyr, and for those who even now follow his footsteps from the floor of the Cathedral into the Canterbury pulpit, his example, like that of all the prophets and martyrs who have died in the service of the Lord, is at once inspiring and daunting.

But then so is Christianity, as is America itself. "I know not how philosophers may ultimately define religion," Theodore Roosevelt once remarked, "but from Micah to James it has been defined as service to one's fellowmen rendered by following the great rule of justice and mercy, of wisdom and righteousness."

Wise words for all of us, whether we are hearers or, like Sam Lloyd, speakers of the words that carry across National Cathedral, through the nave, and perhaps—just perhaps—out the west doors into the world below.

Jon Meacham, executive editor at Random House, is the Pulitzer Prize–winning author of American Lion: Andrew Jackson in the White House *and the recently published* Thomas Jefferson: The Art of Power.

Preface

Sam Lloyd, Dean and Preacher

John Shenefield

Sam Lloyd was formally installed as the ninth dean of the Washington National Cathedral on April 23, 2005. His last Sunday as dean was September 18, 2011.

At the very core of his Cathedral ministry was preaching of the highest quality and deepest impact. The Canterbury pulpit has seen many great preachers deliver powerful sermons: Martin Luther King Jr. of course, but also Paul Tillich, C. Day-Lewis, Francis Sayre, James Forbes, Nathan Baxter, and not least of all five presiding bishops of the Episcopal Church, five archbishops of Canterbury, and three Supreme Court justices.

But never was language deployed in the service of creative imagination more eloquently, nor the message of a generous-spirited and thoughtful Christianity delivered more powerfully, nor the hearts and minds of congregations influenced more profoundly than by the some 150 sermons preached by Sam Lloyd during the six and a half years of his deanship.

A great sermon makes the preacher the cocreator with God of a potent religious experience, using the precision and poetry of language to draw something compelling out of texts on a page, and deriving influential, sometimes unforgettable, real-life messages that can move us to tears, or to action, or to deep inner reflection, in all those ways quite literally making us better people.

Great beauty in the form of a cathedral building or a string quartet or a finely wrought poem, for instance, can induce in even the most resistant among us a sense that—to quote one of Sam's sermons—God may be near. For many, Sam's vivid words play that very same role. His sermons reach beneath the surface of our day-to-day reality to highlight the hints and guesses that riddle our lives; they remind us of the longing and yearning we human beings feel, the restless nostalgia, as many have imagined, for a world we have lost but yet hope and struggle to rediscover.

And to hear him in the Canterbury pulpit not just once or twice but Sunday after Sunday has been a marvel and a privilege we at the Cathedral shall sorely miss and never forget.

Over that time we heard the profusion of recurring themes, and came to recognize them as part of an organic course of contemplative worship, articulated in surprising and eloquent variation, the truest voice of a Christianity speaking persuasively to our contemporary world that many of us have ever heard.

One of Sam's central themes was the need for reconciliation in our world, in our nation, and in our city. There, he taught us, the Cathedral has a special role: It serves as a "third place," where citizens and communities and faiths and races can meet to build relationships and understanding through an array of human contacts that may, in the end, blossom into friendship and trust.

That thought linked closely to another familiar theme: God is about caring for the poor and left out; Jesus came to bring good news to the poor. It is not enough to acknowledge the problems of poverty and exclusion in prayers on Sunday morning; one must live one's life every day trying to break down the causes and doing something to treat the victims.

And Sam charges the more fortunate among us to let God break into our lives which are already dangerously filled to the brim with success and profit and trivial hyperactivity. Only by creating such openings can we ever have a chance to take the deep breath necessary to reach for something more substantial and less fleeting than mere busyness.

These and so many other thoughtful themes are presented in language rich and vivid, full of drama and poetry, dancing together with literary allusions, historical references, and sometimes deeply personal reminiscences. And then, of course, there is that wonderful sense of humor woven into the mighty themes, the distinctive human touch that skillfully brings the congregation and the preacher closer together and opens the mind for a deeper and more sympathetic understanding of the whole sermon's message.

In these sermons of a great preacher, Sam is also a great teacher. And what a pleasure it is to be in his Cathedral classroom.

No one comes away from listening to one of his sermons without learning something new and important and exciting. His enthusiasm for what he is teaching is palpable and infectious—from the evocative Southern literature of Robert Penn Warren and William Faulkner to *The Brothers Karamazov* and the timeless novels of the world's great cultures, to the reflective spirituality of poets such as Gerard Manley Hopkins and T. S. Eliot. C. S. Lewis belongs on his special list. And then there is Michael Mayne, former dean of Westminster Abbey, who, having retired to Wiltshire, England, found in the water meadows of the Avon endless lessons about life. Mayne's *Learning to Dance* is one of Sam's touchstones, and now one of mine.

What an extraordinary six and a half years of memorable sermons! In sum, they are telling testimony to the potency of Dean Lloyd's voice from the Canterbury pulpit, reflecting his strong and inspirational leadership and his steady determination that his—our—Cathedral would make a difference. That is why a small selection of his Cathedral sermons has been collected in this volume, so that the true miracle of his preaching may be shared far more broadly.

John Shenefield is the former chairman of Morgan, Lewis & Brockius LLP and a lifelong supporter of the National Cathedral. He served for ten years as chair of the Cathedral Chapter, its governing board.

Introduction

Sermons from the National Cathedral: Soundings for the Journey

Samuel T. Lloyd III

Though I had been stepping into a pulpit regularly for more than twenty years, the chilly March morning in 2005 when I first ascended the stairs of the Canterbury pulpit of the National Cathedral remains etched in my memory. Each step higher opened a broader vista of massive piers and soaring arches arrayed in procession into the distance. The worshipers I had gazed upon directly from other pulpits seemed in this vast space to be seated half a city block away.

The massive stone pulpit, a century-old gift from Canterbury Cathedral, jutted forward like the prow of a ship into the crossing, where the building's vertical and horizontal arms meet.

The founders of this young American cathedral envisioned it as a crossroads itself where religious faith and American public life could meet. And, indeed, over the years distinguished preachers and spiritual leaders would address the nation from its pulpit—Martin Luther King Jr. preaching his last Sunday sermon, Archbishop Tutu calling for an end to apartheid, Billy Graham honoring the life of President Ronald Reagan, and the Dalai Lama calling for a world of peace and harmony. This was to be a church for the nation.

I remember the moment when I began to take seriously the possibility that God might have been calling me to this post. Walking up the concourse at Reagan National Airport on my way to search committee interviews I glanced aside through the broad window toward Washington and caught a view that stopped me in my tracks. Across the Potomac River, I saw looming above the city the majestic Cathedral, etched against the blue sky, serene as an ocean liner on a sea of green. It dominated the skyline, as if to declare that for all the urgency of the business of government in the nation's capital, there was a Purpose deeper and more enduring at work in the world. Taking up a ministry at this intersection of faith and civic life, and living daily in the tension between God's vision for the world and the realities of politics and history, seemed utterly compelling.

One of the most telling moments in cathedral life occurs countless times daily as worshipers and visitors make their way through the west entrance into the nave itself. If you linger in the back nearby you can actually hear the murmurs of awe as their eyes are swept inexorably upward by pillars reaching toward heaven. Many find themselves suddenly immersed in a vision of harmony and sacred order beyond anything they have encountered. It is as if they taste something of eternity and with it a yearning, perhaps for the first time, to be caught up in the life of a mysterious God.

Into cathedrals come the curious, the seeker, the weary tourist, the spiritually hungry, and the broken-hearted as well, and they sometimes later recount stories of finding a long dormant faith stirring in them, or simply a yearning "to be more serious," as poet Philip Larkin once put it.[1] They meander the long aisles and side chapels; they study the stone carvings and gaze at the hues of blue and crimson spilling through the stained glass windows. And those who come to worship on Sunday or at daily evensong may find themselves overwhelmed by the grandeur that surrounds them, and perhaps catch a glimpse of God's glory in an anthem sung by the bright-faced choristers, a line of a hymn or prayer, or a spark of illumination in a sermon.

Among the most crucial minutes in a congregation's life are those when the preacher steps into the pulpit and articulates in honest, credible words the truths of the Christian faith. The preacher is there to bear witness to the mysterious Love at the heart of the universe—an unfathomable, yet utterly engaged God. And echoing in the back of the minds of nearly every sermon listener at one time or another is the question "Is it true?" Is this immense claim true—that Love is the ultimate reality in the universe, that this God knows us personally, that our world and lives have a destiny, that we are accountable for the lives we live, and that ultimately we have nothing to fear in this life or beyond? When I take my place in the pulpit I often preach as if, as C. S. Lewis once put it, God is "in the dock," being challenged and tested by a skeptical society.[2] Of course my job is hardly to defend God, but to build bridges for contemporary listeners, to help them over the course of twenty minutes to see the preoccupations of their days in the light of the new world of God's kingdom.

The gathering of worshipers in the Cathedral on Sundays was like no other I had served. Because of its mission as a national church there had never been an official congregation. Week by week, pilgrims and visitors would stream in from Portland and Des Moines, from India and England, as well as from the broad Washington area. Tour buses full of teenagers or seniors would drop off their charges for the service and collect them soon after. That inevitably meant that a new "congregation" made up of worshipers from far and wide gathered for each service—a challenge both to the preacher and all the clergy as they sought to create a spirit of welcome and communion. With time, we at the Cathedral launched a permanent congregation. The addition of this ongoing community of prayer and hospitality at the heart of our life brought new depth and energy to the Cathedral's ministries.

I arrived at the Cathedral in January of 2005 in what was a hard time for our country. The United States was mired in two wars. Americans, still recovering from the shock of the events of September 11, 2001, were bitterly divided politically, and were facing a world where faith itself had become a divisive force. The air waves seemed to be dominated by anti-intellectual fundamentalism on one side and an increasing secularism on the other. The times called for a generous-spirited, open-minded, intellectually alive Christian faith, a way of being religious that is deeply rooted in a faith tradition and profoundly open and welcoming. Generous-spirited Christianity became our theme, our strategy, and our goal in our programs and services and especially in the sermons from the Canterbury pulpit.

This was also a time when a tidal wave of religious change was washing over our country. American spirituality was and is becoming increasingly individualistic, more private and eclectic. The impact of the information age on every aspect of life in the twenty-first century, including religion, is undeniable. Clergy often hear a telling phrase, "I am spiritual but not religious." "I am on my own quest," many are saying, and "I am capable of assembling the resources for my own spiritual life."

In many of the sermons in this volume I offered an implicit response to this newest privatizing of the spiritual quest. While churches everywhere are in for a time of major self-examination and reassessment, I am convinced that a new work of the Spirit is underway that will emphasize both the individual search for an authentic relationship with God and our need for creative new forms of Christian community to sustain and challenge us. This ancient faith still possesses undiminished wells of vitality waiting to be tapped. These sermons carry as their subtext a confidence that Christianity is entering a new period of struggle and transformation from which will emerge new ways of being Christian and living the Christian life within the church.

A sermon is in its essence an oral event. It exists at one time and place when a preacher steps into a pulpit and for a handful of minutes musters the language to limn what he or she believes God is saying to that community in that particular moment and through that passage of scripture. This volume contains a record of such moments when these words were released into the Cathedral nave in the hope and prayer that the Spirit of God would work through them. I have called them "soundings," from the ancient practice of measuring the depth of water by plunging a weight at the end of a line into the unseen waters below. It was soundings that gave us our earliest maps of the contours of the ocean floor. Each of these sermons has meant to be such a sounding, using the weight of word, image, and story to probe the unseen depths of our lives. They have sought to create provisional maps of mysteries we cannot fully grasp, and to point us to an elusive, yet always present, endlessly loving, yet finally unfathomable God.

A lifetime of my own sermon reading has convinced me that these momentary soundings can have an afterlife on paper. Individual sermons and whole collections have provided inspiration and guidance for my own exploration into God. As a reader of these sermons, you will have a different experience from their original hearers. You will be able to linger over a passage or poem, you can read the biblical text for yourself and discover fresh dimensions on your own, you can weave these reflections into your own adventure in faith and your own responses to the issues and perplexities of our world. In short, these soundings into the Mystery of God can be occasions for the Spirit to move in you as it did in their first utterance and hearing.

I hope you will find in these sermons a sense of the strange new world that comes to us from the pages of the Hebrew and Christian scriptures, a world in which God is at work seeking us out to call us, to heal us, to give us work to do, and to lead us home. I hope you will catch the outlines of a generous-spirited Christianity being articulated and lived out in the life of this Cathedral as a sacred home for the nation. And most of all, I hope that in these rapidly shifting spiritual times in America, you will hear in these words an invitation "to be more serious"—to probe the depths of the good news of Christian faith and to find as you do a Voice calling your name.

Finally, a personal word. My years at Washington National Cathedral were stretching, challenging, and rich beyond telling. I wish to thank my many colleagues, lay and clergy alike, who shared with me the life of this beautiful, complex, holy place. My deep thanks as well to all those who love Washington National Cathedral, from the Cathedral congregation, volunteers, and chapter, to supporters across the country who were unflagging amid years of great challenge. Sheri Jackson, executive assistant without peer, labored tirelessly with her usual warmth and grace to bring this project to conclusion. John Shenefield, chapter chair in my early years, lifelong devotee of the Cathedral and good friend, believed this project worth taking up and shepherded it to fruition. Last and most, there is my wife Marguerite, to whom this book is dedicated. Her love and companionship in those Cathedral years made these sermons, and everything else, possible.

Book One

Reflections on Faith

A God We Can Trust

Matthew 3:13–17; Isaiah 42:1–9

A child wakes in the night and cries out. Alone in the dark, he is full of fear, even in his crib. The world around him seems dark and threatening. Into his room comes his mother, who quietly takes him up, holds and soothes him, and murmurs to him, "Everything is all right." Soon, calm and assured, the child drifts back to sleep. [1]

That scene enacts a fundamental human drama, according to sociologist Peter Berger. We wake into a strange world needing to be reassured that life is trustworthy. In fact, psychologist Erik Erikson says that the first and deepest issue young children need to resolve, and the issue all of us face continually, is that of trust: can life be trusted or not? [2]

Is the mother telling the truth when she says to her child, "Everything is all right"? Answering that question is maybe the most profound task you and I will ever have, because it will ultimately affect everything we do. And any answer we give will be an answer of faith. Is this life trustworthy? Is there a loving God behind this immense universe? Are we loved and known on this planet as it spins through the darkness of space? Can there be hope of healing and new life when things fall apart?

This season of Epiphany in the church year focuses on the shining out of God's light into the world. In the Old Testament lesson we hear a vision of a God who sustains the entire universe:

> Thus says God, the Lord, who created the heavens and stretched them out, who spread out the earth and what comes from it . . . I am the Lord . . . I have given you as a covenant to the people, a light to the nations. . . .

3

And in the gospel we see the experience that launched Jesus' ministry. Jesus is baptized in the Jordan River and hears a voice calling and commissioning him, "This is my Son, my Beloved, with whom I am well pleased."

It is a bold claim of Christian faith that the creator of the universe speaks, calls, and blesses—so bold that these days a good many don't know what to make of this notion.

Last fall, amid much discussion of Mother Teresa's struggles with doubt and spiritual darkness and the public attacks on faith by several angry atheists, someone walking out after a service asked me with real urgency: "Given all the uncertainty about God, what is it that tips the scales toward faith? Why do *you* trust this faith?" he asked. Which is a way of asking: why should we trust that everything is all right?

Questions like these could take hours fully to answer. But I thought I'd take a first stab on this Epiphany morning to articulate why I believe in a God we can trust. For me the answer has three parts.

First, our lives are riddled with what T. S. Eliot called "hints and guesses" that point us beyond the physical world to God.[3] Such as the experience of life as gift. We are on this earth for only a brief time. Out of the workings of some mystery we are given a few decades to be alive amid the fifteen-billion-year history of the cosmos. We did not earn our way into this world, we did not create our capacity to grow, achieve, and live full lives, we did not have to *be* at all. This life is sheer gift. It's hard not to believe in a creator God when we hold an infant in our hands. The greatest shock of all is the fact that we *are*, and that the cosmos *is*.

There are many hints and guesses. Encounters with beauty in nature, and in art, music, and literature, for example, have been powerful pointers to God. I suspect we can all name moments when we were lifted out of ourselves—as we lingered on a beach or mountaintop, as we stood in front of one of Turner's landscapes at the National Gallery and felt swept into a world of radiant beauty. It may have happened as we listened to Mozart, or Crosby, Stills, and Nash, for that matter—times when for a few moments we and the music were one. Listen to this description of one person's experience at a concert:

> A friend persuaded me to go . . . hear a performance of Bach's B minor Mass. I had heard the work, indeed I new Bach's choral music well . . . The music thrilled me, until we got to the great Sanctus. I find this experience difficult to define. It was primarily a warning—I was frightened. I was trembling from head to foot and wanted to cry . . . [I felt as if] I was before the Judgement Seat. I was being weighed in the balance and found wanting. Bach's music becomes the place of her encounter with God.[4]

Philosophers and theologians have used many sophisticated arguments to demonstrate that understanding the world requires pointing to a First Cause, an original actor, a power that holds all existence in being. And that points inevitably to God.

C. S. Lewis always pointed to two key signals, or hints, of God. One was the experience of longing and yearning. We spend our lives with an inner restlessness that keeps us yearning for a peace, a home, a security, a sense of being completely loved, that are always beyond our reach. Lewis called it something like nostalgia for a world we've lost, and it haunts us in such a way that we never stop searching for the home where we belong. That home we spend our lives yearning for, he says, is God.[5]

Another signal for Lewis was moral obligation. Two people may disagree over whether something is right or wrong, but they will both agree that some sense of obligation exists. In an utterly relativist material world there would be no such thing as obligation pressing in on us.[6]

Science itself is full of hints and guesses. Many scientists insist that we live in a universe stunningly fine-tuned to make the emergence of life possible, even on a tiny planet in a minor solar system in one galaxy among billions. Allan Sandage, the astronomer who figured out how quickly the universe is expanding and how old it is, says it was his scientific research that led him back to faith.

> Physicists have stumbled on signs that the cosmos is custom-made for life. It turns out that if the constants of nature—unchanging numbers like the strength of gravity, the charge of an electron and the mass of a proton—were the tiniest bit different, then atoms would not hold together, stars would not burn, and life would never have made an appearance.[7]

Well, all that is my first answer. The world keeps pointing beyond itself. A materialistic understanding of the world where physics, chemistry, and biology explain everything can't account for the world in all its complexity. And it certainly can't explain such experiences as love, beauty, wonder, and compassion. In those moments we are touching a reality beyond the ordinary.

My second answer is that testimonies are countless of people who have experienced life-changing moments of closeness to God. Sometimes we can see more than the ordinary, and glimpse the holiness hidden in every moment. Poet Ruth Pitter once described sitting and gazing at the grass in the field as a young woman when all of a sudden she glimpsed another dimension, that continued to return to her in adulthood and made its way into her poetry.

> I was sitting in front of a cottage door one day in spring long ago, a few bushes and flowers around me, a bird gathering nesting material, the trees of the forest at a little distance. A poor place—nothing glamorous about it. . . . Suddenly everything assumed a different aspect—no, its true aspect. For a moment, it seemed, the truth appeared in its overwhelming splendor. The secret was out,

the explanation given. Something that had seemed like total freedom, total power, total bliss, a good with no bad as its opposite . . . had suddenly cut across [my life] and vanished.[8]

Testimonies abound of people who have experienced God's calling and presence—from St. Paul and Julian of Norwich to John Wesley and Blaise Pascal to Hildegard of Bingen and Martin Luther King Jr. They encountered an overwhelming Other in ways they could not deny.

A close friend of mine still gives thanks ten years later for a night just before Christmas, as he lay in a hospital bed faced with grave heart trouble. There in the dark hours he experienced an intense sense of being loved and held by God. After that experience, his life shifted. He became much calmer, more at ease, less driven. He still chokes up when he talks about the "night visitor" who came and changed his life.

Is it true that everything is all right? Well, now you have two of my three answers. I believe the case for the existence of God is overwhelmingly compelling. But we base our lives on faith, not on proof. None of us can fully justify by argument the lives we live. We live by faith, by putting our trust in some way, some set of values, some way of seeing the world.

Christian faith is a decision to trust that all these experiences point to a God of infinite goodness who holds and sustains the world. And that brings me to the third part of my answer—that this God comes to us, addresses us, and seeks us out through the people of Israel, and most importantly, in the life of Jesus of Nazareth. Without the story of the Jews and what happened through Jesus, we would be left guessing about who or what it is to which all these signs point. But instead God has spoken, God has sought us out.

It happened for Jesus when he was about thirty years old and was baptized. A power of love grasped him definitively in a way that shaped his entire life. As he went down in the Jordan River and emerged, he experienced an overwhelming sense of who he was and that he belonged to One he would call "Father." That was the day when he knew without any doubt that "everything is all right," that there was nothing to fear, not even death itself. "This is my son, my beloved," he heard, "with whom I am well pleased."

And from that day he began his ministry of spreading the word that everyone, absolutely everyone, was beloved by this holy, mysterious God. No lines could be drawn, no groups could be left out of his circle. He had experienced a love wider and deeper than the cosmos itself.

Jesus showed us a surprising God. When I hear atheists describe the arrogant, controlling, cruel, condemning god they don't believe in, I want to say, I don't believe in that god either. When I hear descriptions of a god willing to condemn billions of people to hell for not being Christians, I know I don't believe in that god either. When I hear descriptions of a god who is always on America's side, on the side of the nation with the most clout, on the side of an economy that creates vast gaps between rich and poor, I don't believe in that god either.

The God we meet in our lessons today is a God of mercy, who, in the passage from Isaiah is calling servants and followers to build a world of justice for everyone. This is a God who pursues and nudges, who confronts and challenges, who seeks us out relentlessly, and whose patience never ceases. This God isn't running the show from the top down, isn't controlling every event. This is a God who can't heal the world without you and me, and has sent his Son to show us that we are beloved too, and to call us to spread that belovedness across the city and the world.

Is everything really all right? Is there a love we can trust at work in our world and our lives? Can we trust that at our life's end God will be there to receive us?

Answering those questions is no trivial matter. Jesus never expected his followers to believe it all at first. All he said was, "Come on along, follow me, and if you stay with me, you'll come to trust me and this God more and more." Knowing God doesn't come at the end of an intellectual argument. The promise of this day is that if we will follow this Jesus, learn from him, and stay with him—read the scriptures, come to church, talk to others about our faith, serve those who are in need—we will come to know God for ourselves, and Jesus as our companion. We will hear in our own way the voice from heaven saying, "You are my son, my daughter, my beloved; in you I am well pleased."

Follow Me

Mark 1:14–20

"Follow me," Jesus says. "And immediately they left their nets and followed him." Those are some of the most mysterious words in the whole of scripture. How could it be that Simon, Andrew, James, and John, tough working-class men plying their trade as fishermen, just drop their nets and follow this wandering rabbi?

Faith. Commitment. Follow. Those are big, bold words. But often those words seem pretty far away from the reality of the church as we know it.

By now there has been a great deal written about how the "mainline" churches—the Methodists, Presbyterians, Lutherans, Episcopalians—are becoming the sideline churches as they continue to decline in numbers and influence. They have each lost a third of their members in the last forty years. There was a poll a few years ago in which people in various denominations were asked how much their faith meant to them. As you might guess, fundamentalists and Southern Baptists ranked highest, with more than 70 percent of their people saying their faith was very important to them. After them came the Mormons, much further down, the Catholics, and toward the bottom a cluster including Methodists, Presbyterians, and Episcopalians. Only 42 percent of Episcopalians said their faith was important to them. Deep, passionate commitment seems to come hard for many mainline Christians.

Instead, we've been hearing a lot about the different kind of spiritual quest baby boomers have been on. Dr. Wade Clark Roof, a professor of religious studies, describes this generation born in the late 1940s and '50s as spiritually restless. Their quests are often marked by shifting alliances with religious institutions and the continual search for something else. One writer has described their homelessness as something like the ultimate shopping trip—a lot of window shopping, a lot of dabbling, a little of this, a little of that—something like a "great mall" path to heaven.

The boomers' quest, Roof says, is highly individualistic and antiauthoritarian. People hunger for meaning, but don't want anyone telling them what they should do or believe. They have a consumer orientation: What does this do for me? Everyone seems to be working on their personalized portfolio of ways to find sacred meaning, drawing from various therapies, New Age practices, meditation, and recovery groups.

And by most accounts, the generations younger than the boomers—the gen-Xers and the millennials, as some call them—are just as skeptical of authority and church structures, even though they are more interested in traditional forms of worship.

Over the years, in talking to people about their faith and about their unease over the big words like commitment and following Christ, I have often sensed a real pathos. I've heard many talk about how empty their experience of the church had been growing up, how little real experience of Christian love they had ever found in the church, and yet how they still hunger to be connected to a larger world of meaning.

And my guess is many of us here today share that pathos. At some level we seek a living God, but in an age of hi-tech, scientific analysis, and the unrelenting reality of the TV screen, trusting in an unseen Mystery can be hard. My sense is that we are often afraid to open ourselves too much, for fear either that we will find there really is nothing to all this or that there is more than we ever imagined. It's safer to be cautious.

But what strikes us in the gospel this morning is the sheer impulsiveness of it all. Jesus walks up and says, "Follow." It's a call from beyond them. This was not part of their career plan. Something intrusive, a challenge, an invitation interrupts their lives.

And the biggest shock is that they go along with all this. We're inclined to marvel at their bravery and courage. That's not like us complex, educated people. We have responsibilities. We wouldn't have gotten where we are without being careful, dutiful, minimizing the risks. We're likely to get some professional guidance, a career counselor, a therapist. But something just happens in this story. Something from beyond grasps them.

You may have heard of a book by Malcolm Gladwell called *Blink*, about how many of the important decisions we make come in an instant—whom you fall in love with, what house you want to buy, what kind of work you want to do. Things have been stirring inside you for a long time, but then all of a sudden something clicks. It happens in the blink of an eye. [1]

And did you notice? There is no talk in this gospel of a faith that comes in a neat package. These fishermen aren't asked to believe anything at first—no theological doctrines, no philosophical arguments. Jesus doesn't put in front of them a set of rules and regulations or requirements for admission.

He just says, "Come and follow." It seems that the only way they are going to know what Jesus is about is by going along with him, sharing his life, listening to him, doing what he does. All that faith in Jesus takes for starters is a willingness to trust a hunch, to decide to try it for ourselves. The poet William Butler Yeats said, "Man can embody truth, but he cannot know it."[2] The truth of life is not a package of ideas that will fit into our categories. It is a way of living, of being, that we discover as we enter into it and grow.

It is natural to want to shrink life into nice, analyzable bits. Science seems to have taught us that anything can be understood or mastered, given enough time. But what about joy, or love, or delight, or grief, or despair, or the longings of our souls, or the glimpses we've had of a peace we have no name for? We never fully fathom those.

There is an unforgettable moment in Dostoevsky's novel *The Brothers Karamazov*, in which a high-society woman comes to the wise spiritual leader Father Zossima, asking him to help her recover her lost faith. "How can I believe in God again?" she asks. He answers, "You must learn to love. Try to love your neighbors, love them actively and unceasingly. And as you learn to love them more and more, you will be more and more convinced of God and the immortality of your soul."[3]

What an unexpected twist that is. Not, "First you must have faith," but rather, "Love, and then faith will come." Turn loose of yourself, learn what it means to live like Christ—opening yourself to God and to those around you—and you will find that God is real. Follow Christ, he's saying. Come and live the way human beings were meant to live. Let go of your preoccupations. Link your life to people who need you—at home and around you. Come and be like Christ. And you will begin to find yourself discovering a Purpose and Love you could never have thought your way into.

Over and over the great teachers of our faith have said that we can never know God with our minds. We can know about God, but real knowing requires giving ourselves. That's the problem with the spiritual marketplace of our time—trying a little Christianity, a little meditation, a little of the other religious traditions. These are all deep wells of truth that will take us down into the Mystery. But we have to give ourselves fully to one of them, and we Christians believe that in Jesus we can go all the way down into the heart of God.

And that means what we most need to do is enter into the disciplines and practices of Christian faith. We need to learn the practices of real solitude and real community. We need to take time to pray, to be quiet enough to allow our noisy lives to settle down until, in the silence, we can speak what our soul needs to say and know ourselves accepted and embraced. If you need help in learning to pray, ask for it. Ask for it here, or wherever you call home. And then find a real community—people supporting each other, learning and working together as they grow in Christ's way.

And finally, coming to know Christ for ourselves, calls for serving Christ's wounded—the hungry and the homeless and the immigrant and the victim of war. Jesus said that if we want to see him, that's where to look.

I suppose only half-crazy people decide to go out and stake their lives on an unexpected call, or an impulse. But every now and then it happens.

William Willimon, dean of Duke University Chapel, wrote recently about the first time that Wendy Kopp, a young Princeton graduate, came to his campus to recruit for her new program. It was called Teach for America, and it aimed at attracting the best and brightest college graduates to teach for two years in some of the poorest schools in the country. There had been a few posters around the campus about this unpromising job opportunity, and my friend, the chaplain there, expected only a handful to show up. Instead there were some three or four hundred.

In a low-key way, Wendy Kopp explained to these ambitious, talented college seniors that this really wasn't much of a job. "You'll be working in some of the worst schools in the country," she said. "Many of them won't have any decent textbooks. A fair number of the kids will be from broken families, and some will be hard to handle. It could be dangerous at times. The hours will be long and the pay will be barely enough to live on. It'll probably be the hardest thing you'll ever do."

"So," she said, "if there are two or three of you here who would like to find out more, why don't you come on down and you can put your name on a list. Thanks for listening. Good luck with your careers. Have a great day."[4]

Will Willimon said that these bright, privileged students, with their whole futures laid out in front of them, started jamming the aisles to come down front to put their names on the list—on an impulse. It seems they heard a call.

"Come and follow me," Jesus says. At some level you and I are here today because God has been calling us. God has reached out and grabbed us and brought us here to make disciples of us.

"Come and follow me," he says. That doesn't mean we have to drop our nets and leave home. It meant that for those four fishermen. But if this story is about being called into the great flow of God's life in the world and letting ourselves be caught up in it, then my guess is that that will mean a different story for each of us.

"Come and follow me," Jesus says. You can follow me in Chevy Chase and Adams Morgan, in Tulsa and in Kenya. Listen for what I'm asking of you. Listen in the stirring of a sleepless night, in the words of a hymn we sing today, in the nagging issues at work that won't go away, in the yearning in your own heart for a life that matters.

"Come and follow me," he says. It may mean doing all the same things in your life, only doing them so that Christ's love shines through how you do them. It may mean raising children and writing briefs and meeting with customers. It may mean writing checks, or going on mission trips, or serving meals, or lobbying at the Capitol on behalf of the poor. It may mean doing less every day, instead of more, so that you can hear God's voice more clearly.

The possibilities are endless if we just listen. God is calling.

"Follow me," Jesus said. "And immediately they left their nets and followed him."

The Calling of Holiness

Isaiah 6:1–8; Luke 5:1–11

I wonder if you are ever struck by the strange things we say and do here on Sunday morning—the silence before the service, the dressing up in vestments and processing, the singing, sitting, and standing, the saying certain repeated phrases such as, "The Lord be with you . . . And also with you." It's all pretty elaborate. "Why all the fuss?" you might ask. Why all this formal business called worship?

And there are words we use all the time here that I'm guessing most of you would be hard put to define. Take, for example, the word "holy." "Holy" is a word that speaks of the mystery, the strange otherness and beyondness, of God. It goes back almost to the beginning of the Jewish faith. "Be holy, for I am holy," God says in the Book of Leviticus. "Worship the Lord in the beauty of holiness," one of the psalms says. "You are the holy one of God," Peter says to Jesus centuries later. Just a few minutes ago we sang that old standard hymn, "Holy, holy, holy, Lord God Almighty." What is all this holiness about?

Now let me guess . . . For some of you your hearts may be sinking, at least a little. Maybe you came here this morning looking for practical advice—three steps to better behaved children, four ways to get over a broken relationship, five steps to closing the gap between the rich and poor. And if that's what you're looking for, then chances are that hearing a lot of talk about holiness may not sound so exciting.

But Christian faith is not first of all about being practical and useful. It is about encountering an immense, overwhelmingly mysterious God. It's about glimpsing something so deep, so rich, so grand, that it makes our words seem like tin cups thrust under Niagara Falls, overwhelmed by the reality they are trying to contain.

That's why what is happening in the prophet Isaiah's vision in the Temple in our first lesson is so important. There inside the vast, smoke-filled temple, the veil between this world and eternity parts, and Isaiah sees into the heart of reality itself. "In the year that King Uzziah died, I saw the Lord sitting on a throne, high and lofty," he says. He sees six-winged angels, calling to each other in the words we call the Sanctus, which we sing every week in our Eucharist:

"Holy, holy, holy is the Lord of hosts; the whole earth is full of his glory."

At the heart of reality, the vision tells us, is an endless song of joy and praise. The whole temple shakes at the sound of the words. Who knows what exactly Isaiah saw, except that it was a shattering experience? He saw into the holiness at the heart of everything. It was as if he had looked away from the trees and stones shining brightly around him in the day's light, and gazed directly into the sun itself.

Isaiah encountered God. It was an experience of awe, wonder, and adoration in the presence of a reality vastly greater than any he had thought or imagined. Sometimes we catch glimpses of that holiness in moments of awe and reverence—walking on a beach, or listening to a Beethoven symphony, or holding a new grandchild. My guess is we've all been with people in times of great joy or terrible loss when we knew without a doubt that we were standing on holy ground.

To be holy originally meant to be set apart, to be wholly other. The scriptures were clear that God's ways are beyond our ways, and so the holy things of God were set apart things, and increasingly they were seen as mysterious and even powerfully sacred. Moses stood on "holy" ground when he encountered God. "The Lord is in his holy temple, let all the earth keep silence before him," another psalm says. And God's people came to be called a "holy nation" and a "holy priesthood." All these came to possess some of God's own sacred power.

Just last week I heard a firsthand description of an encounter not so different from Isaiah's. Stuart Kenworthy, who is rector of Christ Church in Georgetown and our close neighbor, spoke in an address to our diocesan convention about his first experience walking into this Cathedral. He was then a Methodist minister serving an inner city congregation in Philadelphia, and he and his wife had come down for the day just to visit this place. He said he remembered wandering around in a state of awe—at the grandeur of the building, the beauty, the arches, and the play of light. It was overwhelming, he said. And he remembers standing near the Holy Spirit Chapel and saying to his wife, "This place is so holy. I would love to be part of a church that knows this as home." And he went on to say that his predecessor at Christ Church, Sanford Garner, another dear friend of this Cathedral, was himself converted as a boy of twelve or thirteen by simply standing in this nave, at a time when there wasn't yet even a roof over the place he stood. But there, gazing up at the vast, unfinished arches, he experienced an overwhelming sense of God's presence.

But for all the depth and holiness of the God of Christian faith, we are living in a time when there seems to be a conspiracy against holiness. In the place of the God Isaiah encountered in the temple we are seeing a steady stream of nice, comfortable, domesticated versions of God. Our age seems to have been on an earnest quest to shrink God down to manageable size.

In a recent book called *Soul Searching*, which is about the religious lives of American teenagers, the authors describe what seems to have become the predominant religion of our time, for teens certainly, but also for adults. It's called "Moralistic Therapeutic Deism." Its beliefs are simple:

1. A God has created and watches over life.
2. This God wants us to be good, nice, and fair to each other, which is what the Bible is really about.
3. The goal of life is to be happy and feel good about yourself.
4. God doesn't need to be much involved in your life except when you need God to resolve a problem.
5. And finally, good people go to heaven when they die.[1]

That is the religion of a nice God who wants us to be pleasant, respectful, responsible people ourselves—a flattened out, lifeless, harmless God, who will never call or confront us with a grander, more demanding vision for our life than we had imagined. Religion is mainly about feeling good, happy, secure, and at peace. And happily God is easygoing, since his job is to solve our problems and help us feel good about ourselves. As the authors put it, "God is something like a combination Divine Butler and Cosmic Therapist: [he] is always on call, takes care of any issues that arise, helps his people feel better about themselves, and does not become too personally involved in the process."

At one time Christians were clear that the purpose of life was to "glorify God." Now the tasks seem to have been reversed. Increasingly it has become God's job to glorify us, to help us find the fulfillment, the success, the happiness we seek on our terms.

We also see God co-opted these days—as the god of the conservative agenda and the god of the liberal agenda. There is a provocative new book that wants to get us to see how subtly God is being co-opted in an array of ways. The long title says it all: *God Is Not . . . Religious, Nice, "One of Us," an American, a Capitalist.*[2] The holy God we meet in our scriptures and in our worship cannot, the authors say, be counted on to endorse the ways that we arrange our lives. God's righteousness, compassion, and justice stand in judgment over every dimension of our lives.

That is why worship is so essential. We need regularly, steadily, to be brought into the presence of this awe-inspiring, strange, even fearsome God. We need to gather in a place that stretches our worldview and opens our eyes to the depth and glory around us. We need to learn and relearn how to adore, to open our hearts in awe and wonder; how to praise God for the beauty of the world and the depths of God's unshakable love; how to offer thanks for every breath we take.

And that is why we need this odd business of worship, even with its strange formality. When we worship here we are on holy ground, and so we are careful how we speak and what we do. We bow in reverence, we make the sign of the cross to dedicate ourselves, we greet the holy in each other when we pass the peace. This is brash behavior, this dealing with the ultimate power in the universe, so we shouldn't do it lightly. Annie Dillard once wrote that if we really acknowledged what was going in church, we wouldn't come here without crash helmets.[3]

For all the intensity of Isaiah's encounter with the holy God, the story doesn't end with his ecstatic vision. Just the opposite. "Woe is me! I am lost, for I am a man of unclean lips, and I live among a people of unclean lips; yet my eyes have seen the King, the Lord of hosts." To look into the holiness of God, to see God's endless love and beauty, is immediately to be struck by how far short we fall from the perfect love he is seeing.

But the story doesn't end there. God acts to close the gap between divine holiness and human brokenness. An angel holding a burning coal touches his mouth and cleanses his sin. And then God speaks to him and says, "Whom shall I send, and who will go for us?" And Isaiah says, "Here am I; send me!"

The same thing happens in our gospel story today. When Peter sees the immense catch of fish comes from being with Jesus, he has his own experience of being overwhelmed by holiness. He throws himself down at Jesus' feet and exclaims, "Go away from me, Lord, for I am a sinful man!" And then Jesus reaches toward him saying, "Do not be afraid; from now on you will be catching people." We encounter this God as holy, which then exposes our fear and inadequacy. And then God reaches toward us to forgive, to heal, and to call and send us to do his work.

I don't think there has ever been a time when our world has more needed to rediscover holiness and all that comes with it—awe, reverence, adoration, and praise. In this country holiness is becoming increasingly rare. The more busy, driven, and self-absorbed we become, the more we lose the sacredness of our lives. And without a keen sense of a holy God, we lose our capacity to see the holiness in each other, in the world around us, and in the most vulnerable.

Human sexuality, for example, has become increasingly a transaction in which two consenting adults provide pleasure to each other. But that is a far cry from the holy vision of sexuality as one sacred human being giving the supreme gift of himself or herself to another in the context of a lifelong commitment. Or, think of the level of violence in our entertainment, and the degree of violence in our culture. Increasingly, it seems that nothing is sacred. And according to Kentucky writer Wendell Berry, in the Bible destroying nature isn't just bad stewardship or foolish economics, it's blasphemy. It is flinging God's holy gift of this earth back into God's face as if it were of no worth beyond what is needed to maintain our wasteful lifestyles.

Our whole world is suffering because of a loss of holiness. As Andrew Harvey, a contemporary mystic, put it:

> There is a worldwide famine of adoration, and we are all visibly dying in it. The desolation, nihilism, meaninglessness, tragic and brutal carelessness and perversity we see all around us and in us is the direct result of living in a spiritual concentration camp in which we are starved, and have starved ourselves, of just that food our hearts, minds and souls need most—the food of worship, of love, of gratitude, of praise, the bread and wine of adoration.[4]

Both of our lessons show us a holy God. And then Isaiah and Peter have a decision to make. Will they follow and learn more and go deeper? Will they say yes to their call?

Why not ask the holy God to speak to you? Why not listen to the words of scripture, sing the hymns, receive the bread and wine, and let God's holiness reach through them directly to you? Perhaps here in this temple you will catch a glimpse of the Lord high and lifted up, calling you by name and sending you out to serve this world in Christ's name.

The scientist-theologian Teilhard de Chardin once said that in the end there are only two options for humankind: adoration or annihilation. Either we honor the holy, and the Holy One, in our midst, or nothing will be sacred any more. The choice is ours.

"Holy, holy, holy, Lord God of hosts. Heaven and earth are full of your glory."

Costly Discipleship

Luke 14:25–33

Things couldn't have been going better. "Large crowds were traveling with Jesus," Luke's gospel says. Jesus is catching on, people are excited, his poll numbers are surging. It looks like he has a successful marketing strategy and a brilliant campaign.

He must have been doing a good job welcoming absolutely everyone. After all, in last week's gospel lesson Jesus talked about a great banquet feast to which absolutely everyone was invited. "Come one, come all" was his theme. He must have understood people's yearnings and desires. The door was wide open, and people were flooding in.

A lot of ink has been spilled in the last two or three decades about what makes people come to church. Some have argued that it's the conservative churches with their high demands and clear rules that have it all figured out. Many have decided that the secret is to be "user-friendly" churches.

Over the summer I had my first chance to visit a megachurch, one of those vast enterprises as big as a shopping mall that draws people in by the thousands every Sunday. It was impressive. The church I visited was about the most welcoming place I've ever encountered. There were smiling, helpful traffic police directing the miles of backed up cars waiting to get in, and there were warm faces greeting you as you emerged from their user-friendly parking garage. Inside you encountered simultaneous services and classes for every age group you could imagine, each with separate bands and musicians. And then there was the full-service cafeteria for any kind of food you might want. The service was held in an auditorium with easy-listening rock music and a helpful sermon. Strange, though—you didn't see a cross anywhere. Read through the brochures, and you could see there were special interest groups for job seekers, single parents, and recovering alcoholics. This was a church brilliantly focusing on making everything as accessible and helpful as possible.

The more mainstream churches are trying to be "user friendly," too. Go to a Methodist or Episcopalian or Presbyterian church and chances are you will hear a great deal of talk about God's unconditional love, that Christ welcomes everyone, with little mention of the hard words like judgment and sin. Church growth gurus say to us struggling mainliners that we need to find out what people's concerns are and make sure we respond to them, so they will stick around rather than continuing their church shopping. So we want them to see that we have uplifting worship and great programs for their kids and a caring environment where they will feel comfortable.

Jesus drew large crowds, and that's what we're after. But for some reason in today's gospel Jesus decides it's time to talk tough. How's this for a church growth strategy: "Whoever does not hate father and mother, wife and children, brothers and sisters, yes even life itself, can't be my disciple." He can't be serious. And it gets worse. In fact, it becomes clear today that Jesus would have been a disaster as a parish minister.

Now, scholars can tell us that Jesus is trying to get the crowd's attention with these harsh words. He doesn't *really* mean to hate your parents; it doesn't imply anger or hostility. He's using ancient Semitic exaggeration to say that you need to keep your loyalties in perspective. And you know there are times when you explain your choice by saying you "hate" one thing and "love" the other. "I hate spinach, but I love tomatoes." It's a vivid way of saying that one thing is right for me and the other isn't.

Now that probably doesn't get Jesus off the hook that much, because hating your parents is still a harsh thing to say. And he doesn't stop there. "If you won't carry a cross you can't be my disciple," he says. And you just better count the cost if you want to come along with me, like a tower builder making sure he can afford to finish the job, and a king who would be a fool to start a war without being sure he had the troops to win it. Oh, and by the way, he says, you can't be my disciple if you don't give up all your possessions.

What are we supposed to make of this? What if we at the Cathedral ran an ad in the Saturday religion page of the *Washington Post* saying something like

> Is your life going pretty well, but you sense you want to be more miserable? Why not try the National Cathedral?
>
> Having a rough time at home and find yourself alienated from everyone in the house? Good for you. You're looking like a disciple.
>
> Sick and tired of all those beautiful possessions you've been accumulating all those years? Come on to the Cathedral and we'll take them off your hands.
>
> Have you ever considered crucifixion? Try the National Cathedral. [1]

This is not a good church growth strategy! Instead of talking about how appealing church is, Jesus wants them to know how hard it may be to follow. After all, by now he is on his way to the conflict in Jerusalem that will kill him. And a few decades later when Luke was writing his gospel, Christians themselves were being arrested and tortured. It was dangerous to have a Christian in your family, so it was no exaggeration to say that being a Christian could pull a family apart. It could be costly, scary business following Jesus. Jesus wasn't being harsh with these tough words; he was being honest about what it would mean to follow him.

What if he's right? What if becoming a disciple, and becoming a full human being for that matter, has to involve struggling with our loyalties, taking up the crosses our life hands us, even giving away some of what we own? What if we will never actually discover who we were made to be until we learn to give ourselves away? And if that's true, all this talk about having a church that "meets our needs" is starting at the wrong end.

Being a disciple begins with the recognition that we are not the center of our lives, that my life is not about me and my needs. It calls for a willingness to risk, to let God do something new and surprising in us. Here in our own complex days, God wants to give us a peace, a clarity—and a richness of life we won't find any other way. But we won't find it by trying to get our own little needs met, but by giving ourselves to a revolutionary love and a healing cause that will pull out all that is best in us.

In today's hard lesson Jesus isn't being cruel. He's just being honest with us about where life is to be found, and refusing it make it sound easy or simple.

I actually think that people these days are yearning for a life that makes some demands on them. This week's *Time* magazine cover story presented a case for universal national service—a vision of every young person being challenged, not compelled, to spend a year or two or three in a servant role of some sort, teaching, tutoring, and working in underserved communities. "After 9/11," the writer says, "Americans were hungry to be asked to do something, to make some kind of sacrifice, and what they mostly remember is being asked to go shopping."[2] Some 27 percent of Americans are volunteering, and the number is rising. Volunteer service organizations are springing up all over the country.

Many young people these days seem to be looking for ways to change the world. One of the most widely assigned books for students entering college in recent years has been *Mountains Beyond Mountains*, the story of Dr. Paul Farmer, the young physician who decided to spend his life setting up clinics focusing on AIDS and tuberculosis for desperately poor people, first in Haiti, and then increasingly around the world. When the author Tracy Kidder asked Paul Farmer, who is himself a Christian, why he lived that kind of life,

Farmer replied, "I don't know. The problem is that if I don't work this hard, someone will die who doesn't have to."[3]

To be a disciple is to be willing to take up the world's crosses, as well as our own. It is to follow this Lord, and in doing that to discover needs and desires we never knew we could have.

That's why the church fails us when it doesn't tell us that Christianity has a cost. When I first moved to a new parish some years ago, I was eager to introduce a course called DOCC, Disciples of Christ in Community, which I believed could open the Christian journey to people in new ways. The main catch to it was that it required an eighteen-week commitment. I ran the idea by some of my parishioners, and they thought I had lost my mind. Eighteen weeks? Are you kidding? People are much too busy for that, and they would never come to a church class for that long. Well, they had me convinced. But we kept talking about it, and a few parishioners went and experienced the course elsewhere, and finally they persuaded me we should try it anyway. To my astonishment, we had to start a waiting list after 110 people signed up. And it happened the next year, and the next.

It turned out there was a hunger people hardly knew they had, to know Christ, to know their faith, to know their own community in ways they never had. And my guess is that you came here this morning looking for more than you knew, for something worth giving your life to, something large and important.

"Count the cost," Jesus says. Be sure you're ready for what you're getting yourself into. And of course, he is right. If we decide to follow him—to a DOCC class, or to Haiti or New Orleans, or to a prayer group or Bible study or a service group down the street, who knows what could happen? Everything that matters asks of us far more than we ever imagined.

That was true of Jesus, of course. He gave everything he had—for us. He didn't just take up his cross and show us the way. He promised that he would go with us when we picked up our own crosses. He said he would carry them with us, that we would never be cut off from him.

And he believed with everything in him that we would find the life we were made for by following this demanding way. Even the hard times we would face would open out into something deep and firm and good when we knew that God was at work through us.

Jesus didn't seem to care all that much about the size of his crowds. It may be that not all that many people are ready for this demanding road. But here's the surprise. He lived and died for us timid ones too, who aren't quite sure about all this, who aren't quite ready. And he won't give up on any of us, ever.

Will You Dance?

Matthew 22:1–14

A few years ago the *Boston Globe* published a story about an unusual wedding banquet. A couple had gone to the Hyatt Hotel in downtown Boston to plan their wedding, and every detail they selected they were determined to be the very best—food, china, flowers, music. They both had expensive taste, and the bill showed it—many thousands of dollars—and half of it was due on the spot as a down payment.

Everything was moving along smoothly until the day the wedding invitations were to go in the mail, when the groom announced that he couldn't go through with it. He just wasn't sure.

Now the hurt and angry bride-to-be had to go back to the Hyatt to cancel the banquet, only to learn that there was no way to get back the down payment. The contract was binding. There were only two options—to forfeit the down payment or to go ahead with the party.

The bride was, of course, outraged at this. But the more she thought about it, the clearer she was that she would go ahead with the party. Now, though, it wouldn't be a wedding banquet, but instead just a big blowout. As a matter of fact, ten years before this woman had been living in a homeless shelter. But she had managed to get back on her feet over time, had taken a good job, and had eventually made a lot of money. Now she had the idea of throwing a big party for her old friends, the down-and-outs of Boston.

And so in June of 1990 the Hyatt Hotel had a party the likes of which no one had ever quite seen. The jilted bride changed the menu to boneless chicken—"in honor of the groom," she said—and sent invitations to the homeless shelters and rescue missions in the city. And so that summer evening people accustomed to finding their meals in the trash bins of the city made their way through the grand lobby of the Hyatt to a meal of chicken *cordon bleu*. Black-tied waiters served hors d'oeuvres to people with rags wrapped around them. Many had their bags of worldly goods with them, reminders of the hard life they were living. But for this night they were treated like kings and queens—sipping champagne, eating chocolate wedding cake, dancing into the night.[1]

Well, in case you missed it, that's a slightly updated version of the gospel story we just heard. A king throws a wedding banquet for his son and then sends his servants to invite the appropriate guests. When they won't come he sends them out again, this time into the streets and byways to invite anyone they can find, and then he has his party.

In the gospels of Matthew, Mark, and Luke, Jesus tells this story and each time a little differently. But what you can't miss is the conviction in all of them that at the heart of life God is throwing an extravagant banquet, and everyone, absolutely everyone, is invited. "Do you want to know what God is like?" Jesus is saying. Do you want to know what life at its deepest is all about? Do you want a glimpse of how we are supposed to live our lives? Think about a bustling, laughter-filled party with platters of food and drink everywhere, and everyone having a ball.

In fact, Jesus constantly used dinner parties, suppers, wedding receptions, and even breakfasts as images of what it means to be with God. The whole world has been invited to a feast, he was saying—everyone is welcome, everyone belongs, no one is left out. There is enough for everyone. No questions asked—about who is virtuous and who isn't, who has their act together and who doesn't, who believes in God and who doesn't. Everyone is in, and for only one reason: a God of unstoppable love wants everyone in.

There is something wild and unruly about the God at the heart of Christian faith. Many have argued that the one thing that separates Christianity from other faiths is not the notion of incarnation—other religions have versions of a god appearing in human form; not resurrection—other religions have accounts of returns from death. No, it's the simple assertion of grace—the notion that God's love for every human being and for all of creation is unmerited and measureless, and it comes with no strings attached.

That's not the version of God many of us picked up through the years. For many that God was a distant, ominous, angry figure who evoked fear more than anything else. This God may forgive, but first we have to sweat bullets, feel terribly guilty, and then crawl our way out of the divine displeasure.

Here's something totally different. This God is throwing a party for the losers as well as the winners, for the sinners as well as the good, for those who have never darkened the door of a church as well as for the ushers and the members of the altar guild. Everyone, everyone is already in.

But now, having said that, we have to face all the ways this story gets irritating and complicated. In the first place, do we really like this notion that everyone is invited to the party, that everyone is in? Not if you watch the way Christians behave sometimes. Christians have become famous for how readily they write off those who differ from them—people who don't agree with their own particular beliefs, ways of worshiping, or moral views.

Many Christians were stunned when two years ago Lt. General William Boykin said of a Muslim military leader in Somalia that "I knew my God was bigger than his. I knew that my God was a real God, and his was an idol."[2] So much for honoring a child of God who happened to follow Islam.

Christians have been among the worst in claiming to know who's in and who's out of the Celestial City. A number of books have come out recently arguing that the greatest danger in the world is monotheism—whether it's Christian, Jewish, or Muslim—because all these faiths seem to move quickly to a rigid view that "we have all the answers" and everyone else should be relegated to outer darkness.

In one of the wisest books I have read in years, *The Dignity of Difference*, the chief rabbi of Great Britain, Jonathan Sacks, puts the danger this way:

> One belief, more than any other, is responsible for the slaughter of individuals on the altars of the great historical ideals. It is the belief that those who do not share my faith—or my race or my ideology—do not share my humanity. At the best they are second-class citizens. At worst they forfeit the sanctity of life itself. They are the unsaved, the unbelievers, the infidel, the unredeemed: they stand outside the circle of salvation.[3]

And then he goes on to say that from this conviction flowed the Crusades, the Inquisition, the jihads, the pogroms, and ultimately, the Holocaust.

So the good news is Jesus is throwing a great party and we are invited. The bad news is that *all* of us are invited. Jesus is describing a party where Irish Catholics and Protestants, Rwandan Hutus and Tutsis, Iraqi Shiites, Sunis, and Kurds are all invited. It's a party where Democrats and Republicans are invited, homeless people and billionaires, gay and lesbian advocates and those who oppose them, "pro-lifers" and "pro-choicers." God has no taste, no standards!

Of course, that isn't to say that all the people at the party agree with each other. It's to say that the God we meet in Jesus Christ is a God who loves difference, complexity, mystery. As Rabbi Sacks puts it,

> The test of faith is whether I can make space for difference. Can I recognize God's image in someone who is not in my image, whose language, faith, and ideals are different from mine? If I cannot, then I have made God in my image instead of allowing him to remake me in his.[4]

Dean Alan Jones of Grace Cathedral in San Francisco summarizes Jesus' vision through an oft-used phrase in novelist James Joyce's strangest work,

Finnegans Wake: "Here comes everybody."[5] That's the vision of God's
kingdom Jesus shows us. That's the vision our church is given to proclaim.
"Here comes everybody."

There's a second troubling dimension to this simple story. It's the fact
that so many turn down the wedding invitation in the first place. In Luke's
version people list their reasons for saying no—I've just bought a piece of
land; I've got to check out the new oxen that just arrived; I just got married.
Sorry, I'm just too busy to come to the party.

If there's a deep, joyful party at the heart of life, most of us wouldn't
know it. We're usually stuck in traffic somewhere. There's no time in our
personal lives and careers for a spiritual life. That'll have to wait. So will
helping our children grow in their faith. Classes, sports, getting into college,
those things are what count. We run out of time before we get to the party.

Then there are those who can't believe the invitation is real. They have
too many doubts about faith even to give it a try—too many bad experiences
with faith, too many boring church services. The famous socialist Norman
Thomas told a priest friend on his deathbed that even then he still couldn't
bring himself to believe in God. To which his friend replied, "It's all right,
God still believes in you." You don't have to believe to come to the party.
Just come hang around, sample the hors d'oeuvres, see if you don't begin to
catch on to the rhythm of the music.

In our gospel today there is a lot of typical Middle Eastern exaggeration
about the bloody consequences of refusing the party invitation. But the point
is the tragedy of it all. To miss out on the sheer delight of knowing God's
love for us is a terrible loss.

Finally, there's the strangest twist of all in the way Matthew tells the
story. Once everyone is in the party, the king spots a guest who doesn't have
a proper wedding robe. And he brutally orders the man thrown out of the
party. "For many are called," Matthew says, "but few are chosen." Whatever
happened to the gracious invitation?

There's a story behind this harsh language. In both Jesus' time and then
especially in Matthew's, many were starting to take for granted the invitation
to God's feast. Sure, they said, we'll come in, we'll follow, we'll join this
new thing called church, but then that didn't seem to change a thing about
their lives. Didn't you say "Come as you are to the banquet?" they would
argue. Nothing required. It doesn't matter what you do or how you dress. Just
come.

No, Matthew says in his version. Being a guest doesn't mean you come
and do as you please. Sure, there's a party, but are you willing to enter into
the spirit of the party? Will you wear your party clothes? Will you join in the
dance? Because if you decide to come in wearing your grubby clothes, if you
decide to remain your own self-absorbed self, act any way you please, drink

too much, offend everyone else, you may physically be at the party, but the party won't be in you.

In fact, you're turning your back on the party. You thought the king would settle for a noisy crowd of people who would just come in and be their same dull selves. Not on your life. This king wants everyone to catch the spirit, to taste this banquet of peace and centeredness and aliveness.

You have to get into the spirit of the party. You have to allow yourself to be engaged—to get to work on developing a prayer life, take a class, find a project to ease the world's pain. Jesus' invitation calls for conversion, for clean clothes. If you let me, Jesus said, I will make you into bright, radiant creatures of joy made for eternity. But that will mean growth and change.

You see, it's possible to come to the party and miss the party. I remember a birthday party given for one of our friends' children, a little boy turning five. Unfortunately, the boy seemed to have gotten up on the wrong side of the bed that day and things hadn't gone smoothly for him, so at party time the little fellow was in an angry, hostile mood. And it never left him. The guests came, the presents were given, the "Happy Birthday" song was sung, but that boy never did allow the party going on right in front of him to gather him in.

This morning you can almost hear the party now. In fact, we're about to share in God's feast ourselves. We're going to pull out some bread and pour some wine and then taste and see the God who holds us all. The banquet is spread. The invitation is out. And the only question is, Will we join in? Will you join in?

Commanded to Love

Matthew 22: 34–46

In the gospel lessons of the last few weeks, Jesus' adversaries keep firing questions at him. Then, wouldn't you know, it's a lawyer who decides to put him to the test. "So, Teacher, which commandment is the greatest?" Cut to the chase, he's saying. Give us your bottom line. What do you really think is the essence of life?

And Jesus answers him without hesitating, "You shall love the Lord your God with all your heart, and with all your soul, and with all your mind. This is the greatest and first commandment. And a second is like it: You shall love your neighbor as yourself. On these two commandments hang all the law and the prophets."

The greatest commandment is the command to love, Jesus says. Love is the key to everything. And God *commands* us to love.

Sounds easy enough, doesn't it? After all, you hear the word "love" just about everywhere these days. Back when I lived in Virginia a couple of decades ago, I saw bumper stickers everywhere with "Virginia is for lovers." I never could quite figure out what that meant.

I remember dorm rooms in the 1960s and '70s with a poster that just had the four letters L-O-V-E on it. And, of course, the radios of that era were filled with love songs, or what I would call, looking back, terrific codependent love songs. They were all about how life will end if we can't have a certain person in our lives to make our lives complete. "I can't live, if living is without you," one said. "All you need is love," we were told. "Ain't too proud to beg," someone else said. "Love me tender, love me true." One after another, these songs declared that the meaning of the universe hung on the meager attention of a beautiful young man or woman.

Of course, things began to get a little raw later, when songs came along like "Gimme Some Lovin'" and "I Can't Get No Satisfaction." But I'll always remember that good, practical love song "If you can't be with the one you love, love the one you're with."

Love in our time is all about feelings. We speak of people "falling in love." It's something that happens that we have no control over. Either we "feel" love toward someone, or we don't. We're the passive recipients, even the victims, of our feelings. That's why the classic expression of love through the ages has been Cupid with his arrow, shooting people so that they hopelessly lose control of their feelings. In recent years, a much admired CEO of one of America's biggest corporations sat for an interview with a reporter, and soon he and the reporter had "fallen in love." And then, victim of Cupid's arrow that he was, he walked away from his wife and family to follow this new love.

Years of premarital counseling have convinced me that most couples head into marriage because they "fell" in love. They hardly realize that falling in love is just the beginning of a long journey in learning how to love. The commitment they often think they are making is not "for better for worse, for richer for poorer," but something more like "we will stay together as long as our love shall last." As long as it feels right.

The catch, of course, is that feelings are notoriously unreliable. They can change at the drop of a hat. Lives get pulled and stretched, and people change. A relationship based primarily on feelings is built on sand.

But neither the God of Moses in the Old Testament nor Jesus in the New seems to have any interest in feelings of love. "You *shall* love the Lord your God," says God; "You *shall* love your neighbor as yourself," says Jesus. In John's gospel Jesus says, "A new commandment I give you, that you love one another." Love is something that Jesus believed could be commanded. We are told to love God with our hearts and minds and souls and our neighbor as ourselves. This love isn't something that we need to feel.

Love in our Jewish and Christian traditions is a practice, a skill, a demanding discipline. It entails an arduous journey out of our self-absorption into caring for the well-being of another. As secular psychiatrist Erich Fromm wrote in his book *The Art of Loving*, loving is an art, the apex of what it means to be human, and it takes the kind of practice required to be an accomplished pianist, or dancer, or scientist. If we want to become full human beings, we must slowly, carefully learn the art of loving. [1]

One of the surprises of marriage is that deep, enduring love is the result of marriage, not its cause. There is not one word in the service about how married people are going to feel about their spouses. They are asked, "Will you love him or her, comfort him, honor and keep him, in sickness and in health, and forsaking all others be faithful to him as long as you both shall live?" With those words they are promising to act in certain ways. It's a matter of the will. Part of the miracle of marriage, though, is that in making and keeping these promises they come to feel more "in love" than when they began.

A woman I was talking to about joining the church once said to me that she couldn't possibly join because she recognized clearly that she just couldn't like everyone around her, especially the people in this particular church. My answer to her was simple: You don't have to like them; you just have to love them. Jesus was never interested in whether a disciple liked someone. What will save our souls is loving each other, moving out of our own self-absorption and personal preferences to care for our neighbor. And then comes the surprise. As we learn to love each other, chances are, we may even start learning to like each other.

Here in today's gospel, Jesus laid down the heart of it all for his followers. Love is the main thing, the *sine qua non*, the essence, the key. When the tough lawyer challenged him to name the greatest commandment, he wanted Jesus to cut through the 613 separate commandments in Jewish law, all the rules, all the guidelines covering every area of life. And Jesus responded with the Israelis' own core command, the Shema, which Jews had been reciting and wearing around their foreheads and nailing to their doorposts for centuries. "You shall love the Lord your God with all your heart and with all your soul and with all your mind."

Then Jesus shocked them. They thought he was finished. But without missing a beat he said, "There's a second commandment that's like it: 'You shall love your neighbor as yourself.'" Wait a minute; where did that come from? Sure, it's a line out of the Book of Leviticus, but since when has that been pasted in with the first? As Old Testament scholar Walter Brueggemann puts it, Jesus is saying you can't say "God" without saying "neighbor"; it's almost hyphenated—"God-Neighbor."[2] To love God means to love your neighbor. To love your neighbor is the active form of loving God.

For Jesus, your neighbor is the one who needs you, whether that person is across the dinner table, or next door, or across the city or the world. Haven't we all come to feel as if the hurricane victims in the Gulf Coast are our neighbors, and in some ways isn't that true of the earthquake victims in southern Asia? And loving this neighbor isn't about swelling music and warm feelings, but unsentimental, concrete acts.

A few years ago I read an account by a Chicago lawyer named Thomas Geoghegan describing his first encounter with a soup kitchen. He was overwhelmed by the unpleasant smells and the terrible shape the men were in, but most of all he was disturbed because he had expected to love the poor and to be filled with a warm glow, and he wasn't.

And so he complained to his priest friend, who replied, "You're not down there for self-actualization." But Geoghegan protested, "I didn't feel any love for them." The priest replied,

So what?. . . The church says nothing about that. . . . Look, these nuns [who run the kitchen] aren't liberals. They are conservative. . . . They don't care about "love" in our modern, interpersonal way. We, the liberals, want love: we go to soup kitchens to be loved. The nuns go there to feed people. That's it. Give them something to eat.[3]

It's that cool, clear, unsentimental love that you find in people whose lives are given to loving. My bet is that you can see it in people who work in homeless shelters here in Northwest Washington supported by the Community Council for the Homeless. I wager that's what you would see in the health-care clinics and soup kitchens across Rock Creek Park, and in the interfaith meetings where people are putting their heads together to push hard for a better school system and affordable housing.

Loving our God-neighbor means changing diapers and doing the dishes and living with the needs of our children. It means speaking to someone who has hurt us. It is telling a friend she's drinking too much. It is putting our career in jeopardy because our family needs us. It is tutoring kids in Adams Morgan or Anacostia. Love is making sure that something other than the bottom line alone drives our business decisions—things like the welfare of employees or the good of the community.

The ultimate issue for all of us is whether we ever learn to love our God-neighbor. Worshiping God is where we begin. We come to places such as this to open our minds and spirits to the One who made us and loves us. But that alone is only a start. It shows us the things that count—compassion, forgiveness, active love. And it opens us to receive Christ's Spirit and love that make those things possible. Church is meant to be a School for Love, a place where we can learn and practice the skills and art of loving. And this Cathedral's mission is to lead us in the most profound worship of God possible, and then to propel us out in service to our God-neighbor.

There's a short story by John L'Heureux called "The Expert on God," about a young priest whose faith has been riddled with doubts for years. One day he happens on a terrible car accident and finds a young man trapped under an overturned car and dying. After a lot of struggle the priest is able to get the young man out from under the car and holds him in his arms as he begins desperately praying that the young man will survive. The priest anoints him and prays more, but it's clear to him the prayers are useless. Still he prays on, but seems to be hearing only his own empty words being hurled up toward heaven.

Then the story closes in this way: "The dying boy turned—some dying reflex—and his head tilted in the priest's arms, trusting, like a lover. And at once the priest, faithless, unrepentant, gave up his prayers and bent to him and whispered, fierce and burning, 'I love you,' and continued until there was no breath, 'I love you, I love you.'"

At long last this priest became "an expert on God." As he embraced this dying man, he moved away from all of his preoccupation with himself and gave himself away in an act of pure love of his God-neighbor. "I love you," he said as he held him, "I love you."[4]

> "You shall love the Lord your God with all your heart, and with all your soul, and with all your mind." This is the greatest and first commandment. And a second is like it: "You shall love your neighbor as yourself." On these two commandments hang all the law and the prophets.

And on these two commandments hang our life's meaning and our world's hope.

When God Throws a Brick

John 3:1–15

Just last week I heard a talk given by a Minneapolis businessman named Ward Brehm, who with no warning at all began to see his life being turned upside down. It all started when his minister stopped him after church one day and asked him if he'd like to go to Africa. "He might as well have asked me if I'd like to go to the moon," Brehm said.

Seeing his resistance, the pastor asked, "Will you pray about it?" Brehm looked him square in the eye and said, "Arthur, you're the minister, you pray about it. I'll think about it."

About two months later this businessman found himself at an airport with a ticket booked to Ethiopia. But there were more surprises ahead. When he finally met up with the group he would be traveling with they were surrounded by a group of "church ladies," as he called them, there to send them off. "This isn't looking good," he thought. Then just before they boarded the group decided to hold hands and pray, right there in the airport lounge. Brehm said he prayed all right, but his prayer was that none of his clients or business partners would walk by and see him.

Well, off he went for ten days in Africa. And, he says, he's never been the same since. "The moment I stepped onto African soil," he said, "my life was altered." He saw a world that before had only existed for him as a set of statistics. In Ethiopia he listened to surviving family members telling stories of loved ones lost during the years of famine; in Uganda he saw people everywhere dying of AIDS. For the first time, the senselessness of people starving to death overwhelmed him. In Brehm's talk he recalled a subsequent Africa trip hiking into parts of Kenya where no one had ever seen a person with white skin. At one point he was lying exhausted in a tent when a

37

scrawny boy crept in and stole a protein bar from his backpack. He of course let the boy snatch it away, but when he peaked out of the tent to watch the boy eat it, he saw him feeding it to his two-year-old emaciated brother with a distended stomach.

Brehm's experience began to scramble the ways he had put his life together. As he puts it in his book, *White Man Walking*, everything he thought he knew about the world, his life, and God was up for grabs. God seemed much closer than back home.[1] Back there, he thought, with all our comfort and privileges, we are usually only able to see God when things fall apart.

And he recalled an old saying, that sometimes God uses a pebble to get a person's attention. If that doesn't work, sometimes a larger rock. And for those who refuse to pay attention, God resorts to a brick. "Africa," he said, "was my brick."[2] Since that first trip in 1992, Brehm has traveled to Africa regularly taking groups, especially of business executives, getting to see and experience what he had discovered.

I said his name was Ward Brehm. But I believe his real name is Nicodemus. Poor Nicodemus is our gospel lesson today. He is an upstanding leader of his community—prominent, respected, well educated. His career has gone well. He goes to synagogue, he prays regularly, probably has well-behaved kids to boot. But for some reason he's restless enough with his life to slip out under cover of night to find this rabbi named Jesus.

It's by any standard a bizarre conversation. There's a lot of talk but not much communication. Nicodemus leads off with a little cozy familiarity: "Rabbi, we know that you are a teacher who has come from God . . ." "We know . . ." You can almost hear the smug pretentiousness. After all, he's a ruler of the synagogue. "You and I know the deal. Everything is under control." And what are they supposed to "know"? Probably that God is nice and safe and not very interesting or creative. People are supposed to keep the rules, be responsible. Live a good life. That's about it.

But Jesus blurts out, "You've got to be born from above, born anew"—which confuses Nicodemus completely. What does that mean? So Nicodemus tries to get a grip: "But how can anyone be born after having grown old? Can somebody go back into the mother's womb and start over?" Our friend is a little literal-minded, you have to say.

And then Jesus just makes it worse when he says, "The wind blows where it chooses, you don't know where it comes from or where it is going." What kind of god is he talking about? Jesus uses two of the most uncontainable, uncontrollable phenomena—birth and wind—to talk about God. In both, something has to happen to you. We don't get ourselves born; a birthing process does it to us. We don't generate the wind; it drives us. Nicodemus can't find God, or the kingdom of God, on his own. He has to start over, be born again. He can't plan it, achieve it, or put it on his resume. It has to come "from above," Jesus says, from beyond him.

This conversation was Nicodemus' brick. God got his attention in a confusing exchange he would never forget. We aren't told what happened to Nicodemus after his night meeting. Apparently nothing immediately. It must have taken some time for it all to sink in. But something shifted somewhere, because he turns up two more times in John's gospel. He's in the Temple later when Jesus is accused by crowds demanding that he be arrested. One man stands up to defend him. His name is Nicodemus.

And at the very end, Jesus is dead, crucified, and there is Nicodemus. This time he isn't there at night as a seeker, but as a disciple, helping to take Jesus' body away.

Whether it's a pebble, a rock, or a brick, God wants to get through to us, but that's not so easy when we are all so competent, goal-oriented, and efficient. It isn't easy for God to get some time on our calendar, to get our full attention, to get us to take a chance on a deeper, different life. I believe that deep down most people would love to have God change their lives, but they either don't expect it or are afraid that if that started to happen it would ask too much of them.

If you've been to any of our Sunday Forum public conversations, you know there have been lots of bricks flying around. Several weeks ago, Tony Hall, who was a congressman from Ohio for twenty-four years, told us about a trip to Africa that changed his life. From the moment he stepped on the ground in 1984, like Ward Brehm he saw a world he never imagined. He encountered a crowd of some fifty thousand who had hiked as much as one hundred miles in hopes of getting food and water to keep them and their families alive, only to find that no supplies had arrived at all. "I began to hear the moaning in the crowd," he said, as adults and children were dying all around him. "I never got over that," he said.[3]

For this deeply committed Christian, the fight against hunger became the passion of his life, and for two decades he visited the most desperate places in the world and was an unstoppable advocate in the Congress for stopping the scourge of hunger.

Then just two weeks ago, Rick Warren, the pastor of Saddleback Church in California and in many ways the most prominent Protestant pastor in America, told us the story of his and his wife Kay's conversion to the cause of eradicating global poverty. It began with something as simple as Kay's reading a magazine article about AIDS in Africa. The photos of the victims were so graphic, she said, that she covered her eyes and peaked through just enough to read the words. There was a box in the middle of the page that read, "twelve million children orphaned in Africa due to AIDS."

"It was as if I fell on the Damascus road [like St. Paul at his conversion] because I had no clue. I didn't know a single orphan." For days she was haunted by the fact of twelve million orphans.

But after weeks, then months of anguish, she realized she faced a fateful choice. "I made a conscious choice to say 'yes.' I had a pretty good suspicion that I was saying yes to a bucket load of pain. In that moment God shattered my heart."

"That's not my work, Honey," Rick Warren replied, when Kay told him about all this. But within months, they had traveled to Africa together, they had dedicated 90 percent of the $100 million Rick had then made on his best-selling book, and mobilizing churches to fight AIDS and poverty in Africa had become their new calling.[4]

When God throws a brick, anything can happen. The wind blows, the Spirit moves, people start getting born from above into whole new lives.

Here at the Cathedral we have been hosting a remarkable work of art, the Keiskamma altarpiece, that shows what a community can do when an immense brick comes its way. It all began in the rural village of Hamburg in South Africa, where AIDS had taken a terrible toll.

Here are some facts: AIDS is the largest health crisis the world has ever faced. When the bubonic plague swept through Europe it killed some twenty-five million people, about a fourth of the population of Europe. Now three million people die of AIDS each year. That's the equivalent of twenty fully loaded 747s crashing every day of the year. It attacks people in the prime of their lives and leaves their children abandoned. In some countries in Africa a third of the population is infected.

In little Hamburg, within a few short years a whole generation of young adults was dying. Hamburg became a village primarily of grandmothers and orphaned children. How could such a devastated community find a way through the grief and despair?

By the grace of God, an extraordinary doctor moved into their community to serve the AIDS victims. Dr. Carol Hoffmeyr brought with her a love of art, and as she made her rounds to the homes of her patients she developed an idea: to invite the women of the village to join in creating a massive altar-piece, an immense work of art and faith to which everyone could contribute.

It was to be shaped in the exact proportions of one of the great works of Western art, Matthias Grunewald's Isenheim altarpiece, which had been painted in response to a terrible plague in sixteenth-century Europe. Only this new work would be created in a women's idiom, embroidery, and it would be filled with the real images of people in their village woven into the stories of Christ's crucifixion and resurrection. One hundred thirty women joined together to weave the stories of their tragic losses into this magnificent tapes-try. Over months of work the altarpiece became a testament to their suffering and loss, and also to their deep faith that God would carry them through. The creation of this work became the turning point of this community in facing their terrible tragedy.

AIDS was that community's brick. In creating the Keiskamma altarpiece the women of Hamburg affirmed a crucified and living Lord had been holding them through that terrible time. It stands here in this Cathedral as a testimony to their remarkable faith and to a Lord who will not let them go.

Well, as I said, bricks are flying these days. God is getting our attention in more ways than we can count. Nicodemus had been hit by a life-shattering conversation that didn't make any sense at the time. But slowly a new way of seeing and thinking began to get through.

And Ward Brehm, Tony Hall, Kay and Rick Warren, and the people of Hamburg found God coming to them, calling them to new work, new ways of living, new relationships, new experiences.

Have you noticed God tossing any pebbles your way lately? Or stones getting your attention? Maybe there's a brick coming at you right now. All these Nicodemuses we heard about today discovered that our God is a restless, relentless God who won't turn us loose. God wants us to be born anew, to let the wind of the Spirit blow through us and fill our sails.

I don't know how God will get through to you—through a trip to Africa or Honduras, maybe; through a health crisis that shatters old plans and makes every day count; through a conversation, a book, a friend, a sermon, a hymn, a course.

I do know, though, that really to know God's love means letting go and making room and being ready to be born anew, only this time with God at the center.

And I know one other thing. . . . God wants you. All of you. And wants us to loosen our grip, open our hands and eyes, and go where God needs us to go.

"I pray that each of you will find your Africa," Brehm writes. Africa is the place where you need to go so that God can find you—whether your Africa is a faraway continent or in Anacostia, whether it is in Springfield or Silver Spring, in your longtime job or heading off in a new direction.

You must be born anew, from above.

Where is your Africa? Where is *your* Africa?

Following an Elusive Lord

Easter is an exuberant season. We spend seven entire Sundays celebrating God's victory over sin and death. There is meant to be a bright, festival feeling to everything we do in these weeks. So much in this season seems clear and confident. Christ is risen, we have a Good Shepherd, God has broken into history. It sounds as if the way forward is clear as can be.

And yet, the faith most of us live with day in, day out is often riddled with questions and confusion. The faith we proclaim here on Sunday often sounds so certain, but the way we believe it and live it can often seem fragile. Listen to a letter received by Philip Yancey, author of a book called *Reaching for the Invisible God.*

> Dear Sir:
>   I know there is a God: . . . I just don't know what to believe of Him. What do I expect from this God? Does He intervene upon request (often/seldom)? . . . I accept that I'm an immature believer: that my expectations of God are obviously not realistic. I guess I've been disappointed enough times that I simply pray for less and less in order not to be disappointed over and over. [1]

Yancey has received dozens of letters such as this one, and I was struck by how much it echoes comments I hear all the time. People come to church with some faith, or some pieces of faith, or some hope of finding faith, but they are often confused. How does this faith actually work? What can I expect from God? As another letter writer puts it, "How can I say I have faith in God when I constantly wonder if He is really there?" [2]

We talk so much in church about trusting God, about following Christ, that sometimes it's good to remind ourselves how mysterious and elusive this life of faith often is.

Even for the so-called experts, faith can be frustrating. Listen to this prayer written by one of the great theologians of the twentieth century, Karl Rahner:

> I should like to speak with you about my prayer, O Lord. . . . So often I consider my prayer as just a job I have to do, a duty to be performed. . . . You are so distant and mysterious. When I pray, it's as if my words disappear down some deep, dark well, from which no echo ever comes back to reassure me that they have struck the ground of Your heart.[3]

In the gospel lessons these last weeks of Easter, Jesus is actually addressing the disciples' anxiety and confusion. He's with them the night before his death, and his words are full of reassurance. "In my Father's house are many rooms," he said in the gospel last week. "I go to prepare a place for you." And in today's gospel: "I will not leave you orphaned. . . . In a little while the world will no longer see me, but you will see me." Orphaned—that's what they are going to feel like, as if their parents have left them. As if they are all alone with this fragile faith.

Faith for the disciples was not a consistent, clear experience of God or Jesus. They kept misunderstanding, getting things wrong, wanting to hold on tight when things were clear, panicking when things got scary. And after Easter the Risen Lord was even more confusing. He's there and then he's gone. Some see him, some don't. Even those who do see him often don't recognize him.

In fact, the whole Bible is filled with the tension between faith and doubt. By one calculation only a third of the 150 psalms are about joyful trust in God. More than half are about darkness and struggle and wondering where God is. One begins, "My God, my God why have you forsaken me?" Another with, "Out of the depths have I cried to you." And another cries out, "Return, O Lord; how long will you tarry?" The Book of Job is one long struggle to understand God's seeming absence and unfairness.

"Truly you are a God who hides himself," the prophet Isaiah says. Somehow that seems to be an essential part of God's way with us. John Wesley, who founded Methodism, and Martin Luther, the great reformer, both wrote of the times when their faith seemed to collapse.

The poet Emily Dickinson described her struggle this way: "We both believe and disbelieve a hundred times an Hour, which keeps Believing nimble."[4]

The Risen Lord we Christians follow is an elusive Lord. God refuses to be managed, to show up on command. The Holy One has an immense stake in our growth, our learning to live and to love, and that calls for God's standing back and creating space for us to live and choose. God works slowly, quietly, usually in unnoticeable ways. And when God speaks it is usually in hints and whispers that we can easily miss.

"God gives us just enough to seek him," novelist Ron Hansen writes, "and never enough fully to find him. To do more would inhibit our freedom, and our freedom is very dear to God."[5]

The fact is, we need our doubts and questions. That's what makes our faith grow. It's also what keeps our faith from becoming fundamentalist and destructive. One of the great dangers in our world is when religious faith does not permit doubt and questioning. The result can be authoritarianism, fanaticism, and even violence. We are seeing in the news every day the destructiveness of those who believe they are in possession of all truth. They lose the awareness that God's ways are not our ways. That God is first and last a mystery of love beyond our comprehension. That the God we meet in Jesus Christ can't be contained, or manipulated, or used as a club in a fight. When the mystery fades, so does real faith. At times God comes to us with great clarity and passion, but God also calls us to walk by faith, to trust in a mystery we can't fully comprehend.

And here's a surprise: It's often in the dark places, the places that seem farthest from God—the cancer, the death, the break-up, the terrible mistake. It's often there that we experience God holding us. Sometimes we can't even realize it at the time. But looking back later we see that there and then we were on holy ground.

God does not save us from the dark. But God goes with us into the dark, even if at the time we are not clearly aware of it.

Our Easter faith says that this elusive Lord is always with us, but we have to acquire new ways of seeing.

I was struck some years ago by a book called *The Snow Leopard* in which Peter Matthiessen described a remarkable trek across the Himalayas which he and his biologist friend took, ostensibly to study the rare blue sheep that live there.[6] But from the start there was also the elusive possibility that they might see the rarest and most beautiful of the great cats, the snow leopard. The snow leopard becomes for him his symbol for finding the mystery at the heart of life, for glimpsing the presence of God.

Only a handful of people have ever seen the snow leopard in the wild. It hides so well that you can stare at it from within a few yards and not see it. And, strangely, the ones who have seen it are those who have not directly gone looking for it, but have instead gone out to study the sheep, since the leopard feeds on the sheep and lurks around them.

And then, once in awhile, the mysterious one comes, and they are all of a sudden aware that they are seeing it. No amount of hard work can bring them this glimpse of the mystery. It only comes as they attend to the mundane tasks that brought them there, and then once in awhile they might catch a glimpse.

For those of us who seek Christ it often happens that way. We can't make him appear. No amount of hard work will do it. All we can really do is be faithful to our daily tasks as disciples, and as we do that keep praying, keep open, keep watching, for traces of our elusive Lord.

I was sitting with a couple at the dragged-out end of months of marital counseling. And finally there was nothing left to say. All the wrongs, all the hurt, all the mistakes on both sides were out, lying on the floor all around them. And she, and he, and I sat silent. For a long time. They knew then that the only way ahead was to start again to face what had happened, to forgive, to begin the healing process again. Would they say yes or no? You could sense Christ's presence in the room.

I was in a hospital room another time, as a woman was dying. It had all happened so fast it took our breath away. Her family was still stunned. There had been plenty of anger at God and everyone else too. But in that room at the end there was a peace, a sense that some holy presence was holding her and weeping with her.

We glimpse the wonders of God's world, as we sang in the hymn a few moments ago, in stars and thunder, mountain and stream, in Christ on the cross. We see Christ in the face of a child, or a homeless person on the street.

Those moments are not rare. There, in the midst of the events of our days, is this elusive Lord. Don't you sometimes sense Christ here in the thick of Sunday worship? Aren't there times when a glimpse of peace descends on you, even if only for a moment?

In fact, Jesus promises his disciples that no matter how orphaned they may feel, he will always be with them. "I am coming to you," he says, "because I live, you also will live. . . . I am in my Father, and you in me, and I in you." You see, so often it is hard to sense Christ "out there," as one more presence in our world, because Christ is actually in here, in you and me. We are in Christ as Christ is in us.

Given how mysterious this God is, how confusing it can be to trust when things are hard, I want to offer, with Philip Yancey's help, some guideposts for tracking this elusive Lord.

First, don't try to do it alone. Because all of us doubt and struggle with God's absence some of the time, we need each other's support and help on the journey, especially when the going gets tough. I need your faith to carry me sometimes, and sometimes you need mine.

Second, allow the good in your life to penetrate as deeply as the bad. No matter how difficult the situation, God is giving us so much to be grateful for in every day. Hold on to that when God seems far away. Relish it. Give thanks for it.

Third, find something that allows you to feel God's pleasure. You remember the sprinter Eric Liddell in the film *Chariots of Fire*, who told his sister, "God made me fast. And when I run, I feel his pleasure." What makes you feel God's pleasure? Hold on to that.

Fourth, create time daily to be still, to be open to the Christ Spirit, and to listen for where Christ is speaking to you.

And finally, keep looking for this Risen Lord where he said we'd find him. In the scriptures, in the bread and wine, with his friends, among the poor and struggling who need you.

"I will not leave you orphaned," Jesus says. He comes to be with us, but it will always be in ways that are surprising, unpredictable, unmanageable. Just what you would expect from this mysterious, elusive Lord.

Haggling Prayer

Luke 18:1–18

Every Sunday here at the Cathedral we welcome worshipers from across the country and around the world. And chances are on any given Sunday we will have as many joining us from the Commonwealth of Virginia as from any other. And so to you Virginians here today I want to say that I hope you're okay. It sounds as if things have gotten pretty stressful across the river. I just saw in the *Washington Post* a report about a woman in Manassas, Virginia, who was having some problems with her cable company.

Company technicians failed to show up for their scheduled installation of a new service. Then two days later they came but left with the job half done. Two days later they cut off all service. Determined not to give up, seventy-five-year-old Mona Shaw and her husband went to the local call center office to complain, but were told to wait on a bench outside in the August heat. Finally, after two sweaty hours the customer rep leaned out the door and said the manager had left for the day. "Thanks for coming!" he said.

Do you know the experience—when it seems as if you're dealing with inscrutable corporate powers that are treating you like a nobody?

Well, Mona Shaw decided she wasn't going to take it any more. The next morning she gathered up her husband and a solid claw hammer and said, "C'mon, honey, we're going to the cable company." And then when she walked into the office things got a little out of control. BAM! She smashed the customer rep's keyboard with the hammer. Then BAM! She hit the monitor. BAM! The telephone was next. People scattered and screamed, the police showed up, and off she went to the police station.[1]

I have to say, Virginians are a scrappy bunch!

My guess is that Mona Shaw is a lineal descendant of the widow we heard about in our gospel lesson this morning. This widow has her own problems, dealing with a crooked judge who couldn't care less about insignificant people like her. We don't know exactly what brought her to the judge. To be a widow in that society was about as vulnerable a position as you could have, and chances are she had lost her house or property. But this pushy, pestering woman was going to fight for what was right.

"Grant me justice," she demands again and again. She bothers the judge, irritates him. She pursues him on the streets of the city; she hounds him until he can't take it any more. She insists on what she believes is right, until finally the judge gives her what she demands. Her chutzpah carries the day.

Jesus told the disciples this story, our gospel lessons says, so that they "would pray always and not lose heart." If a mean-spirited, crooked judge will finally give in to a pushy widow, he was saying, how much more will a loving God respond to our prayers.

I don't know about you, but for many people prayer is one of the most confusing parts of faith. Does God hear our prayers? If so, why does it so often seem that our prayers go unanswered? What difference do our prayers really make? And what about all the prayers thrown at heaven down through the bloody stream of history? What ever happened to them?

Praying puts our faith on the line. Is there a God or not? Does this God really listen and care? Can or will this God respond to what we pray? Some have suggested that even if prayer doesn't change God, it can change us. Is that it? Is prayer only a way of talking ourselves into a new attitude and trusting things will work out for the best?

Recently many people I know have been praying for a close friend with cancer, and still he died three weeks after the cancer was diagnosed. I have prayed for broken marriages to be healed, for illnesses cruelly afflicting young people to be cured. And, at least, so far those prayers have gone unanswered. People around the globe have prayed for peace in Iraq and an end to the killing in Darfur. Not much progress there.

We could all make a list of unanswered prayers. Somerset Maugham in his autobiographical novel *Of Human Bondage* movingly portrays his main character Philip, born with a clubfoot, one day coming across the text from Mark's gospel that says, "Whatever you ask in my name you will receive it." He thought immediately that he could be healed. He imagined the freedom he would have at last to play soccer, how fast he could run, how people would stop staring at him because of his strange limp. And so he got down on his knees that night and prayed with all his heart to be healed. And then as he woke in the morning he hopefully touched one foot to the other, and realized that nothing was different. That was the night his religious faith ended.[2]

Earlier this week, the Cathedral offered an interfaith Pray for Peace concert, with rock stars such as Jackson Browne and Graham Nash, and leaders of the major faith traditions. In a press interview before, a skeptical interviewer asked an obvious question. "Why is this a prayer service? Do you really think these prayers will help bring peace?" It's a reasonable question. Haven't people been praying for peace for years now?

Of course, many people report that, in fact, their prayers have been answered—some 41 percent in a *U.S. News* and Beliefnet.com poll. But why are some prayers answered and not others? A couple from India miraculously escaped down the stairways of the World Trade Center on 9/11, and after that, converted to Christianity, with the husband becoming an evangelist. But what about the prayers of the other three thousand who perished?

There are plenty of guesses about why prayers seem to go unanswered. Maybe we are asking for the wrong thing, or maybe sometimes our faith isn't strong enough, or maybe God is giving us something another way, instead. Maybe God is doing us a favor by saying "No." As the writer C. S. Lewis once put it, "If God had answered all the silly prayers I've made in my life, where should I be now?"[3]

In fact, the Old and New Testaments are filled with accounts of prayers that were not answered—from Moses and David to the prophet Jeremiah, to Jesus himself, who in the Garden of Gethsemane prayed that he would be spared the death he faced. Prayer is a mystery.

Still, Jesus saw it as essential that we pray and not lose heart. Biblical prayer is like the prayer of that old widow—aggressive, demanding, insistent, shameless. Theologian Walter Wink says it's more like haggling in an outdoor bazaar than the polite lists of concerns we usually offer in our churches. It is Mona Shaw without the hammer. It is Jacob in our Old Testament lesson wrestling all night with the mysterious God-figure, insisting that he won't let go until he receives a blessing.

Yes, prayer means haggling, arguing, pushing, demanding. But here's the strange part. God already knows what's on our minds and hearts. God already wants for us more than we can ask or imagine. But the haggling is our way of being with God in the struggle of our days. Like a child with a parent, we pour out our needs and hopes and wants—not to give God new information, or to get something out of a divine Santa Claus. We do it as our way of being with God in it, working with God, sharing in God's own ache and struggle over our world.

For the sake of our freedom and dignity, God chooses to be limited in power and not to treat us as pawns in a chess game. What life would this be if every person's wishes and desires were answered? Instead, God calls us to live in a world where random events happen both beautiful and terrible—a world of Mozart and Hitler, of beautiful sunsets and destructive hurricanes, of healthy children and the daily deaths of thousands of children from AIDS and hunger. And it's a world where God's will is often not done—because of our human greed and selfishness and violence.

God responds to prayer, but with baffling unpredictability. Presumably, God could act alone without us, or, on the other hand, could leave it all up to us. But instead, God seeks to work with us, within the world and within our own spirits, to lead us and bless us and respond to our heart's desires. God is not a divine potentate, but a Loving Parent, a companion and friend, who wrestles with us and for us.

Prayer matters. In our prayers we open a new space, a new way for God to work in the world through our love, desires, and actions. It opens up a new force field, a new way for God's Spirit to move.

When I pray for my friend, I am God's companion, God's co-worker, caring for my friend. When we pray for peace, we envision a world that has not yet come, and we join our yearning with those of others across the world. And in doing that, we become small islands of peace and hope ourselves, and small channels of God's love that can become rivers and then oceans.

Prayers take time to be answered, sometimes years, even centuries. I know parents who have prayed fifty years for a troubled child. They do not lose heart. Who can count the prayers of American slaves over their nearly two centuries of slavery, or the activists in the civil rights movement, or the Christians in the Gulag in Siberia, or the native people of South Africa living under apartheid? They knew God was with them. But the forces arrayed against them were overwhelming. Still, they prayed and didn't lose heart. They called out to God, they found in God grace and strength to carry them. And, ultimately, over decades they prayed their way to freedom. Every prayer was an act of defiance—tough, shameless, demanding—an act of trust that the God of the universe was in their struggle with them.

Remember that we do not pray as deists or theists to a remote and abstract God beyond us, but as Christians who believe in a God in heaven who is also physically present on this earth inside human beings. And that means that our prayers will have real power to the extent that they lead to our own concrete actions.

We have to "put skin on our prayer," as someone has put it. If our friend or colleague is going through hard times and we offer a prayer for her, but never pick up the phone to call her, we will be praying as theists, not Christians. How is God supposed to heal her? By sending an e-mail from heaven? If we pray for peace, but do not forgive those who have hurt us, how can God actually bring peace? If we pray for the homeless, but make no effort to better their lives, that approach is theist, not Christian.

Writer Philip Yancey reports traveling around the world seeing Christians involved in remarkable ministries—in prisons and rehab centers, as surrogate mothers to children with AIDS in South Africa and as health workers specializing in leprosy in Nepal. He attended a conference in Wisconsin fighting sex trafficking and a Salvation Army conference for what is the third largest standing army in the world, only this one is mobilized to help the poor. He visited a vast complex in Roanoke, Virginia, that through the help of sixty churches grew into a shelter, education center, and clinic. Yancey interviewed the leaders of these ministries and learned that many of these projects began with what he calls "a crisis of prayer."

"God, why don't you do something about the AIDS orphans in Johannesburg or the homeless in Roanoke? Don't they break your heart?" they prayed. And inevitably, they found themselves echoing the prayer of the founder of World Vision: "Lord, may my heart be broken by what breaks your heart."[4] And those that prayed that prayer became the answers to their own prayers.

In a few moments we will offer our prayers for today. They are part of our haggling, pestering, wrestling, with God and for God, for the healing of our world. Let's pray them with all our heart. And then let us pray, "Lord, may our hearts be broken by what breaks your heart."

The key is that we pray always, and do not lose heart.

Does God Care?

Luke 13:1–9

The letter arrived in his mailbox completely unannounced. Novelist Reynolds Price had written a moving spiritual memoir about his struggle with excruciating cancer of the spinal cord, which had led to the loss of the use of his legs. Several years later a young medical student named Jim Fox, himself diagnosed with a vicious cancer, had picked it up and decided that Price was the one to ask the most urgent question of all: "Does God exist and does God care?" Price wrote a response in a little book called *Letter to a Young Man in the Fire*, and he included part of Fox's letter in it:

> I want to believe in a God who cares because I may meet him sooner than I expected. I think I am at the point where I can accept the existence of a God (otherwise I can't explain the origin of the universe), but I can't yet believe he cares about us. [1]

Does God exist and does God care? I once heard a professor call that "the only question." Is there a God we can depend on in a world where things go terribly wrong? It's a question that everyone ends up asking at some point, and some people wrestle with it all their lives. Every priest or minister has had to stand in front of a church and gaze into the numb, uncomprehending faces of parents who have lost their infant child, or of friends and family of a young man dead in a car accident, or of the children and husband of a remarkable mother in her fifties who has finally lost a long fight with breast cancer.

My guess is that just about every one of us has known what it means to sit on the mourner's bench and try to make sense of some terrible loss. Where is

God in this terrible tragedy? How could God let this happen? When terrible things happen, we want to understand.

But the questions get harder. What can people of faith make of the horrific events where people perish by the thousands and even millions? Sometimes it's a natural disaster, such as the tsunami that swept through the Indian Ocean in December of 2004, killing three hundred thousand people. When we think of the grief we Americans experienced over the death of three thousand on 9/11, this scale of loss is unimaginable. I read an account of a man standing in a coastal village in Indonesia who was completely devastated, having watched thousands of men and women washed away before his eyes. He just stood there crying, "There is nothing! There is nothing! Where is God? What is God?"[2]

But human disasters can be even worse. What do we make of the ten million lives that perished under Stalin, the six million Jews murdered by Hitler's Germany, and the tens and even hundreds of thousands who are being killed in Darfur? In Elie Wiesel's book *Night*, which is an autobiographical account of his experience as a boy in the Auschwitz concentration camp, we see a group of prisoners gathered around to watch two men and a boy be hanged at once. For half an hour they watch the three struggle between life and death, and as they struggle Wiesel hears a man ask, "Where is God? Where is He?"[3]

How do we reconcile all this with belief in a loving God? Evil isn't a problem for an atheist's worldview. If you believe in an absurd, uncaring universe you have no conflict. But for Christians the challenge is real. Archibald MacLeish in his play *J.B.*, about suffering and faith in God, puts the issue this way: "If God is God, [that is, if God is all-powerful], he is not good. And if God is good, he is not God [because he must be powerless to stop the suffering]."[4]

There have always been simplistic answers to why suffering happens. Sometimes you hear it said with confidence that this tragedy must be God's will, as if God chooses to torment his children. Sometimes you hear that God causes suffering to teach a lesson, or to punish evil. One of the comments I have heard many times is that suffering is somehow part of God's plan for this person; that suffering and loss are secretly part of some good God has in mind. Some say bitterly that God is indifferent to human tragedy, or there's no God at all. But none of these responses is adequate.

The scriptures themselves don't offer clear explanations. In the Old Testament, suffering is often seen as a penalty for wrongdoing. God tells Israel, "I will punish you for all your iniquities." God calls Israel in the Book of Deuteronomy to choose life or death, blessing or curse. Turn away from God and you will suffer, the texts say repeatedly.

And there is at least some truth to that. Societies that become absorbed with greed and injustice do eventually decline and perish. Nations that insist on polluting the air and water will one day pay a terrible price. Societies that encourage the use of guns as ways to solve problems will become more dangerous and violent themselves. Those who eat too much, or smoke, or gamble excessively, or engage in promiscuous sex are in one way or another putting themselves, their bodies, and spirits, at risk. There are consequences to destructive behavior.

You also hear perplexity in the Old Testament. Psalm 10 cries out, "Why, O Lord, do you stand off? Why do you hide yourself in times of trouble?" And in Psalm 22 we have words that Jesus himself cried out from the cross, "My God, my God, why have you forsaken me?" Where is God's justice and fairness?

The Book of Job in the Old Testament presents an unyielding rejection of the notion that bad things happen to bad people and good things to good. Job is a virtuous man in every way, and every possible thing that can go wrong with him does—the loss of his family, his property, his health. His friends come to console him and to try to figure out what he must have done wrong to bring all this on himself, but he insists that he is a good man. So he demands that God explain. By the book's end he never gets his explanation, but instead catches a glimpse of an immense, mysterious living God who will never abandon him.

Nicholas Wolterstorff is a philosopher at Yale whose son died at age twenty-five while climbing in the Alps alone. In his book *Lament for a Son*, Wolterstorff traces his wrestling with his loss and his refusal of all the clear answers.

> I cannot fit it all together saying, "[God] did it," but neither can I do so by saying, "There was nothing he could do about it. . . . I do not know why God did not prevent Eric's death . . . I do not know why God would let him fall . . . I cannot even guess. I can only, with Job, endure. "[5]

Jesus' friends in our gospel lesson don't understand, either. Some Galileans had been protesting, and the government officials had tracked them down and murdered them in the Temple. And soon after that a tower under construction at Siloam collapsed killing eighteen workers. The workers were killed by a natural disaster, like the victims of earthquakes and tsunamis. Were the victims evil? No, Jesus says, there is no correlation. As he says on another occasion, "God makes the sun to shine on the good and the bad; his rain to fall on the just and the unjust." Bad things happen to good and bad people.

So Jesus turns the question on its head. It's not a question about who deserves or doesn't deserve what. It's a question about your relationship with God. Turn to God, Jesus says to his listeners, repent, learn to trust God through good times and bad. That's the only thing that really matters.

I don't believe there is any way of holding together faith in a loving God and the suffering we see in this world without Christ's cross. We are taught to think of God as all-powerful, all-knowing, as the supreme ruler of the universe, in charge of everything.

But Christians believe that the one full revelation of God we have ever had was in the life, death, and resurrection of Jesus. There we didn't see an omnipotent ruler making things happen, we saw someone who was pure, unbounded love, who didn't command and impose his will but who called and invited, forgave and healed, confronted and encouraged.

God is Christlike. God is love. And love means not controlling, not micromanaging the world. Rather, God holds it, embraces it, and works within it, sometimes in surprising ways we call miracles, to seek to lead human beings into the communities of wholeness and equity for which they were made.

God chose not to create a world of puppets under divine control, but free creatures in a world that operates on its own terms. That freedom means that earthquakes happen, and so do beautiful sunsets. It produces brilliant athletes and physically challenged children. It's a world of remarkable brain cells, and also cancer cells. It makes possible a Mahatma Gandhi and an Osama bin Laden.

In fact, maybe the best analogy for God's way in the world is that of a parent. Parents cannot control what their children do or become. They love them, teach them, support them when they fail, confront them when they need it, but then they have to give them their freedom. It is a risk to let them walk to school or ride a bike or go off to college. They can't prevent car accidents, or calamities in college, or bad choices as adults. To love is to risk, to let go, and to be vulnerable to pain when one we love suffers. And God is like that.

Christians became convinced that when Jesus hung on that cross on that hill outside Jerusalem, it was God hanging there. It was God's declaration that when we suffer, God goes through the anguish with us, that when evil comes, God will bring healing and new life out of the worst that can happen. "I know what you are going through," God says. "I know what it is costing. I know I've called you to life in a dangerous world. But I am going through it all with you, and I promise you that there is life and more life for you."

"Where is God?" the angry prisoner cried again at Auschwitz as the crowd continued to watch their friends hanging on the gallows. And this time Wiesel says, "I heard a voice within me answer him: 'Where is He? Here He is—He is hanging here on this gallows.'"[6] On the cross God is united with us in our worst agony and loss.

"We're in it together, God and me," Wolsterstorff writes near the end of his book as he makes his way back from bottomless grief. "Every act of evil extracts a tear from God, every plunge into anguish extracts a sob from God."[7]

Jesus meant what he said. The question isn't why is there suffering? The question is whether we will trust this God who hung on a cross, and whether we can see that this God cares endlessly?

William Sloane Coffin, who was chaplain at Yale and minister at Riverside Church in New York for many years, had to endure the death of his own college-age son. Young Alex had been drinking and on the way home ran through a barrier and plunged into the waters of a river outside Manhattan. The night after he died a woman made the comment to Coffin, "I just don't understand the will of God." And Coffin let loose with the pent-up passion of a grieving father:

> I'll say you don't, lady! Do you think it was the will of God that Alex never fixed that lousy windshield wiper of his, that he was probably driving too fast, that he probably had had a couple of "frosties" too many . . . , that there were no streetlights and guard rail on the road?
>
> And in the sermon he preached for his son's death he declared, the one thing that should never be said when someone dies is, "It is the will of God." Never do we know enough to say that. My own consolation lies in knowing that it was not the will of God that Alex die; that when the waves closed over the sinking car, God's heart was the first of all our hearts to break.[8]

Today we are not given any explanation of human suffering. Instead, we are given Christ's Body broken for us, his Blood shed for us. Repent, Jesus says. Turn to the God who can make all your suffering and confusion bearable. Respond in love to the victims of the world's calamities. Hold fast to the God who is holding fast to you.

That is God's answer to the worst we face—no formulas, no theories. Just Jesus giving us his life, giving us God's life, and promising that nothing can ever separate us from that love.

The Silence of God

Luke 17:5–10

Listen to the words of one of the most admired Christians of the last hundred years:

> Lord, my God, who am I that You should forsake me? The Child of Love—and now become as the most hated one—the one You have thrown away as unwanted—unloved. I call, I cling, I want—and there is no One to answer—no One on Whom I can cling . . . Where is my Faith—even deep down right in there is nothing, but emptiness & darkness. [1]

Those are the words of Mother Teresa of Calcutta, written several decades ago, and just published in a collection of her writings called *Mother Teresa: Come Be My Light*. Mother Teresa was, of course, the winner of the Nobel Peace Prize and someone revered as the model of self-sacrificing compassion because of her decades of ministry among the sick and dying on the streets of Calcutta. She has been admired not only for her remarkable work, but for the seeming depth and joy of her faith.

Now we have this book that details the many years of Mother Teresa's spiritual despair and her sense of God's absence and abandonment. Discussions about religion, already one of the hottest topics in America, heated up all over again over the last few weeks as atheists claimed her now as one of their own, and theologians hastened to put her experience in a broader spiritual context.

Clearly the publishing of these notes and letters has touched a nerve. Doesn't faith require clear convictions? Can great believers have great doubts? What is religious faith anyway?

One problem is that the language of faith itself often seems to promise clarity. People hear in church talk of what God is "saying" to us, or "calling" us to do. Isn't it our job to listen when God "speaks"? And prayer is often described as a conversation or dialogue, although many people I know grow weary of a conversation when it seems as if they are the only ones doing the talking.

And doesn't it seem unfair that back in biblical days God seemed to speak clearly? "Sure," I can imagine you saying, "Moses was a great hero leading the Jewish people to freedom. If I heard a voice speaking to me out of a burning bush, I'd be a hero, too." And if I had been in the crowd around Jesus when a voice came down out of heaven declaring, "This is my Son, my Beloved; listen to him," well, I think even I could get my act together and follow.

But things have changed. People don't hear voices much any more, or if they do we either think they're fooling us or they need professional help. Now we read those old biblical stories with a sense that story and metaphor have enriched the way events from long ago have been remembered. In fact, my hunch is that one of the chief challenges for faith these days is the mystery of God's seeming silence.

You may remember the film *Love and Death* in which the Woody Allen character at one point turns his eyes toward heaven and pleads with God to give him an answer to his question. He gets nothing but silence. And so he begs again, saying he would be willing to settle for just a few words. Again, only silence. Finally, in desperation he says he'll take anything, even a cough! And the deafening silence sends him away stewing in frustration. Allen taps into a hidden fear underneath prayer and the life of faith for many. Is anyone there? And I think it's that fear and frustration that feeds our reluctance to pray and the cautiousness of our faith.

And so when we learn that maybe the most famous Christian of our time experienced long stretches of God's absence, it gets our attention.

In 1946, after seventeen years as a teacher in Calcutta with her order of nuns, Mother Teresa experienced an intense calling to give up teaching and work in "the slums" of the city with "the poorest of the poor." But soon after her work had begun, she began to go through what she described as "dryness," "darkness," and "loneliness," while all the while maintaining her publicly cheerful demeanor.

There was one brief period when her faith blossomed again, but it soon vanished. By 1961, with the help of a wise spiritual guide, she came to accept this emptiness and darkness as part of her own calling. "I have come to love the darkness—for I believe now that it is part, a very, very small part, of Jesus' darkness and pain on earth."[2] As one Roman Catholic commentator puts it, "I've never read a saint's life where the saint has such an intense spiritual darkness."[3]

Mother Teresa's letters pull back the veneer of a seemingly perfect spiritual life, the kind we expect in our spiritual heroes. In this case, they show a very human woman called by Christ, and yet confused and devastated by how elusive her faith seemed to be.

Doubt, struggle, and the absence of God are nothing new for people of faith. The psalms, which are the Bible's Prayer Book, are full of complaints that God has deserted his people.

Lord, why have you cast me off, why do you hide your face from me? (Psalm 88)

How long, Lord, will you hide yourself from my sight? (Psalm 89)

There are many references in the Old Testament to God "turning his back" on the Hebrew people, a way of speaking of God's mysterious absence. And, of course, Jesus, hanging on the cross, seems to have experienced complete abandonment by God: "My God, my God, why have you forsaken me?" (Mark 15:34) The great mystics such as John of the Cross believed that experiences of "night," or darkness, or the absence of God are inevitable stages in the life of faith. We need them to help us let go of the small, inadequate images of God we keep concocting for ourselves.

John Wesley was perhaps the greatest Christian of eighteenth-century England. In a time when the church had grown rigid and dry, Wesley traveled by horseback all over England preaching to miners and laborers in crowds of thousands, and breathing new life into the tired Church of England. Listen, though, to this letter to his brother Charles, written in a dark time:

And yet this is the mystery, I do not love God. I never did . . . Therefore I never believed in the Christian sense of the word. Therefore I am only an honest heathen, . . . And yet to be so employed of God! . . . I am borne along, I know not how, that I can't stand still.[4]

Wesley's life was a muddle of mistakes, an unhappy marriage, terrible misjudgments, of dark nights of the spirit. But he proved to be the greatest witness to Jesus Christ of his century. Maybe knowing and loving God isn't about a clear, neat package of beliefs, unstoppable faith, and flawless achievements.

In fact, the journey of faith takes us through the terrain of mystery, through times of clarity and confusion, of presence and absence. God is the incomprehensible one, the vast presence inside and outside us, who holds all existence in being, and who can't be captured in our images and ideas. We are in God as fish are in water. We can no more analyze God than a fish can the ocean. As St. Augustine put it, "If you understand, it is not God."[5] God will always be elusive.

Faith is an act of trust—trusting in God in spite of our doubts and confusions. The opposite of faith is certainty, not doubt. It is not about a well-ordered set of convictions and an entirely satisfying relationship with a clear God. In fact, we need uncertainty and doubt. "If there is no room for doubt," Frederick Buechner once said, "there is no room for me."[6]

Something bad happens to religion that has no room for doubt. It becomes arrogant, rigid, all about self and certainty. Religious scholar Karen Armstrong says in fact that the problem with religion today is certitude, the absolute certainty that one is right, in full possession of the truth. Absolute certainty gave us 9/11. We need less certainty, more mystery, more trust, more humility.[7]

After all, Jesus put no preconditions on his disciples about believing certain things. "Follow me," he says, not "believe these things." Live my way, learn what trusting a mysterious, loving God in this complex world means. That's what faith means—taking the step to come along—back to church, into a class or ministry, into an AA meeting, offering forgiveness in spite of your uncertainty or anger. Faith is trusting, risking, betting on the love and power of God, and then finding the confirmation along the way.

In our gospel lesson for today Jesus has been explaining just what it will take to follow him—loving your enemy, forgiving seventy times seven. It sounds overwhelming, and so the disciples cry out in exasperation, "Increase our faith!" Make our faith stronger, clearer, more confident!

But did you catch his response? "If you had faith the size of a mustard seed you could say to this mulberry tree, 'Be uprooted and planted in the sea,' and it would obey you." A mustard seed is infinitesimally small. But if you have even that much faith, you can move a huge mulberry tree, and in Matthew's gospel Jesus says you could move mountains. What matters is not how big and strong your faith is, but what God can do with even the smallest amount of trust we can offer.

And that, we now see, was Mother Teresa's story. It is moving and sometimes heartbreaking to read her accounts of her broken, limping faith, and the long dryness and sense of God's absence. In her letters she is no superhuman saint, but one of us, a good and faithful woman doing what she believed Jesus had called her to do, wrestling with her own darkness and despair. And yet, what great good she did.

I found myself asking questions as I read the account of her inner struggles. Should she have stayed so long in Calcutta among the desperately poor? Might she have had a deeper sense of God's presence if she had moved on to a less exhausting ministry? And yet, in giving up even the sense of assurance and joy in God's presence, she touched the lives of so many thousands of suffering people. It looks as if she sacrificed even her spiritual life for the sake of those she served.

We Christians believe that a great, mysterious God is continually seeking us and speaking through the experiences of our world—in the beauty of nature, the comments of a friend, our delight in a child, in the suffering we see in the news and the guilt at our failure, and, above all, as we read the scriptures and receive the bread and wine. God's presence and absence, God's closeness and baffling elusiveness in our life together, all make up the ongoing journey into discovering God's love for us.

"Increase our faith!" we probably all would say. But it only takes a mustard seed's worth, not something heroic and demanding up front. Just a little at a time, enough to keep on the journey, enough to keep growing, to keep listening for God's leading, and enough to be doing the only thing that really matters, learning how to love. With that mustard seed faith Mother Teresa poured herself out in love, and it moved mulberry trees and mountains. That's something we can do too.

God, Science, and the Life of Faith

Isaiah 40:21–31; Mark 1:29–39

The day was dimming. My fellow backpackers and I had been hiking all day, and had finally pitched our camp at eleven thousand feet. We were cleaning up after supper when a friend began yelling for us to "come look, come look!" And so we dropped everything and gathered at the bluff edge where three immense fourteen-thousand-foot peaks loomed over us. The sun was almost gone, and everything was bathed in deep red and purple hues. Soon, the sky was darkening enough for the stars to begin appearing. We settled in to watch, and one by one the lights came out, until the night sky was teeming with glittering stars. We tried to help each other trace the shape of the Big Dipper and Orion. Some of the stars were so thickly clustered that they looked like mystical clouds. It was breathtaking.

I remember feeling overwhelmed that moment with the immensity of the universe—God's splendor shining down from millions of light-years away. It must have been something like what Isaiah in our Old Testament lesson today must have been feeling when he had God speak some of the most beautiful words in the scriptures:

> Have you not known? Have you not heard?
> Has it not been told you from the beginning?
> Have you not understood from the foundation of the earth?
> It is [the Lord God] who sits above the circle of the earth,
> and its inhabitants are like grasshoppers;
> who stretches out the heavens like a curtain,
> and spreads them like a tent to live in;
> who brings princes to naught,
> and makes the rulers of the earth as nothing.

To the despairing people of Israel in exile, with their own nation in ruins, Isaiah offered a vision of a grand ruler of the cosmos, who reigns over both nature and history. Because of this God, Isaiah says, you can hope again.

It's not hard to sense God's presence in the night sky on a beautiful evening, or in the vast sweep of the universe, but for the last five centuries the sense that God is present in our physical world has been disappearing, especially among many scientists. In fact, things have been going badly between religion and science since at least the sixteenth century.

Copernicus and Galileo, brave scientists of those early years, discovered something that was to shake the world—that the sun, not the earth, is the center of our solar system. Galileo spent the last eight years of his life under house arrest for trying to convince the pope of this new cosmology. Sir Isaac Newton in the early 1700s shook the world by introducing the notion that the solar system and our own life here on earth operate by immutable laws and mathematical formulas, not simply by acts of God.

And then along came Charles Darwin two centuries later, who set the world on fire with his declaration that all life, including human life, emerged over millions of years of evolution, not in the six days described in the creation story in Genesis. This led to the famous Scopes Monkey Trial in 1925 in Dayton, Tennessee, pitting fundamentalists arguing for the Bible's six days of creation against the new scientific view. As a result of that battle much of the scientific world began to dismiss religion as a primitive leftover from a time of superstition. And it drove people of faith in two directions. Fundamentalists saw science as a threat to their literal understanding of the Bible, and so reacted vehemently to disturbing new insights. But there were many religious people who welcomed scientific exploration as the unfolding discovery of how God's world really works.

That war between religion and science rages on even as we speak. Now it's framed as a battle between Darwin's theory of evolution and something called "intelligent design." The advocates of intelligent design argue that evolution is just another theory, entirely unproven and full of holes. And because of this they insist that students should learn about other "theories," such as the notion that there is an intelligent designer behind the world who created and shaped everything.

Intelligent design advocates argue that some things, such as the human eye, are "irreducibly complex," so much so that they couldn't have emerged through evolution and natural selection. So there had to be an initial designer to put all the pieces together.

School boards and courts have gotten into the act. In Dover, Pennsylvania, for example, the school board ordered that a teacher in every science class read a statement insisting that evolution is only a theory, not fact, and that intelligent design is an alternative explanation. Soon afterward the board was voted out of office.

The intelligent design argument can sound pretty reasonable, can't it? But in fact it represents a confusion of categories, a thrusting of religion into a domain that should belong to science alone. Science exists for the unfettered pursuit of understanding through observation, experimentation, formulating theories based on the evidence, and testing them. But intelligent design makes claims that can't be tested because they are based solely on conjecture and faith. That doesn't mean there isn't truth in this idea of God as creator and sustainer of the world; it just means that this isn't science. And then there is what seems to me the deepest flaw in intelligent design. If God is shaping every part of the universe directly, why has God built in hurricanes like Katrina, or the AIDS virus, or malaria germs?

Many scientist argue that science and religion are two separate but compatible realms—what the evolutionary biologist Stephen Jay Gould called "non-overlapping magisterial." [1]

Science speaks with authority, Gould says, in the realm of what the universe is made of and why it works the way it does. And religion holds sway over questions of ultimate meaning and moral value.

Both science and religion can claim too much. Science can claim that we humans have outgrown religion, that everything in our existence can be explained in terms of physics, chemistry, and biology, a view called "scientism." Carl Sagan, for example, in his famous television series *Cosmos*, declared that the cosmos is the sum total of all there is or ever will be.[2] How does he as a scientist know that? That in itself is a faith statement, and its claim ignores the most profound parts of our existence—sacrificial love, awe, compassion, yearning, gratitude, delight.

But religion too can claim too much. It isn't religion's job to explain how the world works. It is to help us to know what, or who, is behind it all. It is to tell us why we're here on this earth and how we should live.

Writing in *Time* magazine not long ago, Francis Collins, director of the National Genome Research Institute and a person of faith, said, "I see no conflict between what the Bible tells me about God and what science tells me about nature. If God chose to use the mechanisms of evolution to create you and me, who are we to say that wasn't an absolutely elegant plan?"[3] Religion and science need each other. As Albert Einstein put it, "Religion without science is blind. Science without religion is lame."[4]

In fact, science can offer tantalizing hints of how God has shaped the cosmos. For example, some scientists are pointing to the stunning balance of forces in the original Big Bang that was necessary for the universe to expand and for life to emerge. The English physicist Roger Penrose once estimated that the odds against a cosmos as suitable as this one to human life to be one in ten to the three-hundredth power—a figure larger than the number of atomic particles believed to exist in the universe.

But to use this as definitive proof of a designer goes too far. We should see these as hints of a harmony we can only glimpse, pointers to the fingerprints of God for those who have discovered God for themselves in a journey of faith. And Christian faith invites us to know this God personally, directly, not simply as an idea, a theory, but as a person, a loving Father, a life-giving Mother, a Companion, a Savior, a Presence at work to lead, heal, strengthen, and sustain.

We heard in our gospel today stories of Jesus healing. He heals Simon's mother-in-law, and then crowds thronged around him as he healed many more. The God of the universe, the gospels tell us, is deeply engaged in bringing wholeness and healing, peace and new life, to individual human beings such as you and me.

And that is the God who meets us in our passage from Isaiah:

> Have you not known? Have you not heard?
> The Lord is the everlasting God,
> the Creator of the ends of the earth.
> He does not faint or grow weary; his understanding is unsearchable.
> He gives power to the faint, and strengthens the powerless.

Those words reach beyond anything science could tell us. They declare that we are living in the middle of a miracle of generosity and love beyond anything we can imagine. This is a God who cares about the powerless, the weak, the broken, a God whose heart reaches out to the victim of Katrina, to the starving child in Mozambique, to the struggling and heartbroken here at home. And then Isaiah describes how God can come to their aid:

> Those who wait for the Lord shall renew their strength,
> they shall mount up with wings like eagles
> they shall run and not be weary,
> they shall walk and not faint.

John Claypool, an old friend and one of the finest preachers of the last generation, once gave a sermon about how this passage helped him through the darkest time in his life.[5] His nine-year-old daughter had been stricken with leukemia, and after an eighteen-month fight entailing excruciating pain she died. Two weeks later John climbed up in the pulpit to give testimony to how he had survived that terrible ordeal and what difference his faith had made. He used the words I just read to say that God has three different ways of coming to us in crisis.

Sometimes, he said, help comes in the form of pure strength and ecstasy, enabling us "to mount up with wings like eagles." Sometimes we are given an almost supernatural power to cope with a crisis and endure. But he reported that that never happened for him in this terrible ordeal.

Sometimes God comes with the energy to go to work on a problem—"to run and not be weary." God gives us the inspiration and intelligence to find a solution. The doctors and the Claypools were doing everything they could to fight what was happening. But again, nothing worked.

But Isaiah tells us, he said, that God has one more way—the capacity "to walk and not faint." For those looking for spectacular rescue, that may not sound like much. After all, who wants to creep along, inch by inch, just barely staying conscious and avoiding fainting? It may not seem like much, he said, but that was the form that God's help took. Sometimes there is no way to soar, no way to run. All you can do is trudge one step after another, barely holding on. The hardest thing he faced in all this, he says, was his own helplessness. "All I could do was stand there by the bed and give [my daughter] a sip of water now and then and rub her and assure her, and it seemed like so little in the face of such an immensity."

Down at the bottom, when his life was at its lowest, John Claypool found that God was giving him the one gift he could not survive without—the gift of endurance, the capacity to walk and not to faint.

We meet this living God in the depths of our spirits, in a dimension far beyond what science can touch. We sense this God on a starry night, or in times when peace and joy come unexpectedly, in times of prayer and worship, in yearning for a just world for everyone.

Thanks be to God for all that science can teach us. We must let science be science. But thanks above all for the great faithfulness of the God who comes to us to renew our strength, so that we can "mount up with wings like eagles," we can "run and not be weary," and even when things are at their hardest, "we can walk and not faint."

The Night Visitor

If Nicodemus had come to the National Cathedral, I imagine he would have sat about three-fourths of the way back, somewhere over on the side. Some Sundays he would have slipped in early to have a few minutes of peace and quiet to let his racing mind throttle down at least a little. He would have loved the anonymity of this vast place with its immense arching grandeur, a good place to be left alone to wonder about God and his own life. And my guess is that he would have slipped out quietly at the end, with nothing more than a nod to the priest at the door.

The Nicodemus we heard of in our gospel this morning is our contemporary—looking for answers for his life but playing it safe. He wants to find God but he isn't at all sure what would happen if he did. He's looking for something more in his life but is reluctant to take a risk.

"Now there was a Pharisee named Nicodemus, a leader of the Jews. He came to Jesus by night." So John begins the story of a proud, cautious man who wants to meet this teacher from the hills of Galilee. This Pharisee is a powerful figure—a "leader of the Jews," maybe one of the Sanhedrin, the "Supreme Court" for the Jewish people.

Jesus is making quite a stir. Many see him as dangerous. But others say he knows God. He speaks with authority. And Nicodemus wants to see for himself, but privately, by night, when no one would spot him, no one would know of his meeting with this noisy outsider.

If it weren't so profound, Nicodemus' conversation with Jesus would sound ludicrous. They keep talking, but there isn't much communication: "Rabbi, we know that you are a teacher who has come from God . . ." "We know," the words of an insider, maybe a little smug, a little pretentious. Let's talk, Jesus, teacher to teacher, Marine to Marine. *We know* what's up here. *We know* how God works and doesn't.

But Jesus' response sails right past that cozy beginning. "I tell you, no one can see the kingdom of God without being born from above."

Where did that come from? So much for a friendly little chat. We aren't talking about a safe journey to know God just a little better. Jesus says, You have to be born from above, or born again—the Greek word can mean either.

Born again—that's a controversial phrase for many, I imagine. It's been badly used by some fundamentalists to shut down thinking and exploration and growth. One moment, one decision for Christ and you have a package of answers. You can flip open the Bible for a set of oracles for every detail of your life. You don't need to question any more.

But of course Jesus was opening up life's possibilities, not closing them down. He wanted to deepen the mystery of life, not shrink it. You have to start over, he was saying, with a life and energy from beyond you. You want to have your same old life just the way it is, and God, too. But it won't work that way.

Years ago C. S. Lewis wrote, "The terrible thing, the almost impossible thing, is to hand over your whole self—all your wishes and precautions—to Christ. But it is far easier than what we are all trying to do instead. For what we are trying to do is to remain 'ourselves,' to keep personal happiness our great aim, and yet at the same time to be 'good.' We are all trying to let our mind and heart go their own way—centered on money or pleasure or ambition—and hoping, in spite of this, to behave honestly and chastely and humbly. And that is exactly what Christ warned us you could not do."[1] You need to start over, Jesus said. Born again.

Several years ago I read an account of a series of conversations the famous French existentialist Albert Camus had with a Methodist minister named Howard Mumma. Mumma was serving an American church in Paris in the 1950s when he noticed in the back of the church a man in a dark suit surrounded by admirers, and eventually the two met and developed a close friendship.

There had always been rumors that Camus was drawn to Christian faith, but he had never converted. Mumma remembers him saying one evening, "The reason I have been coming to church is because I am seeking. I'm almost on a pilgrimage—seeking something to fill the void I am experiencing . . . I am searching for something the world is not giving me."

Camus knew the Bible well, and of all the characters there the one he was most drawn to was Nicodemus. In talking about Nicodemus one day Camus asked Mumma, "What does it mean to be born again, to be saved?" And Mumma replied, "To me to be born again is to enter anew or afresh into the process of spiritual growth. It is to receive forgiveness. It is to wipe the slate clean. You are ready to move ahead, to commit yourself to new life, a new spiritual pilgrimage."

Mumma reports that at that Camus looked at him with tears in his eyes and said, "Howard, I am ready. I want this. This is what I want to commit my life to."[2] Shortly after this conversation happened, Camus died in a car accident.

Born again—it's an offer Camus found compelling. It sounds daunting, but it's an invitation and a promise that there's a richer and deeper life ahead.

Of course, Nicodemus has no idea what Jesus is talking about. "How can anyone be born after growing old? Can someone enter a second time into the mother's womb and be born?"

But Jesus then confuses things even more: "No one can enter the kingdom of God without being born of water and Spirit. The wind blows; you hear the sound. You do not know where it comes from or where it is going." Water, wind, Spirit—those are the keys to this new life. John the Baptist was baptizing in the Jordan River, with water of washing, cleansing. Rebirth means naming where we've been caught, our self-absorption, our drivenness, our narrowness, confessing it, then starting again.

Rebirth happens in the Spirit, which is to say we don't do it ourselves. It comes from beyond us, like the wind. You know what wind is. It's the air that's around you all the time, like God's presence. You don't notice it because it's in everything. But sometimes the air starts moving. You can't tell where it comes from, or where it's going. Rebirth is like that. God moving, stirring.

Sometimes a person comes into our lives. We fall in love, or make a friend, or find a mentor, and life takes on a new shape. Sometimes we read the right book at the right time, and all of a sudden everything shines with a different light. I could name three or four books that have done that for me. Sometimes an event happens—the alcoholic has a car accident and quits drinking; the close brush with cancer makes the old priorities look shallow; a terrorist attack makes you rethink your career plan. Wind, spirit blow in our lives.

It happened for writer Anne Lamott on a day when life looked completely hopeless. As she describes the moment in her autobiography *Traveling Mercies*, a friend turns up and takes her on a walk, which turns lighthearted and refreshing, and it leads Lamott to say this:

> It's funny where we look for salvation and where we actually find it. . . . This is the most profound spiritual truth I know: that even when we're most sure that love can't conquer all, it seems to anyway. It goes down into the rat hole with us, in the guise of friends and there it swells and comforts. It gives us second winds, third winds, hundredth winds. It struck me that I have spent so much time trying to pump my way into feeling the solace I used to feel in my parents' arms. But pumping always fails you in the end. The truth is that you don't rise up until you get way down—the mud, the bottom. But there someone enters that valley with you, that mud, and it saves you again.[3]

Rebirth. New life.

And we aren't born again only once. It happens again and again as we start clinging to our lives again and have to learn to let go. It happens when life knocks us down again, and God again reaches into the valley of the shadow of death and picks us up.

It may bring with it God's summons to give our time to a cause that matters, or our money. It may mean a decision actually to plunge into classes and let this Christian faith take you to a new place. It may mean asking why we were put on earth—what is the gift only you or I can give to the world?

One of the most thrilling things to me about this National Cathedral is that it is a Nicodemus place. This awe-inspiring place is big enough for every-one—for visitors and tourists, for lovers of beauty and seekers, for people of little faith and much, for the already committed and the tentative. And we gather here in confusing times, when, for example, the word "Christian" is a word being wielded by politicians on both the right and the left, when the word itself is a promise of hope for many and a cause of fear for others. We live in a driven, anxious society, and we come seeking hope, clarity, and peace.

And to this Nicodemus place Jesus speaks the same word. You must be born anew. Be open to where God is taking you. Look for what fresh winds might blow here, what new word God may speak to you in these times.

One thing is clear: This new birth isn't planned. It isn't something you can set out to do. It is, to use our gospel's term, "from above." Something happens to you, gets hold of you, when you're not looking.

Well, at the end of our lesson, poor Nicodemus still doesn't get it and says, "How can this be?" And at that Jesus takes him to the heart of the matter: "God so loved the world, that he gave his only Son, so that everyone who believes in him may not [be lost] but may have eternal life." Martin Luther called this the gospel in summary.

I can't give you four easy steps to a new life, Jesus is saying. God is doing something so much grander than that. The Creator of the universe loves you—yes you—enough to hang on a cross to set you free. The answer to your search is to accept that love, and to let yourself be led by the Spirit's breeze.

We aren't told what happened to Nicodemus as a result of his nighttime meeting. Apparently nothing did immediately. It must have taken some time for it all to sink in. But something shifted somewhere, because we see him two more times. He's in the Temple later when Jesus is being accused by crowds demanding he be arrested. One man stands up to defend him. His name is Nicodemus.

And at the very end, Jesus is dead, crucified, and there is Nicodemus. This time he isn't there at night as a seeker, but as a disciple, helping take Jesus' body away.

The man who came with his questions, who couldn't make heads or tales of it all, somehow gets it by the end. Nicodemus said "yes" to God. He followed Christ. He was born anew. It made all the difference.

And it can for you too.

The Miracle of Forgiveness

Matthew 18:21–35

I will never forget a riveting talk given in a forum at a parish I served in Chicago some years ago. A distinguished Shakespeare professor was asked to talk about a faith struggle he had been through, and he told us of the tragedy of his son's death as a result of a careless dentist. His son had had a heart murmur, something the dentist knew, but the dentist forgot to take the necessary precautions to protect the boy, and an infection settled into his heart that within days had killed him.

This gentle father stood before that forum and talked of how, after getting through the initial shock and grief, his deepest desire was for revenge. He described how badly he wanted to hurt back for what had been done to his son and his whole family. What else could set the world right after that man had so wrecked it? He said he thought of suing the dentist, but what kind of money would that be, money gained by the loss of his son? How else could he hurt him, he wondered? What could ever make up for that loss?

How do we deal with the hurts, the wounds that come our way? How do you? Some time ago I sat over lunch and caught up with a friend I hadn't seen in nearly twenty years. There was much ground to cover, but our talk quickly focused on the trauma he had gone through over the past four or five years. In that time, he had come to find out, his wife had been involved in a series of extramarital affairs, had managed to spend up virtually all the family savings, and caused great pain to their children.

Even though my friend had known the full story for over two years, the rage and shock were still raw. He said to me, "I know I need to forgive her, but how could I even begin? How do I forgive?" With wounds such as these, or with wounds much smaller, the question is the same. How do I forgive?

Today's gospel lesson is the second in a row in which Jesus talks about the fundamental human need to forgive. For a species such as ours, riddled with selfishness, short tempers, cruelty, and betrayal, forgiveness is not a luxury. We cannot live without it.

You may know the old story about a woman who was having her portrait painted. When it was finished she complained, "It doesn't do me justice!" The artist then replied, "Madam, it isn't justice you need; it's mercy."

Mercy is the deepest need of us all. The past bears its full share of failures, disappointments, and wounds. So the question is, what power will the past play in our lives? Are we going to continue to be bound by the painful parts of it, or can we find our way to freedom?

In fact, Jesus put forgiveness at the center of everything. It is at the heart of the Lord's Prayer, "Forgive us our trespasses as we forgive those who trespass against us." Often when he encountered someone in need of healing, the first thing he would say to them is "Your sins are forgiven." He told stories of prodigal sons and lost sheep and lost coins, which are all stories of forgiveness. And of course he died on a cross saying, "Father, forgive them, for they do not know what they are doing."

In our gospel lesson this morning Peter asks Jesus, "Lord, if another member of the church should sin against me how often should I forgive? As many as seven times?" In other words, how much is enough? What are the limits of my having to forgive? When do I get to say that's it, I'm not going to try any more?

But Jesus replies, "Not seven times, I tell you, but seventy times seven," which is his way of saying it never ends. There is no real life without forgiveness. Forgiveness for Jesus isn't simply an isolated act but a way of life.

Of course much of the worst cruelty of the last century has been because of people's unwillingness to forgive. Many historians say that the Second World War might never have happened if the Allied powers had been less vengeful toward Germany after defeating it in the first Great War.

The Israelis and Palestinians have been locked for decades in a bitter conflict, and the violent attacks and reprisals, the wounding and being wounded, seem endless. Both sides have been damaged immeasurably. And yet . . . to remain locked in the resentments of the past only makes shaping a new future impossible.

Into this bitter web of wounding comes Jesus calling us to the miracle of forgiveness. It is a miracle because it shatters the chain of cause and effect. It sets people free from prisons of hatred and recrimination. It heals relationships and creates the possibility of new life.

We should be clear what forgiveness is not. It doesn't mean saying the offense never happened. It did. It isn't saying that everything is right away okay, because often it is not.

Forgiving is not forgetting. Memories linger, and they should. It is about remembering that a person is more than this act that has hurt me, and it means remembering that I too have a history, that I have hurt people as well.

Forgiveness doesn't depend on the other person's being sorry. Sorrow makes it easier, but forgiveness isn't about the other person, but about me. It is about changing how I see and relate to someone who has hurt me.

Forgiveness doesn't mean there shouldn't be punishment or consequences or restitution. Society has laws for our life together and they need to be honored.

And finally, forgiveness doesn't mean staying in a destructive situation. The struggle to forgive also calls us to refuse to be wounded continually, either by an unjust government, or an abusive spouse, or a destructive relationship.

Forgiveness has its own clear message: "I am furious at you for what you have done. It has hurt me and continues to. BUT, I refuse to stay trapped in my rage. I am going to forgive you because I know that you are more than what you have done to me. And I know that we both need God's forgiveness. I want to let go of this, and begin again with a clean slate, and leave the rest in God's hands."

At its core, forgiveness is about discovering who I am in relation to God and everyone else. It's what Jesus is getting at in the parable he tells in the gospel this morning of a palace servant who was forgiven a vast debt of ten thousand talents and then refused to forgive a much smaller amount.

Forgiveness, Jesus is saying, begins not with an act but a recognition— that all of us are in debt, all of us need mercy.

And so the heart of forgiveness is a profound act of letting go. The word for forgiveness in Greek and the Aramaic Jesus would have spoken means, "to release," "to let go," "to surrender." We decide to release our grip on the hatred, rage, and hurt, and claim our place in God's ceaseless love and forgiveness.

The steps are simple. First, face up to the hurt and decide to take your time in this work of forgiveness. Second, when the pain washes over you, keep letting go of it as much as you can. Slowly it will get easier. And most importantly, pray for the ability to forgive, and pray for the person who hurt you. Try to see that person in the light of God's love. Ask for the healing power of Christ to give you the power to release the anger.

We have to be willing to stay at this forgiveness thing. Seventy times seven, Jesus said. Sometimes it can take years. In one of her books writer Anne Lamott describes her struggles to forgive her mother through the years. "I prayed for my heart to soften," she wrote, "to forgive her and to love her for what she did give me—life, great values, a lot of tennis lessons, and the best she could do. Unfortunately, the best she could do was terrible. . . . And my heart remained hardened toward her." [1]

And so, Lamott says, for the first two years after her mother's death, she kept her mother's ashes in her son's closet. But slowly Lamott was able to move them to a corner of the living room. And that was for her a major event. She says that Jesus understands that things like forgiving a mother take time. "I don't think he was rolling his eyes impatiently at me while she was in the closet. . . . I don't think much surprises him: This is how we make important changes—barely, poorly, slowly. And still, he raises his fist in triumph."[2]

That's the power the world needs for our healing. That's the power my Shakespeare professor friend discovered on the far side of revenge, as did my friend whose wife had betrayed him. Today is the day of the annual Unity Interfaith Walk, which arose in response to the events of 9/11 seven years ago. Several hundred people of many faiths come together to face the divisions of the past and to mark their determination to see healing and reconciliation. We Christians call that forgiving seventy times seven.

I read recently than on the day that the Civil War ended, a group gathered outside the White House and President Lincoln came out to speak to them. A band was there ready to play. The president spoke briefly about the horrors of war and then joked some, as he often did. People were elated. Lincoln talked too about how important it was to heal the nation's wounds and bring everyone together again. Then he called on the band to play something. The crowd was prepared for "The Battle Hymn of the Republic," which had become their theme song. But instead the president asked the surprised band director to play "Dixie." "That tune is now federal property," he said, and it's "good to show the rebels that with us in power, they will be free to hear it again." For a long moment everyone stood there stunned, looking at each other. The band hadn't performed it in years. But after a lengthy pause it began to play, and they say there wasn't a dry eye in the crowd.[3]

"How many times must I forgive?" Peter asks.

Peter is looking for limits—limits on his relationships with his neighbors, limits to the demands of God's love.

But Jesus refuses. There is no counting. Because there are no limits on the times we will hurt and be hurt. No limits on the love that forgives you and me. And no limits on the power of Christ to heal the past and to set us free.

Holy Laughter

Genesis 18:1–15; Matthew 9:35–10:8

Our Old Testament lesson for today is about something you don't encounter very often in scripture—laughter. So I thought we should start this morning with a story or two, although you might think these come from the bottom of the barrel. Here goes . . .

After a church service, a little boy told the minister, "When I grow up, I'm going to give you some money." "Well, thank you," the minister replied, "but why?" "Because my daddy says you're one of the poorest preachers we've ever had."

Here's another. John Coburn, one of the most admired leaders of the Episcopal Church a generation ago, served in his younger years as the rector of a small church in Amherst, Massachusetts. As he was standing in line after his last service, telling people good-bye, an elderly lady in the congregation who had been there forever came up to him in tears. Coburn leaned down to console her, saying "Don't worry, Mrs. Jones. Rectors here just get better and better." "No, that's just the problem," she said. "They get worse and worse."

It feels good to laugh, maybe especially when it's at the clergy's expense. For some reason, there is very little actual laughter in the Bible. It has been called the world's least amusing book. But today in our Old Testament lesson we have the most famous case of laughing in all the scriptures. In the entire New Testament, laughter only turns up twice. One was in our gospel text last week when Jesus visits the home of a leader of the synagogue whose little daughter has died. And there in the midst of the gloom Jesus promises life in the midst of death. And everyone around him laughs. That's the laugh of cynicism and disbelief.

Holy Laughter

Laughter turns up a second time when Jesus in his teaching says, "Blessed are you who weep now, for you shall laugh." This is a promise that the laughter of joy and surprise are coming. It's a promise of God's unexpected goodness coming out of even the worst of times.

But the great biblical story of laughter is the story of ancient Sarah and her husband Abraham. Sarah is ninety years old, hunched over, no teeth, her face creased with the ruts of her years. She and Abraham had been living an ordinary life in Mesopotamia when God called ninety-nine-year-old Abraham to take his family to a new land. Now years later the Lord tells the old man that he and Sarah will have a son. Sarah, whose ear has been cocked at the tent entrance, bursts out laughing.

What would you do if you heard that a ninety-year-old lady in the geriatric ward is going to give birth, and Medicare is going to pay for it? Abraham himself must have let out a toothless cackle, and the laughing must have gone on nonstop. How ludicrous can you get! They must have been laughing because part of themselves actually did believe it, but they also didn't want to be taken for fools. It made no sense. It was absurd.

"Why did you laugh?" the Lord asks Sarah. "Is anything too wonderful for the Lord?"

"Who me, laugh? You must be kidding. A ninety-year-old, childless woman is told she's going to have a baby. I don't see why I should laugh."

"No, but you did laugh," the Lord says, "and just for that I'm going to name your baby Isaac, which means 'laughter,' just to remind you that the joke is on you." Before long Isaac is born, and Sarah laughs again.

This story of Abraham and Sarah begins in a world of weeping and sadness. They had known tears of disappointment and dashed hopes over those childless years. And when the good news and the laughter arrive, the darkness doesn't disappear for good. They will have hard times ahead, when God will again seem far away and strange. But here in this moment the promise of a child breaks into the darkness, like a glimpse of a far country so strange and new that all they know to do is to laugh with amazement.

We all know weeping that comes with disappointment and tragedy. Our friends here today from Indiana have come with what must be heavy hearts over the flooding in their state and across the Midwest. We are aware of the toll that war, hunger, and heartbreak take every day. But the laughter of joy, of comedy, points to the conviction that God always has a new future yet to give.

In fact, one of the earliest ways Christians talked about Easter was that it was the practical joke God played on the devil by raising Jesus from the dead. Theologians called it *Risus paschalis*, or the Easter laugh. And so, especially in Easter Orthodox traditions, the week after Easter would often be filled with parties, picnics, feasts, and joke telling.

Christian faith is at its heart a comedy—it is about a joy and laughter that point to an ultimate "happy ending" that we see in the death and resurrection of Jesus. And for those who have caught a glimpse of the resurrection, everything looks different and charged with hope.

Methodist Bishop William Willimon declares that "among all of God's creatures, human beings are the only animals who both laugh and weep—for we are the only animals who are struck with the difference between the way things are and the way things ought to be. In those priceless moments when we are struck with the incongruity of the world, humor results. A stern, smug gentleman slips on a banana peel and ends up sprawled on the sidewalk—we laugh; W. C. Fields throws a pie in the face of a pompous woman in an evening gown—we laugh."[1]

Laughter allows us not to take ourselves too seriously. Since we can relax in the confidence that everything ultimately rests in God's hands, we are able to see ourselves as the foolish, self-important people we often are, and to be reminded of the gap between our estimation of ourselves and the reality.

Maybe that's why there are so many church jokes. Most worship and church life are carried on in the mode of high seriousness, and it becomes easy to think God is depending on our own earnest perfection. But then you come across a few bloopers from some church bulletins that put things back in perspective.

> Ladies, don't forget the rummage sale. It's a chance to get rid of those things not worth keeping around the house. Don't forget your husbands.
>
> The sermon this morning: "Jesus walks on water." The sermon tonight: "Searching for Jesus."
>
> Remember in prayer the many who are sick of our community.
>
> Don't let worry kill you—let the church help.
>
> At the evening service tonight, the sermon topic will be, "What is Hell?" Come early and listen to our choir practice.
>
> For those of you who have children and don't know it, we have a nursery downstairs.
>
> Potluck supper Sunday at 5:00 pm. Prayer and medication to follow.

To laugh at the foolishness we get ourselves into is to be able to let go of taking ourselves too seriously. It's to lighten up, to recognize that there is more going on in God's world than our own earnestness, even to sense that there is a grace and mercy bigger than us that we can depend on.[2]

Abraham Lincoln loved to tell stories. Once at a cabinet meeting he read from a humorous book. The cabinet members were amazed, and no one smiled. "Why aren't you laughing?" Lincoln asked them with a sigh. And he told them that with the fearful strain he carried day and night, if he didn't laugh he would die. And he said they needed that medicine as much as he did.

In fact, the whole Christian story has been seen from its earliest days as something like a grand comedy. St. Paul talked about the foolishness of God. "We preach Christ crucified, a stumbling block to Jews and a folly to the gentiles." By any normal standards, Jesus' own life was a holy joke. He was the king who looked like a tramp, the prince of peace who seemed to be the prince of fools. Fyodor Dostoyevsky wrote a novel imagining Christ as a Russian prince and called it *The Idiot*. Some of you of a certain vintage will remember the musical *Godspell* that presents Jesus as the leader of a three-ring circus traveling around in acrobat tights.

And of course Jesus' teachings and stories have a comic feel to them. Frederick Buechner translates one of his famous lines this way: "It is harder for a rich person to enter Paradise than for a Mercedes to get through a revolving door."[3] Jesus told about strange hosts who invite everyone off the streets to their party, of a father who throws the biggest party for the bad son who has squandered everything. He tells about an idiotic shepherd who strolls off to find one lost sheep and ignores the ninety-nine with the good sense not to wander away. Scholar Elton Trueblood decided to write a book called *The Humor of Christ* when he found his son laughing out loud when he heard the story about a man being so concerned about the speck in another person's eye that he failed to see the beam stuck in his own.

But the deepest comedy, and the greatest reason for laughter, is really the Christian story itself. Most people I know expect just about anything in life except the possibility that beyond the darkness they see around them there could be brightness and light. They are prepared to do their best and cope with what comes. What they aren't prepared for is the sheer wild joke of a God who promises a joyful end.

For five days last fall Archbishop Desmond Tutu was with us at this Cathedral for our centennial celebration, and one of his most striking qualities was how much he laughed. It was sometimes more like a giggle. At other times he was slapping his knees and clapping his hands he was laughing so hard. And apparently he's always been that way—even in the dark days of apartheid and the draining years of building the new South Africa. It's the holy laughter of someone who knows that God is at work in this immense divine comedy, and no matter how dark things can become, God intends to draw us into the light.

By all accounts the city of Washington is more polarized than it once was. But people here remember the old days when a Lyndon Johnson or a Ronald Reagan would sit down with leaders of the opposition party after a hard day of politics and laugh and tell stories. People tell you that for all the troubles of those times, Washington was a better place. Laughter puts things in perspective and can soothe hard feelings.

A final story. An Amish boy and his mother visited a large shopping mall and were dumbfounded by everything they saw, especially two shiny silver walls that moved apart and then back together.

"What is this, Mother?" the boy asked. Never having seen an elevator she said, "Son, I have never seen anything like this in my life. I don't know what it is."

The two watched as an elderly man hobbling on a cane made his way over and pressed a button. The walls opened and he went in. Then they closed. The boy and his mother saw small numbers lit up above the doors, going up and then down. Then the walls opened again and out walked a handsome twenty-four-year-old man.

The mother, with her eyes never leaving the man, said quietly to her son, "Go get your father."[4]

Don't we all long for youth and beauty and joy? The joke of the story is that we will never find that in a magical elevator. And the real joke is that there's another kind of joyful surprise waiting for those, whatever their circumstance, who follow this seemingly foolish, jokester Lord.

"Go spread the good news," Jesus says to his disciples in our gospel lesson. "Tell everyone there is a new kingdom of healing and hope breaking in for everyone." Jesus is sending us, too. And at the heart of that kingdom we are to spread are joy, delight, and especially, laughter.

Trusting against the Evidence

Genesis 15:1–12; 17–18

"Is God trustworthy?" In one way or another we humans are asking ourselves that question every day of our lives, whether we realize it or not. Psychologists and spiritual writers broadly agree that at the depth of our beings a constant struggle goes on as to whether we can trust the world we live in and the God behind it. How we answer that question stirring in the back of our minds day in, day out, can have a profound influence on how we "do" our lives.

When a frightened child wakes in the night and his mother assures him that everything is all right, is she telling the truth? We wake every day into a vast, complex world, needing to be reassured. Can life be trusted as we make our way into this new day? It's really a question of faith. Is God trustworthy?[1]

Answering this question, though, isn't easy. Listen to this little parable that psychologist James Hillman believes captures an essential truth of our lives. A father puts his five-year-old son on the steps in front of their house and says, "Jump! And I'll catch you." Happily the boy jumps and is caught in his father's arms. And so the father urges him to climb higher and higher—three steps, then four, and does it again. "Jump!" he says. The boy hesitates now, but goes ahead, and is caught. Finally, he puts the boy on the top step, and as the youngster jumps, the father steps aside, and the boy hits the pavement. He stands up hurt and confused and bleeding, as his father says to him, "That will teach you."[2]

It's a cruel story but, Hillman believes, a true one. We all at times experience life betraying us, sometimes by people who let us down, sometimes by disappointments, hurts, or tragedies we never imagined. And they make us wonder whether we can trust anything at all.

Our lives are a weaving of experiences that often assure us that, at a profound level, "Everything is all right." But they also contain those other signals that life will hurt us, and we'd better be careful. In a world like ours, can we believe that a God of love and purpose is at work—a God who listens, who promises to care for us, who answers our prayers?

That can be a hard question to answer when the evidence isn't clear, or when the pain of life seems to leave little space for God. It's striking how often Jesus, Paul, and the Old Testament writers urge people to trust, to have faith, to hold fast. Maybe the reason is that faith wasn't so easy for them either. A lot of life makes faith look foolish. Read the newspaper, turn on the news, and then think, "Everything is all right." You have to wonder, Is God trustworthy?

Abraham and Sarah in our Old Testament lesson struggled for years with that question. Abram, as he was first called, had been living a comfortable life as a well-to-do, successful patriarch, who was the ripe old age of seventy-five when God called him. Out of the blue it came: "Go from your country and your kindred and your father's house to the land that I will show you," God said, and then he went on: "I will make of you a great nation, and I will bless you, so that you will be a blessing." And, out of the blue, Abram and Sarah immediately packed their bags and left—just like that—trusting in God's promises.

But nothing was easy after that. They traveled to the new land of Canaan, but things were so bad there that they then trekked all the way to Egypt to avoid a famine. And in Egypt they endured fierce dangers that threatened Sarah's well-being and revealed a very dark side of Abraham. God had given them promises, but year after year all they saw was hardship.

The biggest disappointment of their lives had been the fact that they had no children. Sarah was barren, and for a couple not to have a child was to be without an heir or a future. Abraham complained to God, and in response God took him out and pointed to the night sky and said, "Look at all these stars. You and Sarah will be parents of more descendants than all of them put together."

But year after year it didn't happen. So much for trusting God. Finally, though, when Abraham was ninety-nine and Sarah ninety, old enough to be senior citizens in a nursing home, the world shifted for them. Sarah became pregnant, and all she could do was laugh at the sheer wild joke of it all.

This isn't a story about human gynecology. It's the story Israel remembered and told about a God who keeps promises. God's promises to Abraham and Sarah go on for decades without coming true. God calls people to lives of faith and trust, but they don't get to see where it's all leading, how it will all turn out. They are just called to stay faithful day by day. The light of Christ, someone once said, illumines in the night only your next step, but you can't see the surrounding territory. All you can see is the one step ahead.

This Abraham, you know, is Father Abraham. He is the founding father of the three great monotheistic religions—of twelve million Jews, two billion Christians, and one billion Muslims. Even though each religion has its heroic leader—Moses, Mohammed, and Jesus—Abraham is acknowledged as the fountainhead of all three, with the declaration that God wants to bless all humankind. If only all three traditions could affirm that God's promises are for all, that we are all children of Abraham. And wouldn't the world be a safer place if they learned to trust God's promises and not their own certainty and rightness, and to live together with the modesty and humility of brothers and sisters in faith?

All three religions declare that God plants promise and hope in unlikely, desert, barren places. A seed grew in the barren womb of a ninety-year-old woman. The seed of the people of Israel took shape in the desert wilderness. The seeds of faith Jesus planted grew eventually into the mighty trees that came to be the church. And the seed planted on the bitter cross, after three days of death, became a promise of resurrection and new life for the whole human race. That was God's ultimate promise. You can trust me, God was saying, no matter what.

Yes, but . . . , we say. How can we trust in the midst of disappointment, unanswered prayers, and sorrow? Faith *includes* doubt. The opposite of faith is not doubt, but certitude. We live by trust—trust that there are some three hundred million stars in our galaxy when none of us is going to count them, trust that there are electrons when no one has ever seen one, trust that our companions and friends will not betray us, trust that the mysterious Creator God who called us into life wants to bless us. We live every moment of our lives by trust, by faith, but that faith always includes uncertainty.

Christian faith in the trustworthiness of God would be impossible in the face of the evil and cruelty all around us, if it didn't carry at its heart the conviction that God suffers with us, and seeks us out relentlessly, hung on a cross to heal us, and promises us yet more new life beyond even death.

It is a hard thing to believe in a promise—to live by it day after day. It is hard to trust in a promise when you don't have the power to make it come true. The challenge we face, as someone put it, is to give ourselves 100 percent to something when we are sometimes only 51 percent sure, sometimes less.

There are options other than trusting. We can throw in the towel to fatalism or cynicism. We can give up on this story that feeds all the great monotheistic religions. We can decide that the human race for six thousand years has been foolishly wrong, as some of the popular atheist writers of our day are trying to say. We can play life safe, manage our lives cautiously, and enjoy what we can. But what an adventure we will miss.

You see, our struggle to trust God is crucial for our spiritual growth. God has chosen not to make things clear. God has called us into a world that operates in freedom and on its own terms, where sometimes God's will is done and often it is not. It seems that our spiritual growth demands that we not know ahead of time how things will work out, not be able to have God perform on demand in our prayers, that we not know if we have trusted in vain. God wants us to risk, and love, and struggle through the complexities of life in this world.

Abraham and Sarah are our father and mother. But Jesus is our savior. His life and death and resurrection make our daily risks possible. Because he risked everything, we can risk daily in our trusting. He promises that if we risk everything, when we jump from the top step we will leap into the arms of the one he called Abba, Father.

One of the most moving records of trusting God I've encountered was written by a young Dutch woman named Etty Hillesum, who died in Auschwitz in 1943. In her diary, *An Interrupted Life*, we can watch her amazing growth in faith and trust, even as the reality of the death she would face closed in. One night, in Amsterdam, before going to the prison camp, she wrote:

> God, take me by Your hand, I shall follow You dutifully, and not resist too much. I shall evade none of the tempests life has in store for me, I shall try to face it all as best I can. But now and then grant me a short respite. I shall never again assume, in my innocence, that any peace that comes my way will be eternal. I shall accept all the inevitable tumult and struggle. I delight in warmth and security, but I shall not rebel if I have to suffer cold, should You so decree. I shall follow wherever Your hand leads me and shall try not to be afraid. [3]

Those are words Abraham and Sarah might have spoken—words of trust. After all, God promised old Abraham and Sarah descendants as numerous as the stars. And here we are—two billion Christians, a billion Muslims, twelve million Jews—all of us children of Abraham and Sarah. That's a God we can trust—in spite of everything.

Grace

Luke 15:1–3; 11b–32

It was midnight, and his brother should have been home two hours ago. My friend was back from college, and his parents were looking more and more worried. His younger brother had gone out with his buddies, and given the troubled times he was going through, that was always something to worry about.

All their lives the two brothers had divided up the roles. My friend was older, so he took the good boy role—responsible, dutiful. And that apparently left for his brother just one other choice—the bad boy role—and he stepped into it with gusto, getting himself into trouble in and out of school, and eventually into trouble with alcohol and drugs.

It was one o'clock now, and still he wasn't in. My friend went on to bed, leaving the worrying behind. But when he emerged the next morning, he heard quite a story.

At around two the telephone had rung, and there was a garbled voice on the other end, not making any sense at all. His parents didn't think it was their wandering son, but they couldn't be sure. Still, it terrified them with the possibility that something awful was happening. And so their father got into his car, drove the twenty-five miles to Jackson, the big city, and began going to some of the bars and hangouts his son had mentioned. For the next several hours the father drove the streets of the city, stopping at one place after another, asking if anyone had seen him.

The father never found his son that night, but eventually, close to dawn, the boy came home, looking the worse for the wear, but safe. And both exhausted parents were overcome with relief, got him to bed, and then collapsed into bed themselves.

The story of that night has stayed with me all these years as I've thought of that father roaming the streets of Jackson, refusing to give up on his lost son.

We Christians have a word for what happened that night. The word is grace—as in "Amazing Grace." It was just about St. Paul's favorite word—"The grace of our Lord Jesus Christ," "Grace and peace be with you," "My grace," God says, "is sufficient to you." But for all the times we hear it in church, my sense is that few of us know what it means.

C. S. Lewis and a good many others have claimed that grace is Christianity's unique contribution to world religions—the notion that there is a Love behind the universe that is completely unearned, unstoppable, inexhaustible. There are no eight-fold paths Christians must follow as in Buddhism, no code of laws that must be obeyed to draw close to God, no levels of holiness we have to achieve. Jesus came to declare something downright scandalous—that there is nothing we can do to make God love us more than we are already loved, and nothing we can do to make God love us less.

Think for a moment what an ungraceful world we live in. Our lives are driven by a meritocracy of achievement. You're as good as the work you do, the money you earn, the level to which you rise in your profession. No pain, no gain. No such thing as a free lunch. Demand your rights. Get what you pay for. There is little grace when you can't pay your mortgage, when you're caught speeding on I-95, when your child is competing to get into college. If a CEO has a string of bad quarters, he or she is gone. If a baseball manager makes a big mistake in the playoffs, he might as well pack his bags.

And the religion many of us have encountered has shown little grace. Get all the rules right, you often hear. Behave yourself. Don't commit any sins, because if you do you'll make God angry and you'll end up in hell. Much of it has been a religion of morality, observance, and propriety. Ask most religious people what they need to do to get to heaven and they'll reply with something like, "Be good."

But Jesus turned that whole way of thinking on its head. For one thing, he didn't seem particularly drawn to pious people. He hung out with rowdy fishermen, a sleazy tax collector, a social revolutionary or two, a woman of ill repute. His followers were largely a lot of losers—lepers, blind men, people down on their luck and out of work.

That's what has the pious Pharisees and scribes grumbling in our gospel lesson today. "This fellow welcomes sinners and eats with them," they complain. And so Jesus tells them a parable, probably the best-known and most loved story he ever told.

I recently heard of a priest visiting a man in the hospital who was near death, and the man said he had never had much use for Christianity, but wondered if the priest could just take a few minutes and tell him what it's all about. And the priest paused for a moment to think, and then said, "Well let me tell you, there was a man who had two sons . . ."

It's the heart of the Christian story. A son demands his inheritance from his father and heads out to make it on his own in the world. Then he proceeds to throw himself into "dissolute living," as the story tells it, partying, drinking, squandering his father's savings.

The young man ends up humiliated and desperate, eating what the swine eat, for Jews the most humiliating state imaginable. It all feels like the bitter taste of the morning after. But while he's there in the far country, he remembers who he is. "How many of my father's hired servants have bread enough and to spare, and I perish here. . . . I will arise and go to my father." And as he makes his way back, he prepares his speech asking to be allowed to come home.

As he approaches, the father sees his son and runs out to embrace him as the son falls in his arms. And as the son starts to deliver his speech, the father calls out for the best robe in the house to be brought, puts a ring on his finger, and orders a grand party to begin.

Now I don't know about you, but that's not the way I'd tell that story. I'd have the father waiting with his arms angrily folded, and when the son threw himself down say something like, "Well, I'm glad you've seen the error of your ways. I hope you've learned your lesson." Which is exactly the view of the elder son in the story, the responsible one, who like most of us, wants nothing to do with welcoming his brother home.

Have you ever wondered what it would feel like to be able to collapse into a love like this father's? Maybe for many of us the experience of a far country has been less about wild living than in feeling ourselves alone, isolated in a hard world. Have you known the sense of having to make it for yourself, of bills to pay, a job to find, friends to seek out? Have you ever felt that you were out there just coping, cut off from family and friends, even from God? My guess is that we've all longed to be able to fall into the safe arms of a Love that would hold us.

This story is usually called "The Parable of the Prodigal Son"—the misbehaving boy finally coming home. But that's not really what it's about. After all, it begins, "A man had two sons . . ." This is really a story about a father who cannot keep from giving to the children he loves. This father irresponsibly gives half his wealth to this younger son, and then after the boy has squandered it all, runs out to welcome him home. No demands for apologies, no rehearsal of mistakes. Nothing but a grand feast.

And that, Jesus is saying, is what lies at the depth of our lives. It's a story about grace, the shocking fact that our life and our worth are unearned. Everything is given—the love and support in our lives, even the talents we've used to make our way in this world. *Gratis*. Grace. We didn't produce it. And this Love won't quit on us until we're home.

There are loving arms waiting to embrace us. Can you see how revolutionary this is? We have nothing to prove. The key to our lives is not, "Be good," but simply our learning to ask for help.

After Communion, we will sing "Amazing Grace," written by John Newton, who was for much of his life a slave trader. When he finally let himself face the horror of the life he had been leading, he knew what it meant to be a wretch, to have done terrible damage to the lives he touched. But he had also discovered the grace of God, a grace that sought him out, and never stopped working on him, trying to bring him home.

> Amazing grace, how sweet the sound
> That saved a wretch like me;
> I once was lost but now I'm found
> Was blind but now I see. [1]

Grace is the most revolutionary medicine of all, because if we can take in God's grace, we can be people of grace ourselves. There isn't a family among us that does not need the grace of forgiveness. I forgive you because I have been forgiven, not because you have earned it.

Abraham Lincoln was once asked what he would do with the Confederate soldiers once the war was over. He replied simply and directly that he would treat them as though they had never gone away. He was ready to welcome them back into the fold.

One of the miracles of our time has been the way South Africa threw off apartheid without having it lead to a bloodbath. This was a nation that made grace a public policy. Rather than track down and destroy all the brutal enforcers of apartheid, it decided instead to create a Truth and Reconciliation Commission, so that victims and perpetrators could come and simply tell their stories, confess what they had done or what had been done to them. There were unimaginable moments, as victims of torture and maiming and the death of loved ones came to utter maybe the most freeing words the human race has ever discovered, "I forgive you."

Grace reaches across barriers. Last Monday night a group from this Cathedral squeezed into a packed downtown church for a Washington Interfaith Network (WIN) rally. WIN is an interdenominational organization that works together to advocate for the poor and underserved in our city. It was a night of singing and speeches and preaching and a meeting with the mayor. Clear and challenging words were spoken about what must be done in the city. But what you couldn't miss was the sense of joy in being together, the sense that we were all one in being held in an unshakable Love. A divided city felt like one family. Amazing grace.

In this time of racial and ethnic conflict around the world, a time when racism still haunts our American life, when the gaps between rich and poor, black and white, gay and straight are still profound, I can think of no more powerful message than this one that got Jesus killed—that all of us are loved endlessly and equally by God. And called to come home and grow in that love.

Can there be any more important mission here at this Cathedral than to be a place that embodies that grace—in how we welcome people, in how we love, forgive, and respect each other, in how we serve the city around us? Our world is starving for grace, God's amazing, healing, unearned grace, and that is a gift that only the church can give.

I think of that father, driving endlessly up and down the streets of Jackson. I think of that father in the parable, wondering if he would ever see his son again. And I think of the father-like, mother-like God who loves you and me that way.

When I picture the prodigal son returning home, I imagine him looking up and to his stunned surprise seeing his father, running down the path to greet him, arms spread as wide as a cross.

> Amazing grace, how sweet the sound
> That saved a wretch like me;
> I once was lost but now I'm found
> Was blind but now I see.

Book Two

Events and Issues

Cathedral Life

Installation Sermon

A Voice, a Place, a People

A sermon preached on the occasion of the installation and seating of the Very Reverend Samuel T. Lloyd III as Dean of Washington National Cathedral

Isaiah 55:6–13; John 15:1–11; Ephesians 2:13–22

As I was preparing this sermon I received an e-mail that suggested I have some explaining to do. The message came from a friend who is a dean at a university, and who seemed a little confused as to just what it meant to "install and seat" a dean. "I've been a dean for sixteen years," he wrote, "but have never been 'seated.' I've been told to sit down and be quiet, but never officially 'seated.' So I am anxious to check out the process."

Well, to those who have come here to check out the process, I hope you won't be disappointed. And if what we are doing here perhaps seems to be much ado just to show a dean to his seat, then all I can say is, welcome to the world of cathedrals. Cathedrals by nature do things grandly and beautifully, even seating deans. In everything they do they muster all the resources at their disposal to offer an experience of God and the things of God that stretch our imaginations and beggar our words.

And, of course, this day is significant not simply as a celebration in this beautiful cathedral building, but because it marks an important civic and religious moment. We welcome the dean of Canterbury Cathedral representing the archbishop of Canterbury, the head of our Anglican Communion. The mayor of Washington has sent his greetings. Gathered here today are distinguished bishops from across our church, and clergy and lay leaders from the

Diocese of Washington and beyond. And we are honored to have ecumenical representatives among us here, and to have our interfaith friends from the Muslim and Jewish traditions participating in the service.

All of this signifies the multiple missions of this National Cathedral, articulated in the three touchstone phrases that ring through its life. It is called to be "a house of prayer for all people," "the chief mission church of the Diocese of Washington," and "a great church for national purposes."

One of the most telling moments in this Cathedral's life happens daily at the west entrance as visitors, tourists, and worshipers first make their way in. You can often actually hear the gasps of awe as they step into this holy space. My guess is that many of us here have experienced the spell that cathedrals can cast. Some years ago I had the occasion to spend several months in the shadow of Salisbury Cathedral in England where I first experienced the spell for myself. And there I came across a description by the novelist Susan Howatch of her first encounter with that gracefully beautiful building. She had come to Salisbury in a time of intense personal turbulence, and what happened to her there marked the beginning of her conversion.

> I looked out and saw this fantastic sight . . . the floodlit Cathedral, gorgeous, stunning, out of this world, certainly out of any world I'd been inhabiting. It was radiant, ravishing. I stopped dead and that was the moment when the scales fell from my eyes. I felt I had been presented with some extraordinary gift. I could now see and recognize the overpowering beauty of the Cathedral—which was the sign pointing beyond itself to the reality which was still hidden from my conscious mind. . . . I was being systematically seduced by the Cathedral.[1]
>
> That's the power cathedrals have, and certainly this one.

But we shouldn't forget that from the beginning Christians have recognized the dangers in buildings such as this. The Hebrew prophets believed that their people were at their most faithful when they were pilgrims traveling through the wilderness, before kings and temples tempted them to turn away from God. Jesus himself went occasionally to the immense Temple in Jerusalem, but his own ministry was devoted to wandering from village to village preaching and healing far from any grand edifice. The early Christians of the New Testament were clear that their Lord was in their midst, in the life of the community, in the presence of the Spirit leading them, not in any building. And down through the years leaders such as the twelfth-century monk Bernard of Clairvaux would rail against what he called the foolish extravagance of cathedral buildings.

And yet, cathedrals have been powerful channels for God's love and truth. Into cathedrals come the curious, the seeker, the brokenhearted, and the lost, and there, like Susan Howatch, they catch glimpses of God's love for them. And over the decades this Cathedral has served in vital ways: as a haven for the sacred arts, a forum for debate and discussion, a platform for pastoral nurture and prophetic proclamation, a quiet place for solace and meditation, a destination for pilgrimage and personal transformation, a center for theological reflection and ecumenical conversation. The world, and our faith, would be much the poorer without the ministry of places such as this.

It took nearly a century to realize the dream of a great church in the nation's capital. What a privilege and responsibility have been entrusted to us by those who built this magnificent Cathedral. Now it is our high and holy responsibility to make of the life both within its walls and beyond an offering worthy of the devotion that brought it into being.

In praying and thinking about what lies at the heart of this Cathedral's life, I have kept going back to a moment Rowan Williams, the archbishop of Canterbury, has described. He was visiting an Orthodox monastery some years ago and was taken to see one of the smaller, older chapels.

> It was a place intensely full of the memory and reality of prayer. . . . The monk showing me around pulled the curtain in front of the sanctuary, and inside was a plain altar and one simple picture of Jesus, darkened and rather undistinguished. But for some reason at that moment it was as if the veil of the temple was torn in two: I saw as I had never seen the simple fact of Jesus at the heart of all our words and worship, behind the curtain of our anxieties and our theories, our struggles and our suspicion. Simply there; nothing anyone can do about it, there he is as he has promised to be 'til the world's end. Nothing of value happens in the Church that does not start from seeing him simply there in our midst, suffering and transforming our human disaster.[2]

That is the truth at the heart of everything that happens here in this Cathedral. Amid all the activity, all the grandeur, all the splendor of our liturgies, all the work of volunteers and docents and committees and classes and tutoring and tending to the fabric of this space and paying bills and preaching sermons—at the heart of all of it is the simple embodiment of love that hung on a cross for us and will stop at nothing to heal and reconcile us all, until the world's end. Everything in this Cathedral's life should mirror that.

It is early in my tenure as your dean, and the work of discerning what God is asking of us in this time is only beginning. But today I want to offer you a sense of where I believe this Jesus at the heart of everything is calling us.

First, I believe we are called to be a Voice. There is a disturbing absence of thoughtful religious reflection in our public conversation in America today. In print and on television you can readily hear the views of a narrow and divisive religious fundamentalism. It has become so pervasive in our culture now that a number of parishioners I served in my previous position in Boston were increasingly saying they were embarrassed to describe themselves as Christians among their secular friends.

And yet on the other side of the conversation is a secular culture committed primarily to material prosperity and personal freedom, often drenched in consumerism and violence, dominated by magazines, Internet sites, and television that offer little in the way of a vision of what this life is for. What is missing in our public discourse is a generous-spirited, open-minded, intellectually probing, compassionate Christianity.

What we call mainline denominations—Lutherans, Presbyterians, Methodists, Episcopalians, and others—have lost more than 30 percent of their members in the last few decades, and have lost even more of their public voice. I believe this Cathedral is called to be a major voice of a faith that is firm at the center and soft at the edges, deeply rooted in the tradition and radically open and welcoming, a faith that embraces ambiguity, that honors other faiths, a faith that searches the scriptures deeply, a faith that calls us to personal conversion, a faith that insists that Christ's values be embodied in the social order. That faith needs bold proclaimers and communicators.

This Cathedral is called to be a Voice of generous-spirited Christianity.

Second, I believe we are called to be a Place—a place of reconciliation. These are dangerously alienated times. The city in which this Cathedral stands is divided racially and economically, and is the capital of a nation that is polarized politically. Our world and its many religions are riddled with conflict and division.

And yet, as our lesson from the Hebrew scriptures today makes clear, God's truth is bigger than any one group's truth. "For as the heavens are higher than the earth, so are my ways higher than your ways, and my thoughts than your thoughts, says the Lord."

We Christians are called, as St. Paul said, to a ministry of reconciliation. "Christ has broken down the dividing walls between us," we heard from the Letter to the Ephesians. "He came to preach peace to those who are far off and to those who are near." We have seen in Christ's death and resurrection a love that will stop at nothing to heal our divisions. We cannot turn from that work. Ecumenical collaboration, interfaith dialogue, liturgies, programs, conversations, and discussions that seek the ways of understanding and peace are essential for us.

And our own Episcopal Church is painfully fractured. But the most powerful gift we can offer our world is not the sight of a community where everyone agrees with each other, but one that can worship God and serve the world even with their disagreements.

The church's most revolutionary act takes place week by week as it gathers at the altar for the Eucharist. Because at that moment we are acting out the only real hope our world has. And that is not that we will agree on everything, but that it is possible to be rooted in a reality of love far deeper and stronger than what divides us.

This Cathedral is called to be a Voice, and a Place of reconciliation.

And finally, we are called to be a People—committed to serving a world of immense beauty and goodness and yet riddled with suffering and division. The gap between rich and poor in this country has never been wider. Children in this city are growing up in appalling housing, without health care, and are being sent to schools which in many cases fail them miserably. A billion of our fellow human beings around the world live daily on the edge of death from hunger and preventable disease. Those who come into this beautiful space to glimpse Christ must go out ready to see and serve him in the suffering of the world around us.

And that means that as honored as I am today to find myself being seated in this Cathedral, we cannot do this ministry sitting down. Yes, we must sit to listen, to learn, to explore, to pray. But then we have to stand up, to go to work, to speak the truth, to serve Christ wherever he sends us. This Cathedral is called to form a People for mission and service in Christ's name.

For most of my ministry I have had the privilege of serving in beautiful church buildings, and so for nearly all these years I have wrestled with the tension between the church's beauty and the world's pain. No words have been more important to me than these from Harry Emerson Fosdick, the famous minister of Riverside Church in New York City in the last century. Fosdick led that congregation in building a soaring Gothic church in Morningside Heights. In a sermon he preached before they moved into their new church he warned them of the danger their beautiful building could pose.

> You know it could be wicked for us to have that new church—wicked. Whether it is going to be wicked or not depends on what we do with it.
>
> Very frequently in these recent days people come to me and say, "The new church will be wonderful." My friends, it is not yet settled whether or not the new church will be wonderful. If we should gather a selfish company there, though the walls bulge every Sunday [in numbers], that would not be wonderful. If we form a religious club greatly enjoying themselves, and though we trebled in numbers our first year, that would not be wonderful.
>
> But if all over the world, at home and abroad, wherever the Kingdom of God is hard beset, the support of this church could be felt, that would be wonderful. If young men and women coming into that church could have Isaiah's experience of seeing the Lord high and lifted up, and if they too should answer their divine vocation, saying, "Here I am, send me," that would be wonderful . . .
>
> If in this city, this glorious, wretched city, where so many live in houses that human beings ought not to have to live in, and children play where children ought not to have to play, if we could lift some burden and lighten some dark spots and help to solve some of our community's problems, that would be wonderful. If in the new temple we simply sit together in heavenly places, that will not be wonderful. But if we work together in unheavenly places, that will be.[3]

My hope and prayer for this Cathedral as we journey on together is that it will be known not only as a great and holy building, but as

a Voice—of generous-spirited Christianity;

a Place—of reconciliation and healing; and

a People—following Christ into a world that awaits our care.

That would indeed be wonderful.

An Unfinished Cathedral

Festival Service of Thanksgiving on the Cathedral Centennial

Genesis 28:10–17; 1 Peter 2:1–5, 9–10; Mark 14:3–9

Yesterday, in the course of the festivities for this birthday weekend, we reenacted the service of the laying of the foundation stone of Washington National Cathedral, one hundred years ago to the day. After a long century, all the principal players were back again, and for those of us sitting in the amphitheater it felt as if we had entered a time capsule and been transported to a world where Massachusetts Avenue had just been paved and there were at least as many horse-drawn carriages as cars. There they were again: Bishop Henry Yates Satterlee, the visionary founder of the Cathedral, the United States Marine Band, streams of choristers, dignitaries of church and nation, and of course, "old rough and ready" himself, President Theodore Roosevelt, as blustery as ever.

The Cathedral's own carpenters and masons had assembled a large wooden frame and hoist to hold a re-creation of the foundation stone—what looked like a massive block of granite containing the smaller piece of stone brought all the way from Bethlehem.

We were reminded of the vast crowd of thirty thousand who gathered for that day, how all the churches in the Diocese of Washington had held early services at 9:30 so that parishioners could arrive on Mount St. Alban by noon. And we then participated in an abbreviated version of the service—singing parts of the hymns, hearing some of the eloquent words, all leading to the key moment. As we all sang "O Little Town of Bethlehem," a hymn about God taking on flesh among us, we watched mortar spread and the foundation stone lowered into place—the culmination of more than a decade of intense planning, and the beginning of what would prove to be nearly a century of construction.

"God speed the work begun this day," President Roosevelt boomed out. And to my surprise, and others', too, what began as a simple costume ceremony with bowler hats and long skirts, ended up giving some of us lumps in our throats as we watched the stone settling into place. To remember that moment so long ago, we realized, was to touch something holy about who we are and why we are here.

What a century it has been! Eighty-three years of construction itself, and a hundred and more of creating this Cathedral's life and mission. We would not be here today without the dreamers who first met in Charles Glover's living room to imagine a church for the nation built in the heart of its capital. They and a handful of other lay and clergy leaders believed that this was a gift only the Episcopal Church could give the nation, and that it would be worth several lifetimes of labor and devotion to make it a reality.

One of the most striking aspects of cathedrals is that building them requires generations, and often centuries, of architects and builders, artists and artisans, volunteers and benefactors. A cathedral cannot be the achievement of any one time, individual, or group. In fact, what is in many ways most moving about cathedrals such as Canterbury, Salisbury, or Washington, is something we could call "the cathedral spirit." Beyond the soaring beauty, intricate stone tracery, and the sheer miracle that they were built at all, you can't help but be struck by the fact that people who were neither there at the beginning nor would be there at the end gave their lives to create something beautiful for God.

It makes you think of the words of the theologian Reinhold Niebuhr: "Nothing that is worth doing can be achieved in a lifetime, therefore we must be saved by hope."[1]

Building this new cathedral was difficult from the start. Affordable land in the right location was hard to come by, with several attempts that didn't work. The prospects were looking grim, until at last an opportunity came to buy thirty acres of land beside St. Alban's Church, but the price seemed overwhelming. It became clear that Bishop Satterlee himself would have to sign personally a mortgage, worth some $3 million today—for a project he could not be sure would be realized.

On the Sunday before the agreement was to be signed he had gone for a walk in the woods with "the feeling," as he later wrote, "that this was the last Sunday I should be free for many years." And he went on: "I thought of Admiral Dewey at Manila, and how for the sake of his country he had taken his life in his hands; how, if he had been beaten at Manila, there was absolutely nowhere for his fleet to go . . . Then I felt, 'If Dewey can do this for country, surely I can take a different kind of risk for God.'" And so he signed the contract with "as much nerve and courage as I have ever put forth."[2] He put himself on the line.

Then day after day, year after year, Satterlee worked tirelessly to "nationalize the Cathedral," as he called it, to encourage Americans far and wide to see this as their cathedral and to offer their prayers and financial resources for its completion. Finally, after seven years and hundreds of fund-raising letters and meetings, the debt on the land was paid. In Bishop Satterlee's journal he reflected on what that meant:

> I was led into this project. If I could have foreseen the trials it would bring in the winter, spring and summer of 1903, I should never have had the courage to attempt it . . .
>
> No one will ever realize the long suspense, continuous strain, the necessity of depending daily on God's help, which the Cathedral debt . . . has called forth. My only object in writing about it here is to show that God and not man has begun the building of the Cathedral. . . .
>
> I want to emphasize this fact with all the earnestness I can put into words . . . that the Cathedral Foundation in its beginnings, was built up by God Himself, and I want . . . future generations to realize . . . that the work is blessed and hallowed and carried on by Christ Himself, while we have the privilege of being co-laborers with Him as He builds it up, step by step and stone by stone.[3]

An exhausted Bishop Satterlee died four months after laying the foundation stone. Nearly every cathedral in Europe is associated with a great saint or martyr. Buried now just above the foundation stone in our Bethlehem Chapel, Bishop Satterlee is our founding spirit, perhaps even our martyr, a man who spent himself to build a cathedral for the nation.

Even here, in our earliest years, you begin to see three recurring truths of our life. First, there was never enough money. Because we receive not a penny from either the government or the Episcopal Church, we have had to build this Cathedral step by step, stone by stone, dollar by dollar. We depend for our ministry on people who believe this Cathedral can make a difference to our nation and our world. Second, without fail, God has sent us the right people at the right time for every stage of the journey—lay leaders and clergy, women and men of immense faith, talent, and generosity. And third, at the heart of our life has been a willingness to risk, to devote ourselves to a vision that requires not months, not years, but generations to achieve.

Countless people in our life have embodied this "cathedral spirit." There was George Bratenahl, who served as dean during the first twenty years of construction and chose much of the rich iconography in the Cathedral. And Philip Frohman, a consummate perfectionist, who served as architect of the Cathedral for fifty-two devoted years. There was Bishop James Freeman, who for twenty crucial years pushed the construction forward through a

Great Depression and a world war. And of course in more recent times there was Dean Francis Sayre, who for twenty-seven years presided over the construction of the central tower and the nave, aided tirelessly by Canon Richard Feller, who oversaw every detail of construction. Finally, there were the two great builders at the end, Bishop John Walker and Provost Charles Perry, who led the Cathedral out of a financial crisis that threatened its survival, and then with relentless vision and financial toughness completed it in 1990.

And we should never forget that gifts for building the Cathedral came, and still do, in many sizes—from a few nickels and quarters gathered in a mite box, to a few dollars sent in from a small town in Iowa, to the major gifts that ultimately enabled the work to be completed. It took generations of commitment and generosity to bring us to this moment. That, too, has been part of the cathedral spirit. And if you cast even a glance at the gracious beauty of the grounds on our close you should offer a prayer of thanksgiving for Frederick Law Olmsted Jr., the landscape architect, and Florence Bratenahl, founder of All Hallows Guild.

Of course, the actual work of building required the vision of artists and the skill of generations of artisans—stonecarvers, masons, metal-workers, glass artists—who made of their work enduring gestures of praise. Today we give thanks for it all.

But why did all these people devote themselves so inordinately? What propelled them on in the face of so many obstacles?

We know that for many, building this Cathedral was an act of Christian love, and of patriotism as well. They believed that amid all the grand buildings and monuments in the nation's capital, one should represent the God who loves, and has a mission for, this nation. They yearned for a more united country and a more united church, and they believed this Cathedral could be a force for unity. And they were convinced that the spiritual life of the nation needed to be expressed firmly and powerfully in this seat of worldly power.

At a deeper level, though, I believe they cared passionately that at the heart of this city should be a building and a ministry to help people to live by the two great commandments—to love God with all your heart and soul and your neighbor as yourself.

Cathedrals are acts of extravagance. You know, our guides and docents talk about the "Wow moment." It occurs when a visitor steps inside the West doors for the first time. It takes only a few seconds before you hear the "Wows!" Cathedrals seek to show us a beauty and harmony that overwhelms our mind's familiar little categories. They want us to see that we are part of a cosmos, a grand unity, and they want us to fall in love with the God we are glimpsing there. The real business of cathedrals is seduction, getting us to lose ourselves in a peace and harmony the world cannot give.

Our gospel lesson for today is about that kind of extravagance. Jesus is about to be arrested. His life is nearly over, and he knows it. But before the tragic events unfold, we have this intimate moment. A woman comes in with a jar of expensive oil, and she breaks it and pours it over Jesus' head.

It's an act of extravagance. No more prudent than building a grand cathedral. This well-to-do woman, seeing what was about to happen to her Lord, did the only thing she knew how to do—care for him, console him, and as an act of faith, worship him. Surely, the bystanders say, the poor could have used that money, the equivalent of a year's wages for a worker. Of course. But Jesus defends her impulsive act of devotion. No one needs to tell Jesus about caring for the poor; that had been at the core of his ministry, and by this time he's poor himself, dining with a leper, his friends about to desert him, only a death sentence ahead.

"She has done what she could," Jesus says. Sometimes what is most essential to our humanity is the capacity to worship a goodness and beauty far beyond what we can imagine. The woman is doing this for love. And that, Jesus knows, is where discipleship and service begin.

And so Washington National Cathedral serves as a place of pilgrimage for hundreds of thousands of visitors each year, and for worshipers and explorers who come in search of a glimpse of the mystery and wonder of God. We as a nation need a place where our vision can be refreshed, our hearts lifted, and our strength renewed.

"Love the Lord your God with all your heart and soul and mind and strength," Jesus said. Cathedrals are made for that.

But there is a Second Commandment: "Love your neighbor as yourself." Cathedral life is a waste if it doesn't lead to changed lives and a changed world. "Come," our New Testament lessons says, and "like living stones let yourselves be built into a spiritual house." That is the calling of our time—for us to become living stones ourselves, as sturdy and enduring as Indiana limestone, as we embody God's love in a troubling twenty-first century.

Our world needs more than ever a vigorous voice of a thoughtful, Christian faith. Fundamentalism and now an increasingly virulent atheism are defining religion in the public square. Who will take up the challenge to offer a Christian faith committed to intellectual vitality, to respect for other religions, to building a world of understanding and peace, if we do not? Who will help reclaim the word "Christian" as a word of hope and healing in our society? Our role for the nation demands that we claim that mission as our own, in public gatherings, through worship and public conversations, taking full advantage of digital communication as well as television and print.

Our nation needs this sacred place to pour itself into the work of reconciliation. In our first century, the important truth-tellers laid hold of this Canterbury pulpit to address the nation—among them Martin Luther King Jr. and the Dalai Lama, and none more consistently than our own Dean Francis Sayre. When he traveled to march in Selma, he marched for this Cathedral.

When later Bishop Walker challenged apartheid in South Africa from this pulpit, he spoke with the authority not only of his office but of this Cathedral.

Reconciliation in this time means building bridges—across the city of Washington between black and white, across the globe between Americans and Iranians, in the Middle East between Israel and Palestine, in our own Episcopal Church between liberals and conservatives.

And reconciliation means creating ways to carry on the decades-long work of interfaith dialogue and now interfaith work combating disease and poverty in sub-Saharan Africa. To see God in a poor, wandering Jewish teacher about to go to a cross requires that we see God in every human face, and to know that as Christians we are bound to the work of healing the wounds and divisions of our time.

And so this Cathedral, along with its new congregation and its renewed National Cathedral Association, is committed to being that place of healing we are called to be.

Here is our question for today. One hundred years from now, when our successors in this Cathedral gather for a weekend such as this, what will be the story they will honor from our second century? Will we have built a Cathedral in living stones worthy of "the great majestic pile," as Bishop Satterlee called it? Will our successors speak of our audacity in doing something great for God in our time? Will this transcendently beautiful building have fulfilled its calling to be a sign of hope to the nation and world?

I've heard a certain comment many times since I became dean. "Isn't it great that the Cathedral is actually finished! What a relief, that that's been done for us, and we can just enjoy it!" After one hundred years of this Cathedral's life, of one thing I am certain: this Cathedral is not finished, and will never be. Near the end of Bishop Satterlee's book *The Building of a Cathedral*, which foresaw every detail of the new Cathedral's design and mission, one small paragraph caught my eye:

> Somehow, in the cathedrals of the past . . . there is a sense of incompleteness. Nothing is finished. It is as though the builders were struggling to express a thought that was too great for them, and must leave it for future generations to spell out more plainly than they, Christ's description of a house of prayer. [4]

We have so much to do now in our generation and in generations to come. We are being called to use this space generously, creatively, extravagantly, to fill it with the spirit of Jesus himself, to enable people to encounter the Love behind the universe—and then to join us in serving our world.

We, too, must be struggling to express a thought too great for us. We do not fully know what God desires for us, but we have each other and the legacy of a hundred years of faithful service behind us to inspire and sustain us on our way. What thrilling years of exploration and discovery we have ahead.

Thanks be to God for our forebears, for all those who have shared in the cathedral spirit, known and unknown. Thanks be to God for the awe we experience when we step into this space, and for the love and service this Cathedral summons from us.

My deepest prayer is that we will cling to the vast, visionary, risk-taking spirit that has brought us this far, and to our Lord Jesus Christ who calls us to this work.

May this Cathedral always remain unfinished.

Presidential Inauguration

A New Community

Preached the Sunday before the presidential inauguration of Barack Obama

Exodus 3:7–12; Luke 6:27–36

You can feel the buzz in the air. Something is about to happen in Washington that has the whole world watching. Preparations have been underway for weeks, even months. Grandstands have been built in front of the Capitol and up and down Pennsylvania Avenue. Thousands of chairs have been set in place. Inaugural parties and balls are ready to run late into the night. A half-million people are expected to be at the rock concert on the Mall this afternoon. We hear there may be as many as four million visitors to the city.

The word "historic" can be tossed around too easily these days, but no one is questioning the fact that we are in the middle of something historic. A remarkably gifted African American man will take the oath of office as president of the United States.

From the beginning of its history our country has dealt with what many historians have called the original sin of slavery, the blight on our life that gave a lie to many of our deepest convictions about freedom and equality. Condoleezza Rice a few months ago referred to slavery as America's birth defect.

That blight, of course, cannot end in a single election or inauguration. But I was struck by a political cartoon in the *Washington Post* a day after the election. It showed a small Barack Obama figure walking up the sidewalk toward the imposing columns of the White House. Across the top of the cartoon were scrolled the words from the Declaration of Independence, "We hold these truths to be self-evident, that all men are created equal." And at the bottom of the cartoon it said, "Ratified November 4, 2008."[1]

You could say that it has taken 230 years since 1776 for America fully to embrace its deepest beliefs. Of course this can be no claim that racism, inequality, and injustice have suddenly vanished. But we are a different nation with a president by the name of Barack Hussein Obama, whose grand-parents lived in Kenya, and who grew up in Kansas, Indonesia, and Hawaii. In fact, several people I know who did not vote for Barack Obama still speak with a sense of pride and hope because of what he represents.

And this isn't true just for us Americans. After the election, we saw television images of dancing in the streets in Kenya and across Africa, and expressions of joy and goodwill from around the globe. Listen to an e-mail that arrived the morning after the election from a friend in Britain:

> The scenes on television of black voters who suddenly felt that the electoral system might work for them will stay vivid in my mind, and they do your country huge credit. The post-mortem here is all about why we can't envisage the same sea-change in the UK, but I don't see many people of the stature of Obama, black or white, on our political scene.

The event has even captured the imagination of children. Here's a twelve-year-old child's letter to the new president, one of several published in the *New York Times* yesterday:

> Dear Obama, I have grown up with a very liberal mom and a very conservative dad. Thank you for bringing my parents somewhat closer together, ☺. You are my idol, Mr. Barack—I am partly African American and I am very happy to see an African American leading the country.[2]

In the midst of as bleak a time economically as this country has known in eighty years, we seem to be experiencing a strange sense of hope that seems, at least for now, oddly bipartisan.

In one of the grace notes of history, our country will be inaugurating this new president the day after Martin Luther King Jr. Day. The two events are inevitably intertwined. We can't help but look at this moment in the light of Dr. King. You may have heard the line being circulated around in recent weeks that shows so clearly the legacy that gave us our new president: Rosa sat so that Martin could walk; Martin walked so that Obama could run; and Obama ran so that our children can fly.

Presidents in the past have used their campaigns and inaugurals to launch a theme for their presidencies. Franklin D. Roosevelt promised what he called a "New Deal" for an America immersed in the Great Depression. In 1960, John Kennedy began to talk about a "New Frontier."

Today I want to suggest a theme for this new presidency that comes from Dr. King himself. Instead of a New Deal or a New Frontier, I propose that President Obama take as his theme a "New Community," what Dr. King would have called the "Beloved Community." That is what I believe our country and our world most need.

Dr. King believed that our fate as a human race depended on how we cared for and treated each other. You can hear it in the passage from Jesus' teaching we heard this morning:

> But I say to you, Love your enemies, do good to those who hate you, pray for those who abuse you . . . Give to everyone who begs from you. (Luke 6:27–28; 30)

And you can hear it in what is called Jesus' own "inaugural" sermon when he stood up in the Temple at the beginning of his ministry and simply read this passage from Isaiah:

> The Spirit of the Lord is upon me, because he has anointed me to bring good news to the poor. He has sent me to proclaim release to the captives and recovery of sight to the blind, to let the oppressed go free, to proclaim the year of the Lord's favor. (Luke 4:18–19)

King believed that this country was called to become a "Beloved Community," a society in which every life is of equal worth and every human being is entitled to health care, to a living wage, to education in a good school. This was their birthright as human beings, as American citizens, and as children of God. He believed that a new community to bring this about was possible in America, and that Christians were called to work to make it a reality.

Just days before Dr. King was assassinated in Memphis in 1968, he preached his last Sunday sermon from this Canterbury pulpit, and in it he described his vision this way:

> Through our scientific and technological genius we have made of this world a neighborhood and yet we have not had the ethical commitment to make of it a brotherhood. But somehow, and in some way, we have got to do this. We must all learn to live together as brothers or we will perish together as fools. We are tied together in the single garment of destiny, caught in an inescapable network of mutuality. And whatever affects one directly affects all indirectly. For some strange reason I can never be what I ought to be until you are what you ought to be. And you can never be what you ought to be until I am what I ought to be. This is the way God's universe is made; this is the way it is structured.[3]

Four decades ago Dr. King was seeing a vision as old as Jesus, as old as the seventeenth-century poet John Donne, who said, "No man is an island entire of itself. Each is a piece of a continent, a part of the main." Now our everyday life is demonstrating how interconnected we are. We are held together by the Internet, by global trade, by our dependence on other nations for resources and goods. Our banks are intertwined, our corporations are international. If one nation goes through a recession, poor nations and small villages across the globe feel the impact.

The environmental crisis has linked us globally to our fellow human beings around the world in ways that no other crisis ever has. The fate of the world is tied to the question of whether the United States, China, India, and the other powerful nations of the world will be willing to change their ways of life rapidly, before destroying life as we know it on this planet. If the oil addiction of developed countries isn't turned around soon there will be wars and natural disasters around the globe. We will succeed together, or perish together.

This is an historic moment not simply because of the leader who will be inaugurated on Tuesday, but because this economic crisis has given us a chance to change the paradigm of our nation's life. There is a chance that we can learn new ways of interdependence, of service to others, rather than simply independence. Do you remember John Kennedy's rallying cry, "Ask not what your country can do for you, ask what you can do for your country?" President-elect Obama has already called for tomorrow's Martin Luther King Jr. Day to be a day of service. And that sounds like the beginning of what promises to be many calls to sacrificial service.

We have an opportunity to imagine in our personal and public lives a conversion from a culture of consumption, drivenness, pollution, and anxiety, to lives more peaceful, more responsible and interconnected, more willing even to see our standard of living change in order to protect the environment, reconnect with our own neighborhood, and live saner days.

Several weeks ago we hosted at the Cathedral the well-known African American radio and television personality Tavis Smiley at the Sunday Forum, and I asked him what his expectations were for the new president. "Obama can be a great president," Smiley said, "but he will only be as good as we help him be. We can't abandon him. We in the African American community will need to hold him accountable."[4]

This new president will need the best counsel we Americans can offer, both agreeing and disagreeing. He will need our support and our accountability. And he will need our prayers, our daily prayers, as he leads us through perilous times.

Last year, when Congressman John Lewis preached the sermon for our commemoration of Dr. King's final Sunday sermon, he seemed to be summing up King's vision when he spoke of how we all live in one house. As he put it, black or white or Hispanic or Asian American or Native American, whether we are Democrats or Republicans or Independent, we are one family.

That is the essential insight for our time. There is only one house, the house we will build together as Americans and as world citizens.

And then he told of growing up in what was called a shotgun house, a small, plain, rundown structure with holes in the tin roof and places where you could see the ground under the floor, and surrounded by a dirt yard. One Saturday afternoon, he said, he and a dozen or so of his cousins were playing in the yard of his aunt's shotgun house when a terrifying storm blew up— with lightning, rain, and winds so strong his aunt thought they would blow the house away. The thunder boomed, the rain pounded the tin roof, the wind blasted. His aunt got all the children together and had them hold hands. Sometimes one corner of the old house would start lifting from the foundation, and when it did his aunt had them step to that corner to use their weight to hold it down. When another side lifted, they would do the same. He says, "We were little children walking with the wind, but we never left the house."[5]

Not a bad image for the world we are in right now. The winds are blasting, and it is going to take all of us in this house working together, holding hands, if we are going to come through.

Let us pray for our new president, Barack Obama, for his vice president Joseph Biden, for his cabinet, for the Congress, and for the Supreme Court. Let us pray for President Obama's strength, his wisdom, his safety, and let us pray that a New Community can take shape in our life.

May God go with Barack Obama and with our nation in the months and years ahead.

Anniversary of 9/11

Doubts and Loves

A Sermon on the Tenth Anniversary of 9/11

Matthew 6:19–24

For days now as this tenth anniversary of 9/11 has approached, we Americans have been inundated with images and recollections. In one way or another I suspect we've found ourselves recalling the deep blue sky on the East Coast that morning and the towering inferno of flame and smoke that shattered that serene autumn day.

And we've been hearing testimonies of those who lost someone they loved in the attacks, as well as reading reams of commentary analyzing what 9/11 has meant to us over the past decade. Of course, two of the earliest lessons of 9/11 remain clear. One is that human beings can be brilliantly and brutally evil, and that hatred, pride, and intolerance can wreak terrible destruction. But also, that human beings have a breathtaking capacity for courage and self-sacrifice. For all of the evil committed by the terrorists, we still can be awed by the bravery and devotion of the first responders, the police officers and firefighters, by Todd Beamer and his fellow passengers on Flight 93, and, of course, by the men and women in our military of whom we have asked so much in this past decade.

What you can't miss in the whole saga of 9/11 is the immense power of religion for evil and good. We saw on that terrible Tuesday morning how fanatical, uncritical love for one's religion, nation, or culture can easily became hatred for those of another. Theologian Reinhold Niebuhr believed that the worst human sin is religious sin, when people's actions grow out of an absolute certainty about what is true, which becomes the dangerous intolerance of the religious fundamentalist.[1]

127

The last ten years have comprised a strange spiritual pilgrimage for our country, one that has taken us into hard but in some ways hopeful new territory. Do you remember the sense of togetherness we Americans felt in those early days and even weeks after the attacks? The church pews filled again, families were grateful to have each other and were having more meals together, people were swearing to stop honking horns in traffic tie-ups and to stop getting irritated in the grocery checkout line. (Unfortunately, none of those lasted very long!)

But at the same time fear, anger, and concern for self-defense were rising too. And so began ten years of war, of drastically increased security measures, and of deepening divisions within our country. It has been a long decade. I've wondered in my own mind whether we as Americans have had to go through some of what psychologist Elisabeth Kübler-Ross called the stages of grief.[2] When a patient learns that she is going to die, she will often go through phases of response—denial, anger, bargaining, depression, then finally acceptance. We've seen all of these in recent years. Clearly, we Americans experienced trauma at 9/11, and that trauma led to a wide range of reactions, but after a decade maybe it is time for us to draw some lessons and begin to lay this tragedy to rest.

I can't imagine a more important text for us today than the one from Matthew's gospel we just heard. Peter, it seems, hasn't been much taken with his Lord's notion that forgiveness was at the heart of being a disciple, so he decides to put some limits on it. "Lord, if another member of the church should sin against me how often should I forgive? As many as seven times?" Peter must have thought that was pretty impressive. "How much is enough?" he wants to know. "When do I get to say that's it, I'm not going to try any more?"

But Jesus replies, "Not seven times, but seventy times seven"—which is his way of saying it never ends. Forgiveness isn't an isolated act but a way of life that comes straight from a God whose nature is to forgive. It's the only action Jesus called for in the prayer he taught his disciples, the Lord's Prayer: "Forgive us our sins as we forgive those who sin against us."

Much of the worst cruelty of the last century has been caused by people who have been unwilling to forgive—Hutus and Tutsis, Serbs and Croatians, Sunnis and Shias. The Israelis and Palestinians have been locked for decades in a bitter conflict, and the violent attacks and reprisals seem endless. Both sides in these conflicts have been damaged immeasurably and the opposing groups remain locked in past resentments that make a peaceful future impossible.

It reminds me of the account of a former inmate of a Nazi concentration camp who visited a friend who had gone through the ordeal with him and asked, "Have you forgiven the Nazis?" "Yes," his friend said. "Well, I haven't," the man said. "I'm still consumed by hatred for them." "In that case," his friend said, "they still have you in prison."[3]

Into this bitter cycle of recrimination comes Jesus calling us to the hard work of forgiveness. Forgiveness has its own clear message: "I am furious at you for what you have done. It has hurt me and continues to. But I refuse to stay trapped in my anger. I am going to forgive you because I know you are more than what you have done to me. And I know that we both need God's forgiveness. I want to let go of this and begin again with a clean slate, and leave the rest in God's hands."

For Jesus forgiveness begins not with an act but a recognition—that at our depths we are flawed human beings, that all of us need mercy. It's what Jesus was getting at in the parable in our lesson this morning when a palace servant is forgiven a vast debt but then refuses to forgive a much smaller one. We're all in over our heads in debts for the ways we've hurt others.

I have to say that I do not know exactly what forgiveness would mean as we look back at the evil of 9/11. We can be grateful that our government has vigorously pursued the terrorist cells that carried out the attack. And thanks be to God Osama bin Laden is no longer able to attempt new attacks. But we Americans have work to do in our relationships with the Muslim world.

The world shrank for us Americans that bright fall morning. We saw how interconnected the world really is and that our lives are intertwined with factory workers in Shanghai, customer service operators in India, and terrorist cells in Afghanistan. That day opened us to one of the greatest challenges our human race faces—to be able to see the face of God in those who are profoundly different from us and whose language, culture, and way of life we don't understand.

And one of the most disturbing dimensions of the events of 9/11 was the fact that the terrorists who attacked that day were doing it in the name of their god. Killing for God's sake has been one of the ugliest parts of the human story. The stakes could not be higher for Americans, for Christians, and for the whole human race to embrace the holiness of the other.

Amid all the devastation of 9/11, I believe God was inviting us to step into a larger, more complex and mysterious world. Even in the face of all the grave threats to American security, we are being called to a new humility in understanding those who are different from us. Yehuda Amichai, an Israeli poet who was born under Nazism and lived his life amid the brutal conflicts of the Middle East, wrote a simple poem that seems to me to be a song for our time:

> From the place where we are right
> Flowers will never grow
> in the Spring.
>
> The place where we are right

Is hard and trampled
Like a yard

But doubts and loves
Dig up the world
Like a mole, a plough.
And a whisper will be heard in the place
Where the ruined
house once stood. [4]

As human beings and as Americans we need to embrace the reality that we are finite creatures and only God is absolute. It is through a humble living of our convictions, including our doubts and uncertainties, and a determined effort to respect and even love people different from us, that our world will find its way forward. Writer Karen Armstrong, our Forum guest today, calls that love "compassion," and she has found this compassion at the center of every great religion. It is the key, the goal, even as our nation continues to deal with an extremely dangerous world.

Forgiveness, humility, and compassion are the hope for our world's future. And here and there we can begin to see these essential virtues at work. You can see them in the Heartsong Community Church just outside Memphis, Tennessee, where the pastor, when he heard a local mosque had bought property across the street from the church immediately worked with his church to put up a sign in front of the church saying "Heartsong Church welcomes Memphis Islamic Center to the neighborhood." And soon the church began a series of gestures of friendship and support, including allowing them to use their auditorium worship space while construction was underway. That church lost some members, and the pastor received plenty of outrage in his inbox, but what a grace-filled response to the other communities in this country that have resisted having a mosque at all.

In a recent interview, columnist David Ignatius described a sign of this new way in the transformation that has happened in the U.S. Army in recent years as it has learned to build relationships with the local populations in Iraq and Afghanistan—to listen to them, learn from them, work with them. It's a fresh approach—call it a humble approach, a sign of a new day.

Ten years after that terrible day people are being called to live out their faith in a new global context, plumbing the depths of their own tradition while embracing with humility the vast variety of God's world. And they are being challenged to live by the deepest convictions in all their traditions that compassion, peace, and caring for the other are at the heart of what it means to be human.

You see,

From the place where we are right
flowers will never grow. . . .

But doubts and loves
dig up the world like mole, a plough,
and a whisper will be heard in the place
where the ruined
house once stood. [5]

May God give us Americans and all the nations the wisdom and humility to be people of peace.

Place of Reconciliation

On the Far Side of Revenge

Preached on the occasion of the visit of Archbishop Desmond Tutu for the Cathedral Centennial

A year after the genocide of 1994 in Rwanda, which killed some eight hundred thousand people, Archbishop Desmond Tutu visited a village near the capital of Kigali. Dozens of Tutsi had been slaughtered in a church there by members of the rival Hutu tribe. The new government still had not removed the corpses, so the church was like a mortuary. Outside stood a collection of skulls of the victims, some still with machetes embedded in them. Archbishop Tutu has written that he tried to pray, but instead broke down and wept.

The Hutus and Tutsis had often lived in the same villages, spoken the same language, and were nearly all Christian. But over the decades the two tribes had taken turns dominating the country, and each time one tribe came to power it would carry out an orgy of retribution on the other.

The story of Rwanda is horrific, but the pattern of ethnic, racial, and religious hatred is not rare. We have seen it in Northern Ireland, in Palestine and Israel, in the former Yugoslavia, in al-Qaeda, with the Basques in Spain, the Kurds in Turkey and Iraq, the Chechens in Russia, with the Sunnis and Shiites in Iraq, and with the genocide going on in Darfur.

And, of course, our world is filled with divisions that are not so violent, but destructive nevertheless. Many have said that our country has been as politically divided in recent years as it has been in decades, and people will tell you that Washington, D.C., hasn't been so polarized in anyone's memory. I suspect we can all name marriages and families that remain alienated because of wounds that are years and sometimes decades old. And our own Anglican Communion and Episcopal Church are painfully divided.

135

Martha Horne, the former dean of Virginia Theological Seminary, once described a heated community meeting dealing with the divisions in the Anglican Communion. A visitor waded into the discussion innocently and asked the arguing parties, "What would it take to reconcile the differences among you?" And an angry student shot back, "Reconciliation is not the issue here. The issue is faithfulness to God's word. . . . I'm not interested in reconciliation with someone who refuses to obey God's word." And it has to be said that equally vehement assertions have come from the progressive side as well.[1]

Division, recrimination, violence haunt every corner of the globe. We see the ancient law played out repeatedly: "An eye for an eye, a tooth for a tooth." Philosopher Hannah Arendt called this "the predicament of irreversibility," the ricocheting effect of evil causing evil in an endless and often expanding cycle.[2] But as Martin Luther King Jr. put it, "those who live by 'an eye for an eye and a tooth for a tooth' will one day become a blind and toothless generation." Now in a world of suicide bombers and nuclear weapons, King's vision may prove truer than anyone imagined.

It looks as if the central question of the twenty-first century will be, Can we human beings learn to let go of the burdens of the past, engage our differences, and in doing that create a more hopeful future? Can we be reconcilers? "To reconcile" means literally "to make good again," "to repair." Can we learn to repair the fabric of our world as we make room for the stranger and even the ones we have thought of as "enemy"?

Forgiveness and reconciliation have not always been central tenets in world religions. In fact, Hannah Arendt declares that "the discoverer of the role of forgiveness in the realm of human affairs was Jesus of Nazareth."[3] When Jesus spoke of turning the other cheek, of loving the enemy, of forgiving seventy times seven, he was introducing something new into the human saga. In every daily service here at the Cathedral we echo his vision: "Forgive us our trespasses as we forgive those who trespass against us."

Jesus unleashed a movement of forgiveness and reconciliation by sending out followers who would not return evil for evil, who were willing to absorb wrongdoing and thereby release the present from the prison of the past.

St. Paul in our New Testament lesson says that God has given to Christians "the ministry of reconciliation." We who have been forgiven and accepted in Christ are called to be healers and forgivers ourselves. Archbishop Tutu described God's work as an endless labor of reconciliation:

> There is a movement, not easily discernible, at the heart of things to reverse the awful centrifugal force of alienation, brokenness, division, hostility and disharmony. God has set in motion a centripetal process, a moving toward the center, toward unity, goodness, peace, and justice.[4]

Archbishop Tutu goes on then to say that every act and gesture of forgiveness and healing contributes to this slowly building movement toward a new
world.

Reconciliation has been the center of Desmond Tutu's ministry. His great
phrase, "No future without forgiveness," the title of one of his books, sums
up his conviction not only about his own country but for the whole human
race. In the days of apartheid in South Africa, he knew that reconciliation
first demanded confrontation, and he was a key leader in the fight to establish
a new, nonracist government. And then, with the fall of apartheid, the healing
could begin. And so, April 27, 1994, ushered in a new era in South Africa. At
last, all South Africans could vote, and Nelson Mandela, after twenty-seven
years in prison on Robben Island, became president of his country.

But how could South Africa face the horrors of its past? Everyone agreed
there could be no new South Africa without dealing with the oppression of
the apartheid years. They would need to steer a course between those who
cried "prosecute and punish" and those who demanded "forgive and forget."
Negotiators finally hammered out a process that would require three parts:
confession, a full disclosure of the crimes committed; forgiveness in the form
of amnesty from punishment or further prosecution; and, where possible,
restitution, making amends for what was done.

And so South Africa launched the Truth and Reconciliation Commission
with Archbishop Tutu as its leader. I remember seeing TV reports of Desmond Tutu weeping as he listened to the victims tell their stories of unimaginable torture and of the cruelties inflicted even on children and the old. At
times, Tutu would lead members of the audience in singing a hymn to help
the victim recover composure, and often, even in that secular setting, he
would lead them in prayer.

One reporter described a typical commission hearing taking place in a
packed community hall in a dusty township. A black woman told of the night
the security police smashed down the door and dragged away her son, who
had been active in an anti-apartheid uprising. Some days later a policeman
sent for her to come to the mortuary. In terrible detail she described the
bruised and almost unrecognizable corpse, riddled with nineteen bullet holes.
People wept quietly as she struggled to continue. She said that she did not
know if forgiveness was possible, and that she had to know who had done
this to her son. But possibly, she went on, when she saw the face of the man
who killed him she might be able to forgive. Ultimately she, and a great
many others, were able to release their terrible pasts, and begin to move on.

The brutality afflicted whites as well as blacks. Bishop Tutu has often told
the story of a young white woman, Beth Savage, the victim of an African
terrorist bomb exploded at a golf club during a party. Savage underwent
open-heart surgery and was in intensive care for months, and even when she
was discharged she was so disabled that her children had to feed, clothe, and

care for her. Nevertheless, she was able to say this to the commission: "I would like to meet that man that threw that grenade in an attitude of forgiveness and hope and that he could forgive me too for whatever reason. But I would very much like to meet him."[5]

As exhausting as the work was for the commission and for Bishop Tutu, the result can only be called a miracle. A nation emerged from the worst injustice conceivable, with the black majority at last leading the country, and a civil society and economy still in tact. The cycle of revenge had been broken. Forgiveness had proven to be perhaps the most powerful tool for the future of the human race ever discovered.

In the face of the world's divisions, every now and then we have glimpsed another possibility. Seamus Heaney, the Nobel Prize–winning Irish poet, who has reflected long and hard on the hatred that has torn his country apart, put it this way in a poem:

> History says, Don't hope.
> But then, once in a lifetime
> The longed-for tidal wave
> Of justice can rise up.
> And hope and history rhyme.
>
> So hope for a great sea-change
> On the far side of revenge.
> Believe that a further shore
> Is reachable from here.
> Believe in miracles
> And cures and healing wells.[6]

Every now and then a people have caught a glimpse of what a future might be "on the far side of revenge and alienation." There was the outpouring of generosity in the Marshall Plan after World War II when the U.S. helped rebuild our devastated former enemies; there was the creation of a United Nations to work toward mutual understanding; there was the international response to the tsunami two years ago, and the sense of closeness we felt as Americans just after 9/11. These were moments of what Bishop Tutu calls "ubuntu," when we humans realize how deeply we belong to each other.

Just two years ago the nation watched the Amish community of Nickel Mines, Pennsylvania, respond with forgiveness and compassion to the widow of the man who had murdered five young girls in the local school. They invited her to stay with their community, invited her to the funerals, and shared with her the cash gifts that had poured in from around the country. It seemed to point to a new possibility for human beings. Hope and history for a moment rhymed.

In Desmond Tutu's life and ministry we have been given a picture of the future that God wants for us and our world on the far side of revenge. Maybe the most powerful phrases in the human vocabulary are these, "I am sorry" and "I forgive you" and "Let's start again." What if the religions of the world suffused the world's children with these phrases starting in the crib?

Think what would happen to broken marriages or alienated families if the wounded, angry participants used these words more. Think what could happen if political leaders could learn to say they are sorry when they make mistakes. Think what could happen in our divided church if we fully embraced the call to be reconciled to God and each other. What a sign to the world that would be!

Think what could happen in this country if we finally decided to face the truth of what slavery has done not just to African Americans, but to all of us—setting up an underclass, cutting us off from each other, leaving a gap that runs through the life of our cities and our world.

A movement at the heart of things is underway to reverse centuries of division and hostility—a subtle current that began on a cross, and has been working under the surface for centuries. Now it has surfaced in Desmond Tutu and the people of South Africa as they have shown us that forgiveness in the face of terrible evil is actually possible and not just a nice idea. The longed-for tide has risen up.

> Look at South Africa [Bishop Tutu wrote]. We were a hopeless case if ever there were one. God intends that others might look at us and take courage. . . . There is life after conflict and repression. . . . Because of forgiveness there is a future. [7]

Thanks to Desmond Tutu and his people, we have seen what life can look like on the far side of revenge. What if we began to live that way—at home, in this city, in our nation, and our world? What if?

Religious Diversity

The Spirit of Understanding

John 20:19–23

Living in the middle of a bustling city brings many pleasures, but there can be some rough moments. I remember years ago walking our dog down a street on the south side of Chicago and finding myself being furiously yelled at. Another person's dog was off its leash and went running up to a woman who clearly didn't like dogs. The woman let loose a cascade of fury, and her friend began to swing a stick at the dog. My dog and I were some distance away, but for some strange reason I decided to try to be helpful and calm things down. Big mistake. It took only a few words out of my mouth to bring down a stream of fury on me, too. After a moment or two we all went our separate ways, with her screaming and me seething.

I remember thinking a lot about that woman afterward. Obviously something had made her resent dogs and the people who go with them, and she resented enough other things to have her fury just under the surface. What, if anything, could ever be done to bridge the differences between her world and mine?

The philosopher Ludwig Wittgenstein said that the happy person and the unhappy person inhabit two different worlds. They see and experience different realities. A newly married couple full of hope and eagerness knows a different world from an unhappy, alienated couple drifting toward separation.[1]

It is hard to hear and understand each other across the chasms of our different life experiences. There is now a whole industry of books about the difficulties men and women have understanding each other. Deborah Tannen wrote one called *Why Can't I Hear You?* about how hard it is for men and women to communicate. They speak different languages, Tannen says. Men may be trying to say, "I need you to help me," but it doesn't come out that clearly. And women may be saying, "I need some space for awhile," but the men just don't get it.[2]

Then throw in the different stories that have shaped us. Growing up black or white, Southern or Midwestern, prosperous or barely making it—all of those shape how we see and relate to the world. Pakistanis see the world differently from Americans, Hindus from Buddhists, Native Americans from European Americans. Many worlds, many languages, and often so little understanding.

You may remember the mythic story of the Tower of Babel in the Book of Genesis. Once upon a time, it says, the whole world spoke the same language, and the people in their arrogance decided to build a tower all the way to heaven so that they could be gods themselves. But then God punished them by turning their one language into a profusion of tongues, and as a result human beings became divided by their inability to understand or be understood. Our human differences became a curse as everyone built mental walls to defend their own interests and maintain their own superiority. Our world came to suffer from what philosopher William James called "torn-apartness."[3]

Today we celebrate Pentecost, one of the high feasts of the church year, and the day we call the birthday of the church. Today we remember the coming of the Holy Spirit as God's answer to the torn-apartness of our world and the beginning of a movement called church to spread God's healing Spirit across the world. A massive, chaotic crowd had gathered for the Jewish festival days from every corner of their world—there were Parthians and Medes, they were from Mesopotamia, Asia, Egypt, Libya, Arabia, you name it. It would have seemed like Times Square in New York City, or the streets of Cairo or Calcutta—crowds pushing against each other, speaking in dozens of languages, jostling, and arguing.

But strange events began erupting. The disciples had been waiting in Jerusalem for nearly two months since their Lord's death and resurrection, lying low out of fear, and wondering where their lives were going. When all of a sudden something strange erupted. It was like a rushing wind, Acts tells us. It was like tongues of fire. And then something even stranger happened.

All of a sudden this timid and frightened group was filled with confidence and clarity, and they began to speak in the languages of the crowds. Everyone marveled that they were hearing of God's deeds and power in their own familiar words and phrases. Often people have assumed that the miracle of Pentecost was that the disciples, filled with emotion, ran out speaking in incomprehensible tongues, but it's just the opposite. This was a miracle of communication, of communion, of understanding. People heard. They understood. A Spirit of oneness, of belonging, of mutual comprehension had been unleashed in the human race. "Are not all these who are speaking Galileans?"

they marveled. "And how is it that we hear, each of us in his own native language?"

Luke, the author of the Acts of the Apostles, wants us to see that the torn-apartness of our world was now being healed. This was meant to be the beginning of the reversal of Babel. In the face of all the babbling we do at each other, all the arguing, bickering, and misunderstanding we go through, God's Spirit has been poured out to open our understanding, to draw us into communication, even communion with each other.

Our word "spirit" means breath or wind in Hebrew and Greek. It's meant to suggest that God is in us like the air we breathe. God's life is inside our life. And yet it's easy to miss the reality of God in us. But as the great mystics would say, "We are in God as fish are in water." We are so immersed in God's life that like fish we aren't even aware of the Great Mystery that surrounds and holds us.

But sometimes that Spirit within us starts stirring and moving us in new directions. And sometimes the Spirit begins stirring whole groups and even nations, filling them with energy, giving them visions of what ought to be. Think of the way the Spirit has moved across northern Africa and the Middle East in the last few months that people have called the Arab Spring. The Spirit can move a whole society to a new place, as happened in the civil rights movement and the women's movement.

This is a time when we sorely need this Spirit of communion and understanding. Our nation is facing many problems and challenges, but it seems to be crippled by a spirit of torn-apartness. Partisanship, incivility, and narrow self-interest threaten to undermine the well-being and decency of our nation, even our world.

We as a country still have much to learn, for example, in creating a welcoming spirit for Muslims living in our midst. It has been tragic to see the mean-spiritedness of the burning of the Quran, to follow the angry controversy over plans for a Muslim community center near the site of Ground Zero, to hear of the resistance in some communities to the building of mosques. We need the Holy Spirit to open our American spirits to welcome our fellow children of Abraham as full Americans with us.

And on a larger scale, our nation faces massive threats that can only be met with strong, consistent, courageous public leadership. We Americans continue to stand by and watch as tornados, floods, and droughts rage and the climate of our nation deteriorates. We, the strongest nation in the world, seem incapable of providing leadership in dealing with the largest threat to the well-being of our planet. Meanwhile, our nation careens toward a debt crisis that threatens American economic stability for decades to come, but there seems to be little will to make the political compromises necessary to protect our nation.

Just this week I heard a wise senior observer of our national life here in Washington say that there have been few moments in the last half-century when as much has been at stake that required bold moral leadership as now. He recalled the ways that Lyndon Johnson and Ronald Reagan worked with their political adversaries and the two parties were able to hammer out major legislation, something that seems increasingly impossible in these mean-spirited times.

I was reminded that at the Constitutional Convention of 1787, after four months of debate over what appeared to be irreconcilable differences, it looked as if the Constitution might be doomed. But at that dark moment Benjamin Franklin took the floor and made an historic appeal for cooperation and compromise, as he urged everyone to doubt at least a little in his infallibility. Following his appeal, the delegates made the necessary compromises, and that is finally what it took to give us a Constitution.

There must be a way beyond the torn-apartness of our time—in our world, in our nation and its politics, in our own lives and homes, and that way is what we celebrate today. Two thousand years ago Christ's Spirit began to move, first among a small band of disciples, but soon through churches and leaders and events and movements as God has sought to draw this fragmented, ungracious, contentious human race toward deeper life and communion with each other. Christ's Spirit continues to work in your life and mine, stirring us, opening our eyes, calling us into deeper openness and understanding of the lives and realities outside the bubble of our own self-interest.

"There is a movement, not easily discernible, at the heart of things," Archbishop Desmond Tutu wrote, "to reverse the awful centrifugal forces of alienation, brokenness, division, hostility, and disharmony. God has set in motion a centripetal process, a moving toward the center, toward unity, harmony, goodness, peace, and justice, a process that removes barriers."[4] That is the work the Spirit is doing.

And today, as we welcome new Christians and reaffirm our own baptismal vows, we are agreeing to allow this Spirit to move in us, to heal the torn-apartness in our own hearts, and in our relationships, and to stir us up to be part of healing our fragmented world.

I sometimes think that for all the public challenges our lack of understanding creates, the challenges are at least as great in our personal communication—our quickness to judge, our inability actually to be quiet and listen to one another, our readiness to come back with a retort. Listening itself is an act of ministry, a work of the Spirit, when we are willing to set aside our agenda and take in without judgment or argument what someone else is saying.

I was struck recently by the words that journalist Steve Roberts closed with in a recent Sunday Forum conversation with him and his wife, journalist

Cokie Roberts, about their interfaith marriage. Responding to an invitation to offer advice to interfaith couples, Roberts almost blurted out, "I think candor is vastly overrated. The person who says 'I'm going to tell you what I really think' really means 'I'm going to be hurtful and selfish.' A certain amount of humility is useful."[5]

Humility, understanding, openness, patience—those are the qualities this Spirit of healing is seeking to stir up in us. To open ourselves to this Holy Spirit, to open ourselves to the stranger, the other, whether across the breakfast table or across the world, is to be led deeper into communion, deeper into unity with God and each other. It's the wholeness, the oneness, we were made for.

Come, Holy Spirit, and kindle in us the fire of your love.

A Big Enough House

John 14:1–14

It's one of the most moving and poignant moments in the gospels. Jesus is preparing to leave his disciples to face the death looming before him. And so, for a few chapters, we hear him tell them good-bye. The disciples are anxious, and even sound like children wanting to know where Mommy and Daddy are going. "How long will they be gone?" they are asking. "When are they coming back?"

And so Jesus responds, "Do not let your hearts be troubled. Believe in God, believe also in me. In my Father's house are many dwelling places. If it were not so, would I have told you that I go to prepare a place for you?" These are warm, encouraging, but also confusing words. And then he goes on:

"And you know the place I am going."

"No, Lord, we don't know," Thomas says. "What is the way?"

"I am the way, and the truth, and the life," Jesus answers. "No one comes to the Father except through me."

And so Jesus gives his disciples some of the most beloved words we have for talking about death.

In most of the funerals I have been a part of this has been the passage we read. The words seem so right for good-byes. "Do not let your hearts be troubled: In my Father's house are many dwelling places." One earlier translation says there are many "rooms." And the old King James Version puts it most grandly: "In my Father's house are many mansions."

What moving words—that we all have a home somewhere in God's house, a resting place, a place with our name on it, no matter who we are and no matter our background. And what a wonderful picture of life in God—one

149

great mansion with an unimaginable number of rooms, each one different, each one somehow right as a dwelling place. Or you could even say one vast cathedral with many corners and rooms. It's a big, grand house that God lives in.

But this beautiful text all of a sudden gets complicated. Show us the way to the house, Thomas says. "I am the way, the truth, the light," Jesus says. But then he says, "No one comes to the Father except through me." And all of a sudden this warm, inviting passage about the expanse of God's love seems so narrow as to squeeze out two-thirds of the people on earth and the countless billions down through the centuries who have not been Christian.

All three of the great Abrahamic religions have a strong strain of exclusivity. "Hear O Israel: The Lord is our God, the Lord alone, and you shall have no other gods before me." That's the first of the Ten Commandments in the faith of Israel. "There is no God but Allah, and Mohammed is his prophet," the faith of Islam steadily asserts. When these sweeping assertions are used to challenge the idolatries people fall into when they are seduced by the gods of wealth and success, they are powerful claims. But when they are turned into a denial of other faiths, they become troubling.

If we say that the dangers of our time come from Americans worshiping at the altar of the stock market, or the owning of larger and larger homes, or going into debt to have more things, then we Christians need to hear Jesus say, no, those aren't the way to eternal life, "*I* am the way, the truth and the life." But if we use that same affirmation to declare that only Christians will enter God's many-roomed mansion, we have lost its real meaning.

And so it's the strangest of things that this passage of such beauty and assurance, this picture of God's dwelling place as an unimaginably grand mansion with room enough for everyone, has also produced one of the harshest lines in our tradition when it seems to declare that non-Christians must somehow not be part of God's eternal love. As big as this picture is of life with God, is it big enough?

America, you know, has become the most religiously diverse nation in the world. There are more Muslim Americans than there are Episcopalians by far, more Muslims than Jews. Los Angeles, according to Harvard scholar Diana Eck, is the most complex Buddhist city in the world. You can now spot Hindu temples and Muslim mosques dotting the metropolitan D.C. landscape. [1]

And so one of the big questions we face as Americans and Christians is, How do we live with religious differences, especially in a time when many religions are growing around the world and are often intensely tribal and divisive?

One of the chief impacts of the 9/11 attacks was the fresh realization of how dangerous religious faith can be. The attackers were radical Muslim zealots who believed they were carrying out their destruction as an act of religious devotion. We know, of course, that Christians have been capable of the same thing, in the Crusades, for example, and in the pogroms in which Christians over the centuries have gone on rampages killing Jews. And, of course, there have been countless Hindu-Muslim clashes, Hindu-Sikh and Arab-Israeli conflicts, and many more.

"Dear God, save us from the people who believe in you," someone scribbled on a wall here in Washington after 9/11. Religions are powerful—and dangerous. It's enough to make you ask, In a world that seems to get more interconnected and yet more tribal by the day, is it possible for religious people, and especially Christians, to be forces of healing and civic health?

When I'm teaching a course on our faith someone will often ask, "Can people who aren't Christians be saved?" Sometimes the question emerges out of concern for friends or relatives who are nonbelievers or believers in other faiths. There are many Christians who believe that if you don't accept Jesus as your Lord and Savior you are going to hell, just as other Christian traditions have insisted that only the baptized faithful can ever get to heaven. Given the billions of people across the face of the earth and down through the centuries who are not Christians, the ranks of hell would have to be filling up fast.

"No one comes to the Father but by me." It sounds arrogant and intolerant, but is it? Jesus didn't say, "Believing in me is the way, or having the right ideas about my teachings is the way." He said, "*I* am the way." And who is this Jesus who says he's the way? He is the friend of every sinner, every outsider, and every non-Jew he meets. Jesus surrounded himself with the people who had been excluded and had been rejected by the proper religious establishment. He was the one who believed that caring for the broken and suffering is more important than keeping the laws and thinking the right thing. That's his way, his truth, his life.

It was Jesus who said, "I am the good shepherd who lays down his life for the sheep," and when he talked about keeping his disciples safe with him in the sheepfold, he then said this: "And I have other sheep that are not of this fold and I am going to bring them in also." This doesn't sound like a One Way approach.

In fact, if you dig into that little troubling phrase, "No one comes to the Father but by me," there are hints of a much bigger vision than you think. "No one comes to the Father." It doesn't say no one comes to God, but that Jesus is the one who can take them into an intimate relationship with God as "Father."

Who is saved and who isn't, who's in and who's out? I remember puzzling over that as I made my way back into the Christian faith as a graduate student. Christians believe that in Christ God was reconciling the whole world. My closest friend, and one of the finest human beings I knew, had grown up in a hellfire and brimstone church in a small town in the South, and he literally would break into a sweat any time he walked into any church. Because of his early life, faith for him was impossible, and yet his life was in many ways a model for mine.

The finest teacher I had in graduate school was a secular Jew, who loved Shakespeare and St. Paul. As I heard him talk about *King Lear* or *Measure for Measure*, I found my own faith growing deeper and clearer. I heard Christ through him.

And later as a professor I knew well a Muslim colleague who was one of the gentlest, wisest people I had ever encountered. None of these was Christian; all of them were luminous, even holy, human beings.

At the same time I remember thinking back over my own church experience growing up. There were, of course, many good souls, but there were also many who seemed hypocritical, insincere, angry, or self-righteous, too. This was the South of the 1960s, and many of them were strong segregationists. How could it be that these people were somehow *in* and my unchurched friends were somehow *out*?

Only later did I encounter St. Augustine's sobering words: "God has many whom the church does not have, and the church has many whom God does not have." What became clear to me then was that God is bigger than our formulas, more mysterious than all our ways of drawing the line.[2]

What kind of God could it be, when you think of it, who would consign to everlasting damnation any who do not believe by a certain formula, or who belonged to different faith traditions, or even who don't believe in God at all? What parent would ever choose under any circumstances the eternal suffering of his or her child?

Do all religions say the same thing? No. Even though they often have many things in common, there are profound differences. Do all religions basically believe in the same God? Not if you probe very deeply. There's no blending of these different faiths into one. Are all religions equal? No. Some religions or brands of religions are toxic.

What makes us Christians is that we believe that this God of the entire universe, who has reached out to the human race in every time and place and through countless religious traditions, actually came among us in one human life. In Christ we Christians see that God has taken on our flesh, lived, suffered, and died for us, and promises never to leave us. No other religion makes that immense claim.

But that doesn't mean we don't have important things to learn from the Muslim sense of awe before God, from the Jewish passion for living God's Torah, from the Buddhist sense of compassion and surrender of the self, from the Hindu sense of the sacredness of every part of the world.

If you glimpse the full expanse of God's love, you realize that the question is not who's in and who's out, but who knows this love and who doesn't. The whole human race is in the fold of God's love. And yet the role of the church remains indispensable. Church is where we come to reconnect with the love we see in Christ—to be fed by it, to learn its ways, to find the compassion to live it. What saves us is love—God's love for us and our learning to live in this love. "God is love," it says in the First Letter of John, "and those who abide in love abide in God, and God abides in them."

The test of any person's faith or any faith tradition is this: Does it make your world bigger, more generous, more embracing of God's world, or does it make your world smaller, tighter, more like you?

Could it be that Jesus is bigger than Christianity? Could it be that the Father-Mother love that Jesus shows us has been working in every corner of this creation and in every life from the beginning of time and that there is a resting place in God's life for everyone?

"In my Father's house are many dwelling places," Jesus said. "I go to prepare a place for you." "How do we get there?" Thomas asks. "By following my way," Jesus answers. "What way is that?" Thomas asks.

"Love," Jesus says. "Just love."

Race and Poverty

In Thanksgiving for the Life of Dorothy Height

For the funeral of the distinguished civil rights leader, with the president and many of the great African American leaders of our time

I don't know how many times in the course of her ninety-eight years Dorothy Height might have listened to the passage we just heard, but I imagine quite a few. The words called the Beatitudes are so familiar that it's easy to miss how strange they must have sounded when Jesus first uttered them two thousand years ago, and how strange they still are.

"Blessed are the poor in spirit," "blessed are those who mourn," "blessed are the meek." These words are saying that the weakest, the most broken, the most vulnerable people are on to something that others are missing, and that somehow they are at the center of God's heart and work.

And then all of a sudden, Jesus shifts from talking about people— "Blessed are the meek"—to addressing his followers directly: "Blessed are you when people revile you and persecute you and utter all kinds of evil against you on my account . . . that's the way they treated the prophets before you." His disciples are a ragtag group of fishermen, ex-IRS agents, and people off the streets; they aren't the movers and shakers, the power brokers and the famous. But Jesus is saying to them, "You're the ones who are going to change the world."

"You are the salt of the earth," he says. "You are the light of the world." I'm calling you to be edgy, provocative salt in the system, and gleaming lights of moral clarity to confront the world and guide it. You are salt and light to build a new world.

Today, we are giving thanks for the life of a woman who over nearly a century became an unstoppable force of salt and light for our country. For days now and again this morning, we have been celebrating this woman known as the grande dame of the Civil Rights Movement, its unsung heroine, one of the small handful of its most important leaders. Dorothy Height's eighty years of involvement spanned the lynchings of the 1930s, the activism of Eleanor Roosevelt in the '40s, school desegregation in the'50s, and then the civil rights movement of the '60s and beyond, and demonstrated her tireless dedication to equality and justice.

And Dorothy Height's commitment to social justice led to her determined efforts to overcome gender bias in our society as well, even within the civil rights movement. A pastor friend from Chicago sent me a note this week filled with admiration for this tireless crusader, and in it he recalled her memories of being eased to the periphery among the male civil rights leaders whenever a photo was taken with the president of the United States or any other dignitary. The civil rights leadership, he said, was "a man's world." Nevertheless, this brave, persistent woman won her place in the highest counsels of the movement, and today the president of the United States himself is here to honor her.

Dorothy Height was by any estimation one of the heroes of the last century in America. Today we give thanks for her saltiness, for her bright and unrelenting light, for her steely persistence and indomitable spirit.

Now this remarkable woman's earthly pilgrimage is ended, and we are here to thank God for the gift she has been to this country, to her friends and family, and to her colleagues in the National Council of Negro Women and countless other organizations she helped to lead.

Undergirding Dorothy Height's life and work must certainly have been the faith expressed in our service today. Isaiah speaks of God's call "to loose the bonds of injustice, to let the oppressed go free, to share your bread with the hungry, to satisfy the needs of the afflicted." "You shall be called the repairer of the breach," the prophet says, "the restorer of streets to live in." It's clear those words were marching orders for this remarkable woman.

And the passages from the Christian scriptures today speak of the conviction that death is not the final word in the human saga. "I am the resurrection and the life, says the Lord," we heard as this service began. "I am the Alpha and the Omega," we heard in one of the lessons. Christian faith is grounded in the conviction that there is a power at work in the cosmos and in every human life that evil and death cannot defeat, and that means that we humans can live with hope both in this life and in the great mystery that awaits us when we die.

We know so little about eternity. But the Christian gospels are filled with acts of healing and forgiveness, of raising up the downtrodden, of confronting powers of cruelty and evil. And in them, Jesus kept saying, God's kingdom was breaking into history, and eternal life was erupting in the ordinary.

Wherever hope and healing and justice appear, people are glimpsing eternity itself.

And so we could say that eternity was breaking into history when Rosa Parks sat down on that bus, when those marchers made their way across the Edmund Pettus Bridge in Selma, Alabama, when Martin Luther King Jr. stood on the steps of the Lincoln Memorial to proclaim his great dream, and when Dorothy Height challenged one organization after another to open their doors to everyone.

We glimpse eternal life here and now when hearts are soothed, bodies are healed, when decent schools and health care and safe streets become the norm, when children and families have a chance at succeeding, when guns and violence no longer desecrate our streets. In those moments, God's eternity breaks into time giving glimpses of the healed society, and even the eternity, that await us. And eternal life beyond death must be something like all these moments of healing and wholeness flowing one into another until time doesn't matter anymore, and all things are gathered into God's love.

That's the vision that seems to have shaped Dorothy Height's life—a sense that there is what poet John Donne called "one equal music and one equal love" at the heart of reality. It is an immense claim—that death is not the end, that love and healing will have the final word. And it is faith in that ultimate vision that inspired the prophets and truth-speakers and organizers, and that fired Dorothy Height's own determination.

Now Dorothy Height has entered fully into God's life. Because we know so little of that mysterious future, we have to leave it to the poets to give us at least a vision of it, and so I close with the final words of James Weldon Johnson's poem, "Go Down Death: A Funeral Sermon":

> And Death took her up like a baby,
> Up beyond the evening star,
> Out beyond the morning star,
> Into the glittering light of glory,
> On to the Great White Throne.
>
> And Jesus took his own hand and wiped away her tears,
> And he smoothed the furrows from her face,
> And the angels sang a little song,
> And Jesus rocked her in his arms,
> And kept a-saying: "Take your rest,
> Take your rest, take your rest."
>
> Weep not—weep not,
> She is not dead;
> She's resting in the bosom of Jesus. [1]

Take your rest, Sister Dorothy, take your rest. You have been salt and light for nearly a century, and you have left this world a more just, more equal, more hopeful place. "Take your rest, Sister Dorothy, take your rest." May light perpetual shine upon you.

An Extremist for Love

The Legacy of Martin Luther King Jr.

Luke 6:27–36

It's a surprising thing, isn't it, that a man who died just thirty-nine years ago has a major holiday set aside to honor his life? Here in Washington they are planning a memorial on the Mall to celebrate his life and work—the only person to be honored on our nation's sacred ground who wasn't a president. I would guess that every city and most towns in America have a Martin Luther King street or boulevard, a King post office, federal building, or high school. With amazing speed Martin Luther King Jr. has entered the pantheon of the greatest American leaders, and our Episcopal Church remembers him in its sacred calendar as one of the great Christians in the church's history.

With all those accolades, it can be easy to forget just how troubling a figure Dr. King was in his time. I can tell you, he was no hero in the white world of the small Mississippi town to which my family moved in 1965. I was in high school then, and there were plenty who hated him. Most of my family saw themselves as moderates—certainly not racists, but not inclined to get involved in this troublesome cause. When King's march came through town in 1965, it might as well have been happening in Detroit or Cleveland. Everyone just went about their business, kept their heads down, and waited for it to pass.

A friend of mine remembers a more dramatic scene when Dr. King led a march in Columbus, Ohio. There was fear of potential rioting, and so my friend's father sat all night long in the living room of their blue-collar neighborhood house, with the lights turned out, a rifle stretched across his lap, ready to protect his family. Dr. King was no hero to him.

Martin Luther King Jr. was not a comfortable, reassuring figure. Though he was by all accounts a courtly, gentle man, as a leader he was a relentless, provocative disturber of the peace of segregated America. That was an America that I remember well—of signs saying "colored" and "white" posted on restrooms and in bus stations, doctors' offices, and theaters. He was always controversial. Many people criticized him for pushing too hard and moving too fast. And, on the other side, many civil rights leaders, such as Malcolm X and Stokely Carmichael, denounced him for refusing to call for violent revolution.

Many saw him as the new Moses, who, as we heard in our first lesson, was called to lead his people out of slavery in Egypt to a new Promised Land of justice and hope. People saw him as a prophet like Amos or Isaiah, demanding on God's behalf a just society. But for today the word I want to use for King was one he applied to himself. He believed he was called to be "an extremist for love." He quoted frequently Jesus' admonition: "I say to you, Love your enemies, do good to those who hate you, pray for those who abuse you."

That's extremist, and King actually lived that way. Listen to these words of King that seem almost unimaginable in their courage and resolve:

> To our bitter opponents we say: "We shall match your capacity to inflict suffering by our capacity to endure suffering. We shall meet your physical force with soul force. Do to us what you will, and we shall continue to love you. Beat us and leave us half dead and we shall still love you. . . . We shall so appeal to your heart and conscience that we shall win *you* in the process, and our victory shall be a double victory."[1]

An extremist—that's what he was. A provoker, a visionary, a courageous leader who never stopped teaching the power of tough, truth-speaking, justice-making love.

> Was not Jesus an extremist for love [King once wrote]—"Love your enemies, bless them that curse you. . . ." Was not Amos an extremist for justice—"Let justice roll down like waters and righteousness like a mighty stream." . . . Was not Paul an extremist for the gospel of Christ. . . . Was not Abraham Lincoln an extremist. . . . So the question is not whether we will be extremist but what kind of extremist we will be. Will we be extremists for hate or will we be extremists for love?[2]

The words come from one of his most important writings, "Letter from a Birmingham Jail." In 1963, King and his colleagues decided to take their movement to the heart of the Confederacy, to Birmingham, Alabama, to work for civil and voting rights. They were soon arrested for marching without a permit. A group of "liberal" Alabama clergy had published an open letter calling on King for moderation, for him to allow the battle for integration to continue in the courts and warning him that his movement was going to cause major civic disturbances. They supported his goals, they said, but wished he could wait and be more patient.

And so, sitting in his jail cell, King wrote a firm, thoughtful letter, free of anger and bitterness, addressing his critics point by point.

> For years now I have heard the word "Wait!" It rings in the ear of every Negro with a piercing familiarity. This "Wait" has almost always meant "Never." . . . I guess it is easy for those who have never felt the stinging darts of segregation to say "Wait." But when you have seen vicious mobs lynch your mothers and fathers at will; . . . when you have seen hate-filled policemen curse, kick, brutalize and even kill your black brothers and sisters with impunity; . . . when you suddenly find yourself tongue twisted and your speech stammering as you seek to explain to your six-year-old daughter why she can't go to the public amusement park . . . and see the depressing clouds of inferiority beginning to form in her little mental sky . . . and when you are forever fighting a degenerating sense of "nobodiness"; then you will understand why we find it difficult to wait. [3]

We will have to repent in this generation, he went on to say, not merely for the vitriolic words and actions of the bad people, but for the appalling silence of the good people.

For King, patience and moderation were no virtues. After the passing of the Civil Rights Act in 1964, Dr. King, to the dismay of many of his friends and colleagues, began expanding his agenda. He launched the Poor Peoples' Campaign, demanding jobs and decent wages, health care and decent education. And with great controversy he began to oppose the Vietnam War. On the last Sunday of his life Dr. King stood in this pulpit and spoke passionately of all these concerns—racism, poverty, and war.

Of course, all of those problems persist today. I'll never forget an African American woman in a congregation I served, with a young son just turning ten or eleven, saying to me with tears in her eyes, "I can see it happening. Until now I've been able to protect my boy from all the terrible messages this world gives him about who he is as a young black man. But now it's happening, and I'm starting to see the anger, the acting out, the signs that he doesn't believe in himself."

A few years ago Cornel West, now a professor of Afro-American studies at Princeton, described a typical experience of waiting a full hour for a taxi in New York City, while all around him white individuals were picked up. And he revealed being stopped three times in his first ten days living in Princeton for driving too slowly on a residential street. The burden of race in America is relentless still.

In his book *Race Matters*, Cornel West says that the "fundamental crisis in black America is twofold: too much poverty and too little self-love."[4] And it is "overcome not by argument or analysis—but by love and care."[5]

Racism is both a social evil and a spiritual disease.

And the statistics bear out the costly impact of this racism on African Americans. More than one-third of black males under thirty are involved in the criminal justice system. One out of two African American children lives in poverty, and they are at the bottom of the pile when it comes to education, health care, and hope.

Yet somehow as a nation we still can't fully commit ourselves to address the toll that America's sins of slavery and racism have taken not just on our African American brothers and sisters but on all of us. I know that as a white American male I stand here as the beneficiary of centuries of affirmative action that have given me every chance to build a good life. Can I, can we, not reach out to those who have started so far back in the race and do what we can to give them an equal chance?

We need Martin Luther King Jr. as much as ever. We need his holy impatience for justice, his insistence that we not wait, his passionate commitment to say and do what needs to be done to build a more just society. We need his call to nonviolence, and, in the midst of our war in Iraq today, we need his insistence that our nation find ways other than devastating armed conflict to build peace in our world.

Here in the church we need his clarity that Christ calls us to stand with the poorest in our society, to continue working to rid our hearts and this society of racism, to resist the natural tendency to complacency in our privilege. In our time, when churches have spent so much energy fighting internal battles, it is vital to remember a time not long ago when churches stood for something important and played a vital role in creating a more just society. We as a cathedral, each of us ourselves, need to ask, "What is God calling me to do?"

This past week I visited Cesar Chavez Charter School for Public Policy, located in a struggling neighborhood not far from Capitol Hill, and there I saw Dr. King's dream alive. There were young African American students being treated with love and dignity and with demanding expectations. Their teachers were mostly bright young idealists, many of them in the Teach for America program. Everywhere in the school was an insistent call to excellence and a spirit of love. And walking around you couldn't help but sense the hope—that with enough schools like this around this city and across this country, at least some of the ravages of poverty and racism could begin to recede. King's dream seemed possible.

I don't often quote Barry Goldwater, the 1964 Republican presidential candidate, but he once uttered a memorable declaration that has stuck with me. "Extremism in the defense of liberty is no vice; and moderation in the pursuit of justice is no virtue."[6] I regret the safe, privileged moderation that even at my young age kept me and so many others in the 1960s safely on the sidelines of the struggle for justice and hope, and often still does. That moderation is, for me at least, no virtue.

Let us give thanks to God for Martin Luther King Jr.'s immoderate life and holy impatience. May this extremist for love still inspire and guide us in the work ahead.

Black and White on the Road to Emmaus

Preached at the conclusion of a series of events covering racial reconcilia-tion, this sermon looks at the challenge of race in our country in light of the Easter promise of new life

Luke 24:13–35

We've just listened to maybe the most loved of the Easter stories. Two disciples are on the road from Jerusalem to a village called Emmaus on Easter afternoon, and they are talking about everything that has happened. What an upsetting, confusing time they had been through. Their leader had raised so many hopes that a new world was possible, but in a matter of a few months it had all come apart, and now he was gone.

They must have been devastated, and probably filled with guilt, too. After all, by the end all Jesus' disciples had deserted him. But by Sunday afternoon they had heard reports that their Lord's tomb was empty, even that he was alive again, and didn't know what to think. Could things ever really be better again?

And then a mysterious stranger joined them as they walked and asked what they were talking about. "Are you the only stranger in Jerusalem who doesn't know the things that have happened?" they asked. And then they told him the whole story.

Those disciples knew plenty about injustice, hatred, and loss. They had stared at a brutal cross and a sealed tomb. That always seems to be what the world does to its prophets. Could any hope be possible in a time as dark as this?

For the past week we in this Cathedral have been on the road to Emmaus together. You could call us a company of disciples remembering an event that will always honor and haunt this Cathedral—Martin Luther King Jr.'s last Sunday sermon, preached here four days before he was killed in Memphis. This commemoration, falling in the days just after Easter, has asked us to look back forty years, and to take stock of where we are as a nation in the work of racial justice and reconciliation, and to ask what it means for us as Christians.

It has been quite a week. Last Sunday we heard Congressman John Lewis, one of the heroes of the civil rights movement tell his story and issue a renewed call to the work of racial justice and reconciliation. And the week's reflections have included a lecture, a documentary film on the slave trade, a weeklong conference on preaching in the tradition of Dr. King, and sermons twice each day grappling with the legacy of the great preacher and leader.

Two weeks ago, Easter morning declared that Christ is raised from the dead, bringing hope and new life. But like those disciples trudging along, we have been searching for a hope that has often seemed hard to find.

In recent days, the fortieth anniversary of Dr. King's death has brought a great deal of discussion about race in America. Last week Secretary of State Condoleezza Rice declared that America still must grapple with what she called our "national birth defect"[1] that denied black Americans the opportunities given to whites at the country's founding. That echoes the declaration of many that slavery is America's "original sin," and we still haven't fully faced the consequences of that tragic flaw.

Newspapers and television programs have been offering a report card on our country's racial progress in these last forty years. They point to important successes—the impact of civil rights legislation passed in the 1960s, the growth of a vital black middle class, the emergence of important black leaders, among them two black governors, many black legislators and corporate executives, and now a black presidential candidate.

But the debit side of the ledger is deeply troubling. New statistics came out recently declaring that one in every nine black men between twenty and thirty-four is behind bars. One-third of African American men in their thirties have a prison record. Colbert King in yesterday's *Washington Post* wrote that Dr. King "would be saddened by the extent of instability in black families [noting that 70 percent of black babies are born to single mothers] and by the self-destructiveness of young black men four decades after his death."[2] This reflects what African American scholar Cornel West described several years ago as a "nihilism" that grips significant parts of the black community—what he calls "the experience of coping with a life of horrifying meaninglessness, hopelessness, and (most important) lovelessness."[3]

And maybe just as troubling is the fact that those forty years after Dr. King's death, white and black Americans in many ways still live in separate worlds. The Cathedral canon Pastor Eugene Sutton has argued that black Americans read American history differently. What jumps out for them, he says, is the legacy of slavery, the wiping out of indigenous people, and the continued psychological and physical repression. Most white Americans do not think of "America" in the same way African Americans do.[4]

Over the past week I have come to imagine not just two disciples on the road to Emmaus, but two types of disciples, some black, some white. Each has a different story to tell of their hopes and fears, as they are walking into the future, looking for Easter.

I have just finished a memoir called *Grace Matters*, in which a young white man from Vermont decides to join an interracial Christian community in Jackson, Mississippi. Chris Rice, the author, left college to move there and stayed for seventeen years, which became for him a time of hard work and personal struggle as whites and blacks in the community attempted to bridge the chasm between their stories.

Rice became the close friend and partner in ministry of the charismatic African American leader Spencer Perkins, and their candid conversations probed the hidden corners of race relations. Chris came to understand what a difference it made that his immigrant ancestors had come to America by choice, while Spencer's had come in chains on a slave ship. Chris' relatives had passed down from one generation to the next financial capital, networks of friends, stable family life, and solid places in society. Spencer's ancestors had no money and almost no possessions, their families torn apart generation after generation because of the buying and selling of slaves. Even following their emancipation, they had no vote and almost no chance of getting out of indebtedness to white landowners. His grandmother had died of malnutrition in a sharecropper's shack, and his father, the Christian leader John Perkins, had been beaten nearly to death by a white policeman.

"Part of my privilege," Chris Rice declares, "was that for me dealing with race was optional—I could take it or leave it. I could cross town . . . into a white world . . . and for the rest of my life I probably wouldn't have to deal with race again. Unless I chose to." He came to see that no white person has to do anything to continue to enjoy the privilege of being white. But his friend Spencer, he said, "had to deal with the everyday struggles of race whether [he] wanted to or not"[5]—producing two IDs to cash a check, worrying about being pulled over by the police for nothing, knowing simply walking down the street could frighten a woman walking alone.

Chris and Spencer and the rest of their small community lived daily with their different stories. They worked, prayed, and shared a house together for years. They discovered how differently they understood what each other said and how hard it was to hear harsh truth being spoken in the midst of conflict and disagreement.

They were disciples, black and white, on the road to Emmaus, seeking a new Easter where people of both races could share each other's lives and honor and respect each other.

That, of course, was Dr. King's vision. For him the gap between white and black was immense. In 1968, when Dr. King stood in this pulpit he took on directly what he called "the "boot-strap philosophy" which declared that if black people are to rise out of poverty they will have to do it on their own. But people forget, he argued, that no other ethnic group began here as slaves, and that when they were finally freed they were given no help, and certainly no land. It was like keeping a person in prison for years, then discovering he is innocent, then setting him free without so much as a nickel to help him start again. He pointed out that during those years when newly emancipated slaves were trying to begin new lives with no help from the government, the U.S. Congress was giving away millions of acres to white immigrants from England, building land-grant colleges, offering low interest rates, and giving away millions in farm subsidies. It is a cruel hoax, King declared, to expect a man who has no boots to pull himself up by his own bootstraps.[6]

I have to say that I have been receiving affirmative action all my life— from the stable family I started with, to a public education far better than that received by my black neighbors, to the friends and connections that smoothed my way in school and work, to the ease I have as a white man applying for a job. Affirmative action for African Americans has been controversial over the last forty years, but why should only whites receive affirmative action?

We Americans have work to do to close the gap between black and white in America. In the story of those disciples on the road to Emmaus they discovered that they didn't travel alone. A stranger walked with them whom they would realize was the Risen Lord himself. And as he listened to them tell their stories he used the scriptures to tell them of a God who hung on the cross to heal the wounds and conflicts of their lives, to forgive them, and to give the human race a chance to begin again.

He told them, as St. Paul would later put it, that on the cross God had broken down the dividing walls between all human beings, and had called a new, forgiven people to be healers and peacemakers themselves. That is the Easter Lord who brought us here today, and this Lord is calling us as American Christians to be reconcilers between black and white.

What would it mean if we really embraced the fact that Christ crucified and risen has broken down the dividing walls between black and white, rich and poor, Anacostia and Northwest Washington?

Now, forty years on, it is time to begin again. Let me offer some simple steps for starters. First, we need to build relationships across color lines. My guess is that few whites have genuinely close relationships with African Americans—the kind where they have dinner together, know each other's children, share in celebrations together. Building those relationships takes time and a willingness to risk opening ourselves to new discoveries. And we need to create those relationships across lines of race and class in the church too. Here at this Cathedral we are in the early stages of developing a partnership with Covenant Baptist Church in Anacostia, and already this new friendship is enriching our lives.

Second, whites need to be as curious and eager to learn about black culture as blacks have had to be with white culture. Do we know the literature of Richard Wright, Toni Morrison, Maya Angelou, Ernest Gaines, August Wilson, and Ralph Ellison? Do we experience the power of the spirituals of the African American tradition, as well as the great jazz and popular music?

Third, we can commit ourselves to making the places where we live and work more racially diverse and inclusive. That doesn't happen accidentally. It takes focus, diligence, and often courage.

Fourth, as Christians we are called to feed the hungry, clothe the naked, and work to build a more just society for everyone. That means pressing vigorously for better public schools, for affordable housing, for health care for everyone. In no American city are these more urgently needed than here in Washington.

And finally, we need to wrestle with something seemingly symbolic, but potentially very powerful. We need to be willing as a church and a nation to look back at the dreadful legacy of slavery in America and to say simply, "We are sorry." What powerful, healing words those could be. "We apologize and we want to work to make things better." Next fall the leaders of our entire Episcopal Church will gather here at this Cathedral for just such a service, and we as a church will finally say, "We're sorry, we're sorry, for all the ways our nation has supported slavery, and for the easy peace it has made with the terrible consequences of that slavery that continue to this day."

We Christians have urgent work to do. I was greatly moved by some words from Chris Rice's memoir:

> What if America looked at this agonizing race problem and said, "But you know, there is a people among us who live differently, who haven't given in to the normal ways we operate as races. They go out of their way for the sake of the other—even when it's uncomfortable, costly, and inconvenient."[7]

If Christians were to become those kind of people, the world would have to take notice.

Those disciples on the road to Emmaus arrived in the village in the late afternoon and invited the mysterious stranger to stay with them. At the table he broke bread, shared wine, and the disciples' eyes were opened, and they realized that it had been Christ with them all along the road, listening, teaching, drawing them closer to each other and to God. And then they rushed back to tell their friends that they had actually seen the Risen Lord.

Easter happens when tombs open, old divisions heal, when people learn to forgive and to understand each other, when a society becomes more just and hopeful.

My prayer is that all of us, black and white, can stay on this road to Emmaus, trudging toward resurrection, trusting that Christ himself will lead us into the grace and forgiveness to which we are called.

It is time to begin again. May the Spirit of the Risen Christ, and the brave, prophetic spirit of Dr. King himself, keep us steady on the road ahead.

Mind the Gap

While the Cathedral is intended to serve the nation, it is also a cathedral for the city of Washington, D.C. This seeks to address the city's most enduring challenge—the gap between the rich and poor.

Luke 16:19–31

I must have been eleven or twelve years old when I discovered the gap for myself. I was spending a few days visiting with my grandparents in a small town in Mississippi. One day it came time to take home Precious, the warm, loving African American woman who kept house for my grandparents, and I jumped in the car to go along on the brief drive across town.

I remember being stunned as that short drive took us into an entirely different world. We left behind the well-built brick house, green lawn, spacious rooms, and air-conditioning. And we drove into a neighborhood of rundown, unpainted houses, rough unpaved roads, with beat-up sofas and chairs sitting out on the porches where there would be a chance of a breeze.

And I remember being shocked that a world as dreary and barren as that existed so close to the comfortable world of my grandparents. It was as if parallel universes existed side by side, and between them was a gap as deep as the Grand Canyon.

Today is Cathedral Day. This is our birthday Sunday, when we give thanks for the Cathedral's founding a little over a century ago, and we reflect on our mission as a church for the nation and this city and on what it means to be a Christian in these times. For this Cathedral Day, I want to focus not on the soaring beauty of this building but on the city it is called especially to serve, and on the gap between rich and poor that runs wide and deep both here in Washington, D.C., and in cities and towns across the country.

173

There's a saying you will hear if you ever have a chance to ride a subway in London. An electronic voice comes over the sound system as the train is about to stop, urging people to watch their step getting on and off the train because there's a space between the train and the platform. "Mind the gap!" the voice says. Pay attention to the divide. Danger lurks there.

Today I want to talk about what it means to follow a Lord who calls us to mind the gap between rich and poor that runs through the heart of every American city, and none more dramatically than our nation's capital.

Anyone who has been in Washington long would tell you that there is not one Washington but two. One is made up of magnificent monuments and avenues, of museums and memorials, of grand federal buildings and prosperous neighborhoods. It is the world of Cherry Blossom Festivals and Redskins football and tour buses and lawyers and lobbyists and shopping plazas. This is the only Washington that most visitors seem to know.

But there's another city, one that people discover when they venture outside the zip codes of Northwest Washington and cross Rock Creek Park. It is a city of pulsing neighborhoods with dozens of nationalities and languages, and it is also a largely African American city. This Washington is a place of old neighborhoods and long histories, and one where neighborhoods are now being gentrified, pushing out families that have been in one place for generations.

This city faces immense challenges—from crime and gun violence, to sky-high unemployment for youth and adults, to an AIDS crisis on the level of many African nations, to one of the highest infant mortality rates in the developed world. Public schools are run down, streets are pockmarked with potholes, social services are unreliable, and decent health care is rare. This Washington many people now call a "colony." After decades of effort, its citizens have no voting representative in Congress. In many ways, it is a city of powerlessness.[1]

In our gospel lesson for today, Jesus is giving us a parable about minding the gap. You remember how it goes. There's a rich man who's clearly enjoying the good life. He's dressed in royal purple and fine linen, and he feasts sumptuously every day. And then, just outside the locked gate of his grand house, is a poor man named Lazarus, who's living in a misery that Jesus describes in grim detail—covered with sores, desperate for food, dogs licking his wounds. There is an immense gap between these men.

Hearing a story begin this way would have stirred up a whole set of assumptions for Jesus' listeners. Plenty of prosperous people could point to passages in the scriptures that said that God will pour blessings on the virtuous and faithful. The Psalms say countless times that the Lord will watch over the righteous, and it's the wicked who will suffer. So, from this viewpoint, surely, we are to admire the rich man.

There's more than a little of that in our American mind-set—the Horatio Alger view that if you are willing to work hard and pull yourself up by your bootstraps you can be a millionaire or become president. But as preacher Barbara Brown Taylor has pointed out, that might be true if everyone were standing at the starting line of the race when the gun went off, but some are so far back that they know they can never catch up, they aren't quite sure which way to run, they don't have the right shoes, they never got a copy of the rules, and they're in terrible shape, anyway. And so they get branded as losers, and, if it's been going on long enough generation after generation, they start to believe it.[2]

There's a deeper, more consistent drumbeat in the scriptures that opposes the notion that wealth and virtue always go together. In fact, they say God is on the side of the poor. The prophet Amos describes God as being determined to punish Israel because "they trample the head of the poor into the dust and turn aside from the afflicted." The measure of the quality of our faith, the Old Testament prophets taught, rests on the character of justice in the land, and the measure of justice is how we treat the poor.

And in the New Testament, Jesus is explicit. "Blessed are you poor," he says in Luke's gospel, and "Woe to you who are rich." In Matthew's gospel, Jesus says that we will be judged at the end by whether we fed the hungry and clothed the naked. To refuse to care for the poor is to refuse Christ himself.

Well, there they are, the rich man and Lazarus, separated by a vast gap. Then the story shifts abruptly. Both men die, and the rich man finds himself in the flames of hell while the poor man is in heaven with Father Abraham. Now for the first time the rich man really sees Lazarus and asks Father Abraham to send him like a good servant to bring him some water. Even beyond the grave the rich man can only see Lazarus as a gofer to wait on him.

Dream on, Father Abraham answers. You've had your chance to enjoy the good things; now it's Lazarus' turn. "Besides," he says, "between you and us a great chasm has been fixed."

Bear in mind, there's no hint here that the rich man was a bad person or that Lazarus was particularly good. The rich man went to hell because he passed by Lazarus every day and never really saw him. He went to hell because he allowed his brother to become invisible so that he didn't have to care.

It's the gap that's the problem, the chasm between rich and poor and how it isolates the privileged and blinds them to the sacred connection that binds all human beings together as children of God. The poor become invisible to the rest of us. People learn to look past them and not see.

Mind the gap. The fact is that everywhere you look you see the gap. Of the six billion people in the world, one billion of them will struggle today to find a few morsels of food to get them and their children through the night; another billion will be malnourished and have no health care. And yet it's so easy to skip the news reports on Sudan or Mozambique or Haiti.

Here closer to home, the richest 1 percent of Americans have nearly as much wealth as the entire bottom 95 percent. We know how devastating it is that unemployment in this recession is still near 10 percent in many places, while CEOs continue to enjoy their immense salaries. Mind the gap.

Near the end of the parable of the rich man and Lazarus, we actually glimpse the first sign of compassion in the rich man as he realizes what has happened to him. "I beg you," he says to Father Abraham, "to send Lazarus to my father's house—for I have five brothers—that he may warn them, so that they will not also come into this place of torment."

But they have had Moses and the prophets already, Abraham answers— prophets who said love your neighbor as yourself and give generously to those in need. "I never really listened to that," the rich man says. "But if someone goes to them from the dead, then they will listen." And so the story ends with Lazarus resting with Abraham, and the rich man trapped in the fire of hell. The gap is still there. How can we ever bridge this gap between rich and poor, how can we ever create one city, one nation, and one world?

That is what God has set out to do in sending Jesus Christ into our world. Someone has come to us from the dead to bridge the gap. As Jim Wallis of *Sojourners* magazine once said, "In Jesus God hits the streets." God has entered into the world to bind the wounds that divide us.

Jesus called his disciples to step into that gap and find ways to bring rich and poor together. He called them to serve the least of their brothers and sisters, to feed the hungry and clothe the naked. To do that calls for tutoring and feeding and visiting, but also for challenging the way our city and even our country are working—organizing, writing letters, creating coalitions to build a healed city here and across the country.

One of the great gifts to this Cathedral in recent years has been its partnership with Covenant Baptist Church in Anacostia, a remarkably faithful congregation in the heart of Washington's poorest section. Our partnership meetings several times a year are always inspiring, as we hear of their church's courage and risk-taking and its many programs serving the poor of their community.

We enjoy fine food and energetic talk just catching up, and then we take some time to share what's been going on in our churches, often talking about the struggles both churches are facing. Then we study scripture together, and finally we spend time in prayer. A couple of times we've turned off the lights, lit a candle, and sat in silence for awhile as we prayed.

And sitting in the dark something happens. As the silence and the prayers go on, our differences fade away—differences of location, of resources, of background, and experience. And there in the dark we are one with each other, and with Christ. There isn't a gap any more—between Ward 3 and Ward 8, between Northwest Washington and Anacostia. There is only us, God's people, the people Jesus came to live and die for, and it seems for those few moments as if we have actually crossed the gap into the kingdom of God.

I think Jesus' story of the rich man and Lazarus is really about us. You see, we are the five brothers in the story, the ones the rich man wants to get a message to, and this morning someone has come to us, back from the dead, to get us to see. He wants us closer to God, closer to our fellow human beings across the chasm. And his real hope is that we'll mind the gap, and then reach across it and go to work.

Earth Day

To Save This Fragile Earth

Luke 12:22–31

I didn't think spring was ever going to come. I mean it. Never. Maybe it was the temperature on Easter Day, which, as someone pointed out, was five degrees colder than it had been on Christmas Day. Or maybe it has been these past weeks of April when a gray chill, wind, and rain greeted us anytime we ventured outdoors.

But spring is here. Daffodils have yielded to tulips. Leaves have returned to the trees' skeletons. The grass is green again, and the blossoms and flowers are everywhere. I remember when I lived in Boston a friend saying that in New England spring comes in like a Yankee lady—reserved, proper, slow to reveal her charms. But in the South, spring comes in like a hussy—brash, flashy, showing off. I'm glad to say that Washington has all the signs of a southern spring!

To see the earth come alive around here is to be dazzled. It must be what the poet Gerard Manley Hopkins felt a century ago when he gazed around at spring bursting out and wrote, "What is all this juice and joy?" And the words of another Hopkins poem leap to mind on a day like this:

> The world is charg'd with the grandeur of God
> It will flame out like shining from shook foil. [1]

The rebirth of spring has for centuries been associated in the Northern Hemisphere with Easter. Even the word "Easter" seems to come from the name of an Anglo-Saxon goddess of spring. Christians have seen in the return of life to nature an image of God's triumph over everything that dies. In the flowering of dogwood and rhododendron, we can see pointers to the power that moves through all creation bringing life out of death.

The earth comes alive, and that is itself a sort of miracle. But today as we gather here on this Earth Day we have to face the fact that that miracle is terrifyingly fragile, and that "this fragile earth, our island home," as our Prayer Book calls it, is in deep trouble.

Scientists have suspected for more than twenty years that our planet is warming as a result of carbon dioxide being released into the atmosphere from burning coal, gas, and oil. A decade ago scientific experts were already identifying global warming as the largest challenge civilization faces, though at the time the evidence was still fragmentary. They also thought the warming would happen gradually. But two things have occurred in the last few years. One is that the evidence has become overwhelming that warming is happening and that the impact of human beings is a major cause, and the second is the conviction that the change is happening far faster than anyone had imagined.

Last week we read in the newspapers the reports of the Intergovernmental Panel on Climate Change, bringing together the research of a thousand scientists from seventy-four countries. They declared that global warming is already affecting the earth's ecosystems, and that climate change could lead to widespread drought and vast flooding of coastal cities, driving hundreds of millions of people from their homes. It could lead to the extinction of as much as a third of the plant and animal species, and to widespread malnutrition and disease. The years 2005 and 2006 were, they reported, the hottest in recorded history.

We've been seeing indications of global warming steadily in the news— the melting ice caps on mountains, the shrinking glaciers, and the increasing incidence of coastline cities underwater. Just a few days ago the *New York Times* ran on its front page a picture of an Indonesian village now finding itself inundated as water levels rise. James Hansen, the country's foremost climatologist who, as a NASA researcher has for years run the most powerful computer model on earth's climate, has said that we have a decade to reverse the flow of carbon into the atmosphere or else we will live, and these are his words, on a "totally different planet."[2]

And then just two days ago a group of senior military generals warned that global warming poses a major security threat. It will bring chaos, civic strife, genocide, and the growth of terrorism in Asia, Africa, and the Middle East. "We will pay for this one way or another," General Anthony Zinni said, by reducing greenhouse gas emissions today or with military conflict and loss of human lives later.[3]

In short, we are facing what is being called a "planetary emergency."

"So what?" many might say. Things may get a little warmer here in the U.S., but chances are, if we don't live along the coastlines, we may not be hit too badly. But what kind of response is that? What we are learning is that our human choices, and mainly the choices of the most wealthy nations in the world, are endangering our fragile earth and the well-being of hundreds of millions of people. We—you and I— are part of the problem.

Every now and then I have the privilege of holding an infant, or having a wide-ranging conversation with a three-year-old. When I think of those youngsters, I can't help but wonder what are we doing to the world they will live in, and even more, to the kind of world their children will live in? We are squandering a sacred birthright that has been entrusted to us. We are participating in a massive time of decreation—tearing down mountains to produce coal, spewing poison into the atmosphere, leveling forests that are the purifying lungs our planet needs to breathe. And for what?

The United States, with 4 percent of the world's population, is producing 25 percent of the greenhouse gases that are endangering our world. But we are so addicted to a standard of living and a way of life built on inexpensive oil and coal that we don't want to begin to imagine a way out.

Writer Bill McKibben puts the issue clearly: "If you care about social justice, this is the biggest battle we've ever faced." Climate change may produce hundreds of millions of refugees. He describes wandering through the lowlands of Bangladesh, the home to 150 million people, and contemplating their entire homeland going under water. And these are a people who have done nothing to create the problem.[4]

It's enough to make us think again of Gerard Manley Hopkins' poem where, after singing of God's grandeur, he describes what we have done to this glorious earth:

> All is seared with trade; bleared, smeared with toil;
> And wears man's smudge and shares man's smell.

We humans are on the verge of doing irreparable damage to the nest that bears all of our lives. I continue to be haunted by that 1969 photograph we all know of the earth when it was first viewed from outer space. There it was, a beautiful blue globe, with its swirls of white clouds, floating through the fathomless dark night of space. James Irwin, one of the astronauts who first saw that sight, said, "This beautiful, warm living object looked so fragile, so delicate, that if you touched it with a finger it would crumble and fall apart. Seeing this has changed [us]."[5] Only it hasn't.

You will hear a great deal in the coming weeks and months about this crisis from Earth Day advocates, environmentalists, and, I hope, our political leaders. But today we are asking what that crisis means to us as Christians. We believe that, as the psalmist puts it, "The earth is the Lord's, and all that is in it." Some have called this the Eleventh Commandment. The earth is God's, not ours. We are called to be stewards of it, to care for it lovingly, and to hand it on no worse than we found it.

But, of course, Christians have too often been part of the problem. Beginning in the earliest centuries, Christian faith started emphasizing an otherworldly salvation, where the whole point of faith was to deliver us from the world. In fact, there was a study a few years ago that reported that the more religious people are the less they are inclined to care about the environment. Maybe the most famous example of that was former Secretary of the Interior James Watt, a fundamentalist Christian who, in the 1980s, said that long-range conservation of natural resources was unnecessary because Jesus would be coming soon to end everything.

But Jesus has defined our deepest Christian instincts, as in the gospel today when he points to the lilies of the field and the ravens in the air as models for simple trust in God. In the parable we heard this morning, Jesus pointed to the spiritual destructiveness of piling up more and more wealth only so that we can "eat, drink, and be merry."

And it was St. Francis of Assisi who saw the creation as an array of blood relatives—brother sun, sister moon, brother wind, sister water, mother earth. "Be praised, my Lord God," he said, "in and through your creation."[6] There is one life in all of God's creatures.

The farmer, poet, novelist Wendell Berry says we all live within what he calls the "Great Economy,"[7] the economy of nature. And we must learn to fit harmoniously into this larger whole. Remember, he says, only nature knows how to make water, air, forests, and topsoil. And now we humans are destroying this "Great Economy," tearing apart the harmony we were created to be a part of.

Finding that life-giving balance calls for facing down our massive need to own bigger houses and drive ever more massive SUVs. It means rethinking our taste for out-of-season strawberries flown in from California and apples from New Zealand. It means learning to shape lives less dependent on countless hours driving on highways. It means more energy-efficient homes and office buildings.

But, unfortunately, none of this is likely to make enough difference in the face of this planetary emergency. The answer will have to be public, political, and governmental. We Christians need to be prepared to educate and advocate to protect this fragile earth.

That will call for a massive shift in national priorities, with leadership as strong as that which led us through the Second World War, that put a man on the moon, that conquered polio, and that established basic civil rights for everyone. It will take saying "no" to the powerful economic interests tied up in the way things currently are. It will cost us to do this work of reconciliation with our planet earth. Are we as a nation and a world capable of bearing that cost? I don't know, but I worry.

What I do know is that I don't want to have to explain to my grandchildren, or to God, how we sat by, too addicted to our way of life to make the necessary sacrifices, to change our economy and lifestyle before disasters struck.

We are being called, in how we live, how we act, and how we vote, to protect this earth we have been given. The challenge we face is daunting. But the Easter promise is that God can bring life out of this threatening death. The God who raised Jesus from the dead can raise us from something less than life—our driven, wasteful lives—to life itself, a life that is simpler, more connected to the Great Economy of nature, more rooted in its place, and more committed to renewing and caring for this vulnerable nest, this fragile earth.

Even Gerard Manley Hopkins, who so mourned the desecration of the land in his time, held on to this Easter trust that God's Spirit can kindle and renew us. His poem about God's grandeur and what we have done to it ends this way:

> And for all this, nature is never spent;
> There lives the dearest freshness deep down things;
> And though the last light off the black West went
> Oh, morning at the brown brink eastward springs—
> Because the Holy Ghost over the bent world broods
> With warm breast and with, Ah, bright wings. [8]

That's the promise. The Spirit is moving in our world now to renew the face of the earth. The question is, Will we join in?

Independence Day

A Humble Patriotism

Matthew 5:43–48

On a sabbatical a few years ago, I had a chance to spend nearly two days with my family exploring the towns and beaches of Normandy in France, tracing the events of the D-Day invasion of June 1944. That was when the Allied forces launched maybe the most remarkable military invasion in history, to begin taking back Europe from the Nazis. Hundreds of thousands of British, Canadian, and American troops crossed the English Channel under cover of night and then poured onto the beaches at dawn.

It was enormously moving to walk through the American cemetery overlooking Omaha Beach, where more than ten thousand American soldiers are buried. Row after row of white crosses dotted the landscape as far as the eye could see. This was holy ground, and you couldn't help but feel proud of the way our country fought at great cost to defend the cause of freedom around the world.

A little American history will tell you that not all the wars we have fought have been so noble or necessary, and some have deeply divided us, even the current war in Iraq. But standing on the beach at Normandy, I couldn't help but think how precious freedom is, and how grateful we should be for our country and for the soldiers who have given their lives to protect it. My sense of patriotism ran deep and strong those days.

Three days from now our nation will celebrate the Fourth of July, the nation's birthday, and our most patriotic day. It's in many ways the highpoint of summer, with its picnics, parades, fireworks. For most of my adult life, I've spent the Fourth in a tiny community in rural Tennessee, with a parade including every fire engine in the county, Shriners circling in their miniature motor scooters, horse-drawn carriages with local 4-H Club queens ambling slowly down the street, and two or three marching bands strutting along. People line the streets cheering as the paraders toss candy to the kids. Nearly everyone is dressed in red, white, and blue.

Now as a Washingtonian I'm experiencing D.C.'s parades, picnics, and fireworks on the Mall. Only the celebrations here are anything but small and quaint. Wherever you are in this country, my hunch is that it's hard not to feel patriotic on the Fourth of July.

It has to be said, though, that patriotism is a complex virtue. We have every reason to love our country. It has in many ways fulfilled the dream of John Winthrop, one of the founders of the Massachusetts Bay Colony, who called on the settlers in this new land to be "a city on a hill," a beacon of freedom and hope to the world. In the Declaration of Independence, which was signed on July 4, 1776, Thomas Jefferson and the other signers held up a vision that has continued to have revolutionary power, declaring that all human beings are created equal and are entitled to "life, liberty, and the pursuit of happiness."

But there were troubles in our nation from the start. Many of the signers of the Declaration, for example, were slave owners, and slavery wasn't to be outlawed for nearly a hundred years. In the new Constitution, African Americans had no votes, no legal rights, and for political purposes were counted as three-fifth of a white person. The nineteenth century saw nearly all the Native Americans either killed or forcibly removed from their lands to make room for the white settlers. Women didn't get the vote until 1920.

It was a great vision of liberty and justice that America held out for itself, but America has always been a nation of flawed human beings, including many who have been eager to promote their own interests at the expense of the well-being of their country.

Part of the essential greatness of America has been the way it has welcomed disagreement and dissent. Over the past 231 years of its life, Americans have argued vehemently over just about everything. Not long ago I heard a young teenager, in response to the bitter polarization in this country over the war in Iraq, say, "I wish Americans could still be as patriotic as they used to be." It's easy to forget that deep disagreement is at the core of what it means to be patriotic. It's this very freedom to disagree and debate for which our soldiers have fought and died through the years.

William Sloane Coffin, the former Chaplain at Yale in the divided Vietnam War days, and a tireless American prophet during his years at Riverside Church in New York, has written that "[T]here are three kinds of patriots. Two bad and one good. The bad ones are the uncritical lovers and the loveless critics. The good patriots carry on a lover's quarrel with their country, a reflection of God's lover's quarrel with the world."[1] We love our country enough to want it to fulfill the dream it was founded to embody, and sometimes that will call for passionate argument and even strong opposition.

Coffin goes on to say, "How do you love America? Don't say, 'My country, right or wrong.' That's like saying, 'My grandmother, drunk or sober'; it doesn't get you anywhere. Don't just salute the flag and don't burn it either. Wash it and make it clean."[2] Love your country, he's saying, and work to make it the best, most generous, most compassionate nation it can be.

Christians necessarily have hard questions to ask of our country. Our Old Testament lesson is a vigorous reminder that we Christians are accountable above all to a God who knows no national boundaries, and who calls citizens of all nations to lives of justice and peace. In fact, God's only partiality seems to be toward those who are poor. Listen to what Moses has to say to Israel:

> The Lord your God is God of gods and Lord of lords, the great God, mighty and awesome, who is not partial and takes no bribe, who executes justice for the orphan and widow, and who loves the strangers, providing them food and clothing. You shall love the stranger, for you were strangers in the land of Egypt. [We could translate that, You shall love the immigrant, for your people, too, were immigrants in the land of America.] You shall fear the Lord your God; him alone you shall worship.

Though we love our country, as Christians we are called to love God and God's vision for all human life first. And that means we will have many lover's quarrels with our country—about how it treats the poor, immigrants, and prisoners, and how it relates to the other countries of the world.

In our gospel reading, Jesus is very clear about what he expects from us:

> You have heard that it was said, "You shall love your neighbor and hate your enemy." But I say to you, Love your enemies and pray for those who persecute you.

Those words were addressed not to a nation but to Jesus' disciples. But they are marching orders for Christians in how they seek to influence whatever nation they call home. Where was this vision, for example, in the lead-up to the Iraq war as militaristic Christian leaders seemed to be leading the march to battle? Charles Stanley, pastor of the First Baptist Church of Atlanta, whose sermons are watched by millions of viewers, said, "God battles with people who oppose him, who fight against him and his followers."[3]

Dr. Gregory Boyd, a leading evangelical pastor, has written a book called *The Myth of a Christian Nation*, lambasting his conservative Christian colleagues for trying to build a certain kind of Christian nation—with prayer in public schools, displays of the Ten Commandments on buildings, and an array of take-no-prisoners positions in the many culture wars, outlawing abortion and gay unions. It isn't the political positions themselves that Boyd finds disturbing, but the determination to impose one set of religious views on an entire nation, and demonizing those who oppose them. It is idolatrous, he says, and unfaithful both to the gospel and to America's deepest principles. [4]

The fact is that at the heart of the founders' vision of America was a conviction that there would be no state religion, no Christian America. Thomas Jefferson called this new way a "fair experiment"—to have a nation that embraced religious liberty for all and refused to make any one religion official.

That has been part of the genius of America, and its value can be measured by the fact that religion has flourished in this country in the last two hundred years more than in any other Western developed nation. Maybe most importantly, it encourages religious people to keep a healthy tension between their faith in a God whose love transcends all borders and loyalties, and their own loyalty to their country.

The great cellist Pablo Casals once said, "Love of country is a wonderful thing, but why should love stop at the border?"[5] That's what Jesus would say. There are no borders to Christ's love, and nor can there be for Christians. When it comes to an issue like global warming or immigration, Christians can't ask simply what's good for America. We have to ask what is best for all God's children and what is God's will for the whole human race? The greatest question isn't what will keep the American economy expanding at a certain rate, it is how can America best use its immense wealth for the sake not only of its citizens but the world?

And so patriotism will always entail both pride and love of our country, and also a lover's quarrel with an America still striving to live by its highest ideals. We are called to a humble patriotism, a servant patriotism, a patriotism that loves America, but is also is capable of loving in equal measure all of God's people. Whenever we hear a politician end a speech by saying "God bless America," we Christians should perhaps silently add a second prayer, "And God bless the rest of the world, too."

At the end of Communion we'll have a chance to sing what is for me the most moving of all our national songs, the one I wish were our national anthem. "O beautiful for spacious skies, for amber waves of grain," we'll sing, and we'll celebrate all the beauty of this glorious land we have been given. Then in the second stanza we will sing the words not just of our love of America, but of our lover's quarrel:

> America! America! God mend thine every flaw,
> Confirm thy soul in self control.
> Thy liberty in law.

Those lines make a good national hymn a great one.

Patriotism is a noble virtue, this loyalty we have to our land and to the idea of freedom. But patriotism alone, apart from God's love for the entire human race, can be a dangerous thing.

And so let us give thanks for this nation, for this land of the free and home of the brave. Let us praise God for its purple mountains' majesty and its fruited plains. Let us be grateful that we have the privilege of living in a nation that is the envy of the world for its freedom and prosperity, and that has welcomed millions upon millions of refugees seeking a better life.

And as Christians let us love America with a humble patriotism, and with an awareness that our truest homeland is finally not America, but God.

Thanksgiving

A Thankful Heart

Thanksgiving is arriving this year just in the nick of time. These last few months have been an edgy, unhappy period in our country. Over the summer and fall frustration has been spilling over just about everywhere, with people angry about what's happening with the economy, frightened about the loss of jobs, and anxious about the future. Polls are saying that for the first time in decades Americans believe their children will have less prosperous lives than their own. The recent elections have been ugly, and our representatives and leaders are bitterly divided. In this land of abundance a widespread sense of scarcity has taken over, a grim sense that there aren't enough of life's essentials to go around.

So it's time to step back, take a break, and see if we can get some perspective on what's going on. And I can't think of a better place to turn for guidance than our nation's Thanksgiving Day celebration this week, which is the closest thing we Americans have to a true national holiday. Unlike Christmas, which will come rolling in soon behind it, Thanksgiving doesn't exclude any group from its celebration. It makes a profoundly religious assertion, but it does it in a way that is ecumenical and even interfaith—the affirmation that beneath all the different creeds in our country is one uniting attitude and that is thankfulness.

When we gather next Thursday with friends and family many of our celebrations will begin with a moment of pause. Some will offer words of thanks and maybe even sing the old doxology, "Praise God from whom all blessings flow," some will make signs of the cross, some will simply bow their heads and join hands, some might offer a toast. And for at least a few hours, we Americans will pay attention to the blessings of our lives rather than to our problems. And we will sense what it might mean to view our world and our lives with glad and thankful hearts.

We should be careful not to romanticize that first Thanksgiving feast. It had come at the end of a brutal first year in the New World. The Pilgrims had arrived at Plymouth in 1620 after a grueling two-month voyage on the *Mayflower*. The New England winter was harsher than anything they had ever experienced. By the time the one-year anniversary arrived, half of the Pilgrims who had set out from England were still alive. Everyone had lost someone they loved. The seeds they had brought along to grow their food failed to grow in the rocky New England soil, and starvation was a constant possibility. Only corn brought to them by the native people had kept them alive. By the spring and summer, though, things had become more hopeful, new crops had been planted—this time with fertilizer introduced to them by the natives—and they had begun to believe they would survive.

And so Governor William Bradford called for "a time to rejoice together after a more special manner"[1] and sent out hunters to secure the ducks and geese for the feast. Contrary to what many paintings have suggested, the Pilgrims didn't sit at a long table covered with a white linen tablecloth, with the natives standing around. They stood around a fire throwing meat into steaming pots and ate with their fingers and knives. And in that feast they offered God their thanks and praise for surviving their first year. Their Bible had told them about ancient Israel's harvest festivals, when the Israelites thanked God for the abundance of creation and for delivering them from captivity and leading them to freedom. Now the Pilgrims were celebrating their own deliverance.

What is so striking in this story is that in the midst of the hardest of times, these Pilgrims, rather than turning angry and bitter, raised their hearts and voices in gratitude. They seemed to know something we need to know in this time of our own national discontent. Nathaniel Philbrick has written a superb book about the Pilgrims called *Mayflower: A Story of Courage, Community and War*. He is convinced that it was the Pilgrims' faith that saw them through that hard time. Their trust in God made all the difference, as did their willingness, because of their faith, to see the native people as allies rather than enemies, and that faith and openness turned out to be the key to their survival. Their response to their hard times was not resentment, bitterness, and blaming, but the power and possibilities of thankful hearts.

Gratitude is at the heart of Christian faith. It is the emotion that underlies the whole Christian experience. At the foundation of our faith are not rules and obligations or guilt or fear, but a foundational amazement at all that we have been given, and an unstoppable desire to offer thanks and praise to the Giver. The deepest truth of our faith is that "Life is gift," as preacher John Claypool always put it, and if we can keep our spirits focused on that we can engage whatever comes our way more graciously. If you look at those Pilgrims, you can see that a grateful heart isn't based on lives that have everything people want or need, but on the ability to see the goodness and gifts that are there no matter what.

The truth is that we are on the receiving end of life all our days. And the best gift we can give ourselves is to cultivate gratitude as a way of life. In Rabbi Harold Kushner's book on the Twenty-third Psalm, he describes gratitude as "more than a ritual of politeness or just remembering to say 'thank you.' It is a way of looking at the world that does not change the facts of your life but has the power to make your life more enjoyable." Gratitude, he says, "is a favor we do ourselves more than it is something we do for the recipient of our thanks."[2]

Those first Pilgrims had little control over their lives. The struggles and losses they faced had been overwhelming. They could hardly affect the harsh weather, the failed crops, and all the other things that had gone badly, but they did have the capacity to choose how they would view the events ahead of them. And they chose to see their lives as receivers of God's generosity in bringing them strength and fortitude even in the worst of times. In a time of immense scarcity, they focused on God's abundance—God's care and promise. In their gratitude the Pilgrims personified the truth that in our times of scarcity and worry, there's nothing we need more than thankful hearts.

When I've taught Bible classes in the past, people have noticed how often God insists on being praised, and the Book of Psalms, for example, is filled with one song of praise to God after another. In C. S. Lewis's book *Reflections on the Psalms*, he tackles head-on the notion that God somehow is an egomaniac who needs to be praised just to make him happy. It's just the opposite. We are commanded to praise and give thanks because we need it. A gift is only fully enjoyed when it has been celebrated and the Giver has been thanked. The completeness of our receiving the gifts of our lives is our relishing them and then praising God for them.

Developing a thankful heart expands our spirits and frees us from the comparisons and resentments that can consume our energy. Lewis commented, "I notice how the humblest and at the same time most balanced minds praised most; while the cranks, the misfits, and malcontents praised least. Praise almost seems to be inner health made audible."[3]

In fact, having a thankful heart is pretty close to the key to living, and that goes for all of us, no matter how much or how little we have.

Years ago, *Chicago Tribune* columnist Joan Beck began writing down a list of things she was thankful for and found that she couldn't stop:

> As we gather together to count the Lord's blessings we are grateful, Dear God, for families and farmers and fathers and faith, for summits and summers and Sundays and sunshine, for "It's benign" and "You're hired" and "Your new baby is perfect." . . . We thank you today for MRIs and MVPs and MTVs, for MDs and CDs and TDs, for IRAs and CPAs, for Oprah and opera and op-ed

pages, for beaches and beagles and Beaujolais, for beaus and beavers. . . . We
thank you, God, for no-cavities kids and no-cut contracts, for peacemakers and
pacemakers and homemakers . . . Shakespeare and Sousa and Seurat, and
Seuss, for Pilgrims and pioneers and patriots' dreams . . . , for the decrease in
mortality and the increase in longevity, for medications that relieve mental
illness and blot out pain, for 98.6 and 20/20 and 120/80, for 10K and 401K, for
Lincoln and lilacs and licorice. . . . For a port in the storm and a bridge over
trouble, for dawn after dark, for cocoa after caroling, for healing after hurt and
for life after life, we thank you Lord of heaven and earth. [4]

And on she goes. You see, when you really start being grateful it's hard to
know where to stop.

We Christians are called to be agents of a different spirit in our time, a
spirit of abundance, of gladness even when we seem to have less than we did,
or very little.

I hope we can take the next few days to make our own lists of the little
things as well as the large ones for which we are grateful. And, in response, I
suggest that we do three things:

First, we can offer our thanks and praise, telling God how grateful we are,
putting our trust in God even in the face of our fears and anxieties.

Second, we can pass the generosity on, by allowing God's goodness to
flow through us as we respond to the immense needs we see around us.

And third, we can ask God to guide us in making our family, community,
and country more grateful and generous. We can seek a deeper simplicity of
life, less cluttered with things, developing a deeper clarity in what we need
and don't need and a stronger commitment to building a generous society for
everyone.

Raymond Carver, one of the fine poets of our time, wrestled with the
demon of alcoholism much of his life. And then, thanks to the love of his
new wife, he found his way to sobriety, which was then sadly interrupted by
a fierce cancer. Not long before he died, he left his record of what the world
looks like to a man who is seeing clearly. It is called "Gravy."

> No other word will do. For that's what it was. Gravy.
> Gravy, these past ten years.
> Alive, sober, working, loving and
> being loved . . . Eleven years
> ago he was told he had six months to live
> at the rate he was going. And he was going
> nowhere but down. So he changed his ways
> somehow. He quit drinking! And the rest?
> After that it was all gravy, every minute
> of it, up to and including when he was told about,
> well, some things that were breaking down and
> building up inside his head. "Don't weep for me,"
> he said to his friends. "I'm a lucky man.

I've had ten years longer than I or anyone
expected. Pure gravy. And don't forget it.[5]

Our lives didn't have to be as filled with goodness as they are. And the only response is gratitude. The secret of life is for us to continue to recognize more and more that this life is all gravy. And don't forget it.

Giving Thanks in All Things

Ephesians 1:15–23

One of the constants in my life as a child was the act of saying a blessing before family meals. Giving thanks for the food set before us was always the first step before we could plunge into our meal. The problem, though, was that there was often something set before me that I didn't feel like giving thanks for. Like green peas.

It would be hard to overstate how much I hated green peas. When served them, I would spread them across the plate in the vain hope of making it seem that I had eaten some of them, or I would attempt to cover them up with bread or meat. It didn't help to hear constantly from my parents how good they were for me. Sometimes during the blessing my eyes would gaze at the bowl of peas, and I remember being struck by the unfairness of having to say thank you for the last thing in the world I wanted.

It is hard to be grateful for a lot of things life serves us. That was the substance of a comment I heard in response to last week's sermon about gratitude and giving. "I liked what you were talking about," the person said, "but gratitude is much harder when life itself is hard." What does it mean to be thankful when life isn't going well?

That's a good question to be asking as we prepare for Thanksgiving, which is for many of us one of the best holidays of the year. No worry about presents, none of the same high level of expectations. It is simply a day to be with people we care about, enjoy a feast, and be grateful.

Every year, when I can, I get to a family reunion at a small lake house in some piney woods in the South. There isn't much to do there but catch up with each other after a year apart, eat entirely too much, and watch whatever football game happens to be on. The highpoint, though, is when we gather outside for a simple service of lessons and prayers, and sing those wonderful Thanksgiving hymns—"Come Ye, Thankful People, Come," "We Gather Together to Ask the Lord's Blessing," and "Now Thank We All Our God."

What will it be like, I've been wondering, for people across our country to sing those hymns in this season, when it may seem harder than usual to feel grateful? The nervousness in the world around us is palpable. Paul Krugman, the winner of the Nobel Prize for Economics this year, says that the U.S. economy is suffering from a crisis of faith, a growing lack of trust in all our economic institutions. People are watching their savings dwindle, and the attempted solutions aren't working. I read a news account of a financial consultant who has several clients living in their cars now.

This will be a different kind of Thanksgiving. But there is still something essential about giving thanks, even when times are hard. After all, that's how it all began.

The Pilgrims who arrived at Plymouth, had a hellish first year—of hunger, disease, conflict with the native people, and death. Of the 102 who arrived at Plymouth, only half were still alive to mark their first anniversary in the new land. Nearly all the families had buried a husband, wife, or child in the rocky New England soil by then. The crops they planted from the seed brought over on the *Mayflower* almost all failed, and they were facing starvation. Without the corn brought to them by the natives—two pounds per person per day—they would not have survived the hard second winter.

When the time came, though, to mark their first year, they chose to do it as an act of thanksgiving. These Puritans lived by their Bible and knew about Israel's annual harvest festival. So they thanked God—not for easy lives and a comfortable world, but for providing them enough corn to survive the winter, for God's presence and guiding hand, for being able to put one foot in front of another through the cold, hard days and nights. It was a choice to respond in thanksgiving instead of resentment or despair, and to focus on the gifts that kept coming, even in the hard times.

If we are going to live glad and grateful lives, we will have to do it in a world that is a mixture of good and bad. No one has caught this better than eighteenth-century poet William Blake in these simple lines:

> Man was made for joy and woe
> And when this we rightly know
> Safely through the world we go.
> Joy and woe are woven fine,
> A clothing for the soul divine.[1]

In fact, I have learned from a Catholic writer named Richard Rohr to call this experience of pain and woe "the left hand of God." The right hand of God, he says, is the way God brings us joy, friendship, and love. We sense God's goodness directly. But the other half of life contains disappointment, pain, and agonizing effort. Yet God comes to us mysteriously, hiddenly, in the times of suffering and crisis, so that the hard times, too, can draw us close to God.[2]

On this day when our Forum focuses on the human journey of aging, you'd have to say that getting older is one of those mixtures of joy and woe. The wrinkles appear, the memory sputters, the body starts to creak. But there's another side to this. There's gratitude, which, as Rabbi Harold Kushner puts it, is "a way of life that does not change the facts of your life but has the power to make your life more enjoyable." In his book about the Twenty-third Psalm he has a chapter on the phrase "My cup runneth over" where he describes the pills he takes for blood pressure and the eye drops for glaucoma.

> Instead of lamenting the ailments that come with growing older [he says], instead of wishing I was as young and as fit as I once was, I take my medicine with a prayer of thanks that modern science has found ways to help me cope with those ailments. I think of all my ancestors who didn't live long enough to develop the complications of old age and did not have pills to take when they did.[3]

I have known more people than I can count who have said that in a strange way they don't regret their bout with cancer, as terrible as that experience was. Because after that nothing looked the same, everything was clearer, things shined in a way they didn't before.

"Give thanks in all things," St. Paul says. It's no easy thing to live with this mixture of joy and woe. It is no easy thing to live in an economy that is staggering, that hasn't found its bottom. And yet we must. Years ago there was a book called *The Choice Is Always Ours*, which pnders the fact that we are not free to determine the events that come our way, but we are free to decide how we will respond to them.[4]

It is natural to ask of anything bad that happens a question filled with resentment: "Why did this happen to me?" and in doing that to focus on our frustration and anger. But every situation offers another possibility of asking, "What is the gift this hard time has to give?" which assumes that an infinitely creative God always has more life for us.

This is Christ the King Sunday. Today, we declare that there is a vast cosmic love that holds us in its care. If when you stepped into the Cathedral this morning you had continued walking up the aisle all the way to the high altar, you would have found yourself standing in front of a majestic sculpture of Jesus, sitting on the throne raising his right hand in blessing and holding a round orb, symbolizing the earth, in the palm of his hand.

That's where we all are, our faith says, in the palm of Christ's hand. And to know we belong there is to know that gratitude can never cease, and that

God never stops holding us, seeking to stretch and teach and deepen us. We can't fall out of that embracing hand.

Did you hear the words from the Letter to the Ephesians today? God has seated Christ "far above all rule and authority and power and dominion, and above every name that is named. . . . And he has put all things under his feet and has made him the head over all things for the church."

Christ's love, Paul is saying, rules in this cosmos, above every president and CEO and prime minister. It may not seem that way very often in our troubled world, but that is its deepest secret. Christ's love is at work in this moment in you and me and across our world, and we believe that it will finally draw all of us into a new and healed world.

And that means we can trust that even when things are at their hardest, even as the stock market stays shaky, even as great industries threaten to crumble, we cannot fall out of that loving hand that holds us. And that means that here and now we can be patient and watchful for God's good gifts.

The choice is always ours. Either we live a way of gratitude in these hard times by reaching out and giving, serving, and caring for our neighbor next door and across the city, or we choose lives of fear and selfishness.

I believe God is calling our nation, and us individually, to a simpler, more grateful, more connected life together. What a gift it would be in this hard time if we were to find ourselves staying closer to home and turning to our neighbors, giving in ways we never expected.

A friend of mine a few years ago visited war-torn Croatia and found himself one evening going to a church service in a small town there. The day before he had visited a nearby village that had been recently destroyed. Virtually every building was gone, and the population of fifty thousand was reduced to less than three thousand. The patients in the hospital had all been executed. The small town my friend visited hadn't been overrun, but every person there had close relatives and friends who had been victimized. Unemployment was over 25 percent, and the average wage was $400 per month.

The Protestant Church had been decorated for the harvest season and the service was simple, with people offering their thanks to God for the blessings in their lives. They sang hymns accompanied by violins, guitars, and keyboards. And my friend recognized one of the songs they sang in Croatian, but he knew it in English by heart from his early Sunday school days. It went like this:

> When upon life's billows, you are tempest tossed,
> When you are discouraged, thinking all is lost,
> Count your many blessings, name them one by one,
> And it will surprise you what the Lord has done.
> Count your blessings, name them one by one,
> Count your many blessings, see what God has done. . . .[5]

My friend said that if someone had slapped him in the face he couldn't have been hit any harder than he was hearing those people with almost nothing sing that song.

The weeks and months ahead are not going to be easy for our nation and world. But even in hard times, we can choose to hold on this way:

> Count your blessings, name them one by one,
> Count your blessings, see what God has done.
> Count your many blessings, name them one by one,
> And it will surprise you what the Lord has done.

Book Three

Church Year

Advent

Waiting

Baruch 5:1–9; Luke 3:1–6

Imagine that you enter a room and find on a table a beautifully wrapped Christmas present, with a note attached that says, "This present is for you but don't open it now . . . wait." I suspect that seeing that might evoke several responses—a sense of intrigue and anticipation, but also of frustration or irritation. Why wait? Who wants to? Why should we have to? And here's the real question. . . . How many of you think you would obey the command and actually wait? [1]

I vividly remember as a boy, with Christmas drawing near, dying to know what was inside that large wrapped box under the tree with my name on it. I would join in the general pleading with the parents to let us open just one present early—always to no avail. And I have to admit that on one occasion I might have pulled back the tape just a little when no one was looking to see if I could figure out what was there.

Truth is, I never did like waiting. And my guess is waiting doesn't come naturally to most of you either. And so that puts us at odds with this Advent season that insists on waiting. Just when everyone around us is getting in the swing of all those Christmas songs, like "I'm Dreaming of a White Christmas," and is ready to sing "Silent Night" and "O Little Town of Bethlehem," we come to church to wait. We even sing songs about waiting, like, "O come, O come Emmanuel" or "Come thou long-expected Jesus." How's that? Two hymns basically about a Messiah who's running late and we wish would hurry.

The lessons of the Advent season are all about people who are waiting. The passage from Isaiah we often hear—"Comfort, comfort my people,"—is addressed to the people of Israel who have been living in exile in Babylon for seventy years. That's a lot of waiting. In our lesson today from the prophet Baruch, people are waiting with yearning too: "Arise, O Jerusalem . . . see your children gathered from west to east rejoicing that God has remembered them."

You hear this waiting in our gospel lesson about that strange prophet John the Baptist out in the wilderness calling out, "Prepare the way of the Lord, make his paths straight." The people he's talking to have been expecting the Messiah to come for decades, even centuries. Now, John says, your waiting is almost over.

And in a couple of weeks Advent will take us to a young woman named Mary, who has been told that she is pregnant with God's own child, and she is facing nine months of waiting and preparing for a birth she never imagined.

The great American rabbi of the twentieth century, Abraham Heschel, once wrote, "The inner history of Israel is a history of waiting for God, of waiting for His arrival."[2]

No wonder Advent isn't many people's favorite part of the year. After all, who loves waiting? It's not something that comes naturally to us. I came across not long ago a book called *In Praise of Slowness*. The author, a journalist named Carl Honoré, describes the moment in his fast-moving life when he realized something was wrong. He was in a long line at the airport with nothing to do but wait. Being unable to stand there and do nothing, he started skimming a newspaper and his eyes landed on an article called "The One-Minute Bedtime Story." To help parents deal with their time-consuming youngsters, the authors had condensed classic fairy tales into sixty-second sound bites. Sort of "executive summaries," you might say. At first it sounded good, given Honoré's habit of trying to steer his two-year-old son toward the shortest book to read. His son would often say, "You're going too fast" or "I want another story!" while the whole time Honoré was eager to get to supper, e-mails, reading, bills, checking the late news on TV and the Internet.[3]

Then, as he began to wonder how fast Amazon could ship him the full collection of one-minute stories, it hit him. "Have I gone completely insane?" he asked himself, and began to think, "My whole life has turned into an exercise in hurry, in packing more and more into every hour. I am Scrooge with a stopwatch."[4]

There's nothing wrong with speed, Honoré says. The problem is the way speed becomes an addiction, an idolatry. "No time for that novel you got at Christmas? Learn to speed-read. Diet not working? Try liposuction. Too busy to cook? Buy a microwave."[5]

And he recites the human costs—insomnia, migraines, hypertension, ulcers, and burnout. And there are others. The average working parent spends twice as long dealing with e-mail at home as playing with his or her children.

We've lost the art of anticipating, of waiting for something that takes time, of looking forward to something. All we care about is ripping open the gift the future holds and enjoying it right now. We don't seem to know how to be in the moment, and we've lost the willingness to relish an experience after it has happened before we move on. In short, we want instant gratification, and we measure every moment for its cost-benefit ratio of satisfaction.

It's a part of our national personality, too. In a forum at the Cathedral on the American role in Afghanistan, the Scottish diplomat Rory Stewart, who had spent over a year walking across Afghanistan, expressed his hope that the U.S. would not launch a major new military operation there. His reason was fascinating. Stewart argued that Afghanistan is going to need a low-level presence of American forces for decades to come to help them stabilize. But America historically has not had the patience for that. It tends to rush in to try to fix something, then gets frustrated, and ends up abandoning the whole project. America isn't very good at waiting, he said.

The assumption behind all of this, of course, is that we are what we do and accomplish, and anything that slows down and gets in the way of our doing what we think needs to be done is an affront. We are solo achievers, with the world on our shoulders, and the measure of our worth is the measure of what we accomplish.

But what if we have some foundational things completely wrong? What if our real significance has to do with our involvement in the lives of others? What if we are meant to be not just achievers but also receivers, people created for responsiveness and relationship?

Waiting isn't an unfortunate, accidental piece of life, but something at the center of what it means to be human. How can we have a genuine conversation if we're not willing to wait for the other to speak? If we are made for mutuality and relationship, then waiting is going to be at its center. If we love someone, we have to be willing to be receivers, partners, and collaborators.

Waiting calls for the capacity to live fully in the present, without always pushing toward a future that we somehow believe will bring us the fulfillment we want. It means accepting what the mystics call "the gift of the moment." If we are pressing constantly toward the future, we lose the gift of what is here in front of us just now—the child in our household, the colleague or the challenge at work, the beauty of a day, the support of friends.

Much of the life of faith is about waiting, too. The Psalms speak constantly of waiting for God. "My soul waits for the Lord, more than watchmen for the morning," Psalm 130 says. "For God alone my soul in silence waits," Psalm 62 declares. "Those who wait for the Lord shall renew their strength," the prophet Isaiah announces.

Waiting for God is an essential part of Christian faith. The reality is that we don't possess and can't control God. Virtually every person of faith I have known has felt at times a sense of God's absence, doubts about God's

closeness, confusion about where God is. And everyone I know has had a
sense of searching for God, listening for God, longing to draw close. And
everyone I know experiences their lives at times as broken, lost, empty, or
lonely in ways they can't fix and that won't go away. In a time of jobless-
ness, fear, and people losing their homes, many are struggling. It can feel like
waiting for God, longing for God's guidance and healing and strength. "O
come, O come Emmanuel."

And far from our own comfortable experience, think of the billions whose
waiting for God is immediate and even desperate—the child in the Sudanese
refugee camp, the mother watching her child die of malaria, the grandmother
walking twenty miles a day to carry water back to her family, the Afghan
father wondering in this war what side to choose to best protect his children.

Our waiting for God is intended to be both patient and impatient. The
waiting of the pregnant Mary must have been charged with anticipation but
also involves a patient trust. Sometimes we simply have to wait in a mode of
expecting but not knowing what to expect. The poet T. S. Eliot in his *Four
Quartets* described that kind of waiting this way:

> I said to my soul, be still, and wait without hope
> For hope would be hope for the wrong thing; wait without love
> For love would be love of the wrong thing; there is yet faith,
> But the faith and the love and the hope are in the waiting. [6]

Sometimes all we can do is move forward, not knowing what God will do
but trusting in God to open a way. A long journey through disease, a long
search for a job that hasn't brought results—in the face of these we live in the
moment, we lean into a future we can't see, and we trust.

Then there are times when we should be waiting impatiently, like John
the Baptist when he says, "Prepare the way of the Lord. Every valley shall be
filled and every mountain and hill made low." Get ready, he says. Do what
you would do for any king coming into your territory. Go out ahead and
smooth the road and get ready to receive your leader. In short, get busy. Start
living for the future that you trust is coming.

If you are longing for a world that is not headed toward an environmental
disaster, get to work making that new world a reality now—driving less,
conserving more, using local markets, pressuring the Congress. Start living
the future you're waiting for now.

If you are longing for a school system and a health-care system worthy of
the richest country on earth, start working now to bring that future into the
present. If you are waiting for a world less driven, less exhausting, less tense
than this one, start living that world now. If you are waiting for a life with
more depth, with a sense of purpose to guide you, if you're tired of feeling
cut off from life and from God, start living that intentional life now. Prepare
the way of the Lord by taking the time to sit quietly—fifteen minutes a day—

and name what you are waiting for, where it is you need Christ to come into your life in this season, and pray "Come, Lord Jesus, come."

Of course, the strange fact of our lives is that the God we are waiting for has already come. The birth we anticipate in Bethlehem has already happened, and Christ's own life fills every corner of the universe. Christ is active everywhere, because without him the earth wouldn't turn, the snow wouldn't fall, the oceans wouldn't surge. Without him there would be no Handel's *Messiah*, no Gothic cathedrals, no universities or hospitals or charities that care for the poor. And without him we wouldn't be here today, gathered to experience his presence and to sense his life going on in us right now. No, you can't touch him as his mother did, or hear him as his disciples did, or feast with him as strangers did. But he is here, drawing us into his life in this Advent season.

Just a few weeks ago I caught a glimpse of Advent waiting and Christmas joy all wrapped into one evening. It was a going away party that friends were having for their twenty-nine-year-old daughter with Down Syndrome, who was finally and with immense excitement moving into a group home where she could have what she felt would be a more adult life. Her parents had put on a black tie dinner with sixty or seventy friends to mark this major step. Their daughter beamed in her beautiful dress and was the queen of the evening. She was, as she always is, as exuberantly warm and loving as anyone I have ever met. There were speeches and toasts and many hugs for this remarkable young woman.

As my wife Marguerite and I made our way out into the night, we marveled at what the constant love those parents had given their daughter had produced. Twenty-nine years of active, hardworking, endlessly patient waiting for their daughter to find her own life. Advent waiting had given way to Christmas joy. You couldn't miss the sense of Christ in their household that evening.

Let us wait, patiently and impatiently. Prepare the way of the Lord. Come, Lord Jesus, come.

Making Room for God

Isaiah 35:1–10; Matthew 11:2–11

For those who are counting, there are now eleven days until Christmas. For all of the high spirits of the season, this is about as busy and emotionally demanding a time of the year as we have. There is year-end pressure for many businesses, there are gifts to buy, cards to send, travel to plan, Christmas trees to haul in and decorate, office parties to go to.

And then there's the emotional weight of this time of year—the memories of Christmases past and longings for Hallmark Card versions of what we think Christmas should be and anticipation of times with family.

In the midst of all this busyness the church gives us this Advent season so that we can clear space and make room for God. Last week and this we are looking at John the Baptist, the ornery, demanding prophet appearing out in the wilderness and calling Israel to get ready to receive the Messiah. "Repent," "turn around," he says. Stop what you're doing and prepare the way for God to come into your world and your life. As we heard today, his harsh charges and provocations ultimately landed him in prison. You and I are not ready just as we are to receive God in our lives, he's saying. There isn't space, there isn't room. We've got some changing to do.

Making room for God is in many ways the constant theme of Advent and Christmas. The prophet Isaiah speaks of the valleys being raised up and the mountains made low to create a path for God to come.

When Mary hears the angel Gabriel tell her that she is to bear a child who is to be the savior of the world, she has to consent to this, to say yes. She has to be willing to make room for God in her own body and her own life. That's the way the fifteenth-century monk Fra Angelico imagined it as he painted the moment of Annunciation. The room is portrayed as plain and bare—a virginal room, the art historians say, meant to be a sign of a young virgin woman who was willing to let Christ's life take shape in her.

And, of course, at the center of the Christmas story is the fact that Mary had to give birth to the Christ child in a stable outdoors in Bethlehem, because the world could make no room for him in the inn. In some ways that's always the issue. Do we have room in our busy, demanding lives for Christ to be born in us?

One of the chief spiritual issues of American life is the too-muchness of our days that can keep Christ out. Preacher William Willimon tells of a conversation with a friend who was the pastor of a group of churches in Africa that had gone through tremendous suffering. His country had endured brutal political oppression, and his friend was even in prison for awhile. And so, when he came to the U.S., Willimon welcomed him with open arms and did everything he could to help him.

At the end of the visitor's stay, Willimon was expressing concern for the desperate situation his friend was going back to when his friend said, "Actually, I have more sympathy with your situation. There is just so much here. You have so much freedom, so many things. What is left to offer people? What needs do they have for which the gospel could be fulfillment? I have great respect for those of you who preach the gospel and who minister in the situation of North America. There is so much fulfillment and so little emptiness. The gospel feeds on emptiness."[1]

How can there be room for God when our lives are so full? When our own kingdom is having a good year, we don't yearn so much for God's kingdom to come. When life is good, why bother with something like redemption?

Part of that fullness is choices. Everywhere we turn there are choices. If you don't like listening to the NPR pledge drive, flick to another station. If you don't like Starbucks coffee any more, there is Dunkin' Donuts. If you don't like one church, or one job, or one city, or one spouse, well then, just go find another. We can choose.

I was listening last week to a National Public Radio conversation about the impact of technology on our lives, and the main theme was how steadily we are using our computers and handhelds to fill up every waking second of our brain's attention. One researcher reports that we switch our attention when we're sitting at a computer thirty-seven times every hour. We are eager to check Facebook, texts, and e-mail, because, he says, we get a dopamine rush by clicking to a new spot simply in anticipation that something interesting might be there.

This obsessive leaping from data byte to data byte is diminishing our memory, our attention span, and our capacity to reflect. In fact, he's saying our brain needs boredom, down time, time to muse and think and remember. And with no capacity for wonder and reflection there is no room for depth or for God.

Several years ago when I was away on retreat, I heard some words that have been stirring in me ever since:

> If we have it all together, there is no room for God in our life. But on the other hand, in our brokenness, vulnerability, and need, God finds us irresistible. [2]

I wonder if you find those words as piercing as I do. Isn't all our busy-ness, whether it's the daily rush, or the Christmas frenzy, or the computer click, actually aimed at having it all, having full satisfaction at every moment? Isn't that finally what we most want? I am guessing that many of us here are the sort of Type A, highly responsible, driven lot who live in and around Washington or get to visit here. We are working hard to have it all together!

And having it all together is not needing anyone else. It's to be right all the time. It's to be self-possessed, self-contained, independent, private. It means having money in the bank, a substantial roof over our heads, a career we can count on, and health that won't give out. And if we have it all together, we really shouldn't need anyone else, and certainly not God.

There's a story of a seeker after enlightenment who went to the spiritual master and said, "Show me how to know God." The master listened to him, then took a cup, placed it on a table, and poured water in it until it overflowed. "Stop, why are you doing that?" the seeker said. "Because you are like that. Your life is so full as to be overflowing. There is no room for God in your life. Come back when there is room in your cup."

And there's the rub. For all of our fullness, we are not full. For all of the ways we have stuffed our lives until things are spilling over the rim, the deepest yearnings of our heart—for love, for belonging, for peace, for a just world for everyone, for a purpose in our lives—often go unmet. And so we need to hear that other, paradoxical truth: "In our brokenness, vulnerability and need, God finds us irresistible."

We naturally think of the broken things in our lives as our enemies—the worry, the job loss, the illness, the conflict at home, our failures. But maybe we've had it all wrong. The places that are broken are exactly where God finds us irresistible, because they create space for God to come in. They open us up, they show us we aren't masters of our own performances, that we need love, support, and help that we can't muster for ourselves. We are not God, our achievements are not God, we are souls searching for home, and the light of home shines through our broken places.

And so some of the most important work of this Advent season is to peel away the veneer of having it all together and pay attention to what's underneath.

It's something we need to do as a nation as well. As long as we are intent on being the always virtuous superpower, we are closing God out of our public life. As long as each political party acts as if it is in full possession of all truth and that to think differently from its view is to be morally bankrupt, our politics and our country will have a troubled future. Perfect wisdom is not an available option for political leaders any more than it is for you and me. Our leaders need uncertainty, a willingness to listen, and the capacity to compromise. If we can acknowledge our own limits, our need for cooperation and support in facing our own problems, we will be making room for God's love, justice, and truth in our life together.

And if in these harsh economic times we can address the struggles of the poor and jobless in our cities, the plight of those who are holding down two jobs and are still unable to afford a roof over their family's heads, especially the sky-high unemployment in urban centers, then we will be making room for Christ's love to be born in our cities in the coming year.

Is there room for God in your life? That's the question of these Advent days.

It's the question a man had to face in the fine movie of several years ago, *About Schmidt*. The story opens with Schmidt, who is played by Jack Nicholson, sitting miserably through his retirement party, and we slowly come to see that here's a man who had stuffed his life full of things that never really mattered to him. As his career is ending, he sees how quickly his company files are being tossed out. His wife, whom he doesn't like, dies unexpectedly, and his daughter wants nothing to do with him.

Schmidt is a frightened, lonely man. One day, though, in going through his mail he opens an appeal from an international children's fund, which says that for $22 a month he can help an orphan in Africa and that he can actually write to the child. So on the spot he sends a check, and starts to write letters to Ngudu, a six-year-old Tanzanian orphan. He writes the boy about his wife, his troubles with his daughter, about his lonely, lost life.

At the end of the movie he returns home from his daughter's wedding and finally names the truth of his life: He declares that he's a failure, and that he's never made a difference to a solitary human being. And then he sees an envelope from Tanzania. It contains a note a nun has transcribed for him from Ngudu, thanking him and sending him a picture he has drawn. Schmidt opens it up to see two stick figures, an adult and a child, their arms outstretched to each other as if they're holding hands. And for the first time, tears begin to run down Schmidt's cheeks. At long last, he has stopped covering over the broken places in his life and begun to make room for God.

What about you? Is there room for God in your life this season?

Are there fears, losses, and broken places that you keep pushing away? Pay attention to them—they are where God is seeking you.

Are you burdened about trouble at work or at home? Don't run from it, but listen to what it is saying. Chances are that's where Christ is coming.

Do you see a world that doesn't look much like a savior has come to it? Watch for the broken place that has your name on it.

You see, "If we have it all together, there is no room for God in our life. But on the other hand, in our brokenness, vulnerability, and need, God finds us irresistible."

Mary Said Yes

Luke 1:26–33

The gospel this Advent Sunday is one of the most beautiful stories in the Christian tradition: the Annunciation, in which the angel Gabriel brings Mary the startling news that she is to bear the Messiah. It has all the qualities of high drama—a young girl being called to take part in the salvation of the world.

In much of the Episcopal Church, at least, you don't hear a lot about Mary these days. For our Roman Catholic friends, though, Mary is essential; they refer to her as "Mother of God" and "Queen of Heaven." And the Eastern Orthodox tradition calls her *theotokos*, the God-bearer. But there has been an uneasiness about Mary in the Protestant and Anglican traditions, a concern that all the focus on her as an object of devotion and veneration, expressed in prayers, shrines, and hymns, could be a distraction from focus on Christ. In an old story told by Harvard preacher Peter Gomes, when a former dean of St. Paul's Cathedral in London arrives in heaven, Jesus comes down from God's right hand and says: "Ah, Mr. Dean, welcome to heaven; I know you have met my Father, but I don't believe you know my Mother." [1]

Increasingly, however, Mary is being embraced by all the traditions as the brave young woman who gave birth to Jesus, God Incarnate, who suckled and nurtured him, who taught him compassion and love. And it's that Mary we meet in our lesson today.

Maybe because the scene is so dramatic, artists have for centuries done their best to capture the intensity of the Annunciation. Anyone who has strolled through galleries of Renaissance paintings has encountered countless versions of it. Mary is nearly always portrayed as an idealized image of youthful femininity, carefully composed and beautiful. While reading a book

225

in her courtly Italian room, she is interrupted by the dazzling angel Gabriel. Often the presence of a dove hovering over the scene signifies that what is happening is the work of the Holy Spirit.

For years I have understood the Annunciation as a powerful invitation being offered to Mary. Out of all the people on earth, God chooses this insignificant peasant girl to give birth to the savior of the world. Mary is frightened and overwhelmed, and the question is, Will she agree to do it? The great reformer Martin Luther wrote that "all heaven and earth held its breath to see if Mary would say yes." And finally she does, saying, "Here am I, a servant of the Lord. Let it be with me according to your word."

Lately, though, I've begun to think that I've been missing something crucial in this story. God isn't so much inviting Mary to consider taking on this role as informing her that something immense is about to happen through her. Gabriel doesn't ask her if she would like to be the mother of Jesus, whether she would care to think about it, whether it fits in with her plans for her life. "Behold you will conceive in your womb and bear a son," he says, "who will be called the Son of the Most High." That's what is about to happen!

All this was brought home to me when a friend showed me a remarkable painting of the Annunciation by the sixteenth-century artist Lorenzo Lotto. In it we don't see a composed Mary listening to the angel's announcement. Instead, an alarmed Mary is turned toward us, the viewers, and away from Gabriel; her eyes are wide with fear. Gabriel seems confused himself. Looming over his head, in the sky just beyond the room, is a fierce-looking, gray-bearded God, with his hands and arms outstretched and clamped together, pointing down toward Mary with a gesture you would never want to have aimed at you. God looks more than a little frightening. And at the center of the scene is a cat running across the middle of the floor with its back arched, its front paws in the air, as if it has been electrocuted. Every detail speaks of tension, terror, and alarm. And there is Mary, staring at us, as if to say, "Imagine this! What would you do if you were in my place?"

The Annunciation is the moment when Mary discovers that God is doing something through her. In fact, the surprise of the Christmas stories of Joseph and Mary, of the shepherds and wise men, and of the entire Bible for that matter, is that God is the initiator. God intrudes into peoples' lives, calling them, acting through them, giving them tasks to accomplish.

To Mary it seems not only ludicrous that she should be chosen to take a role in this mission, but also upsetting. First, we are told that she was "much perplexed" by Gabriel's words to her. Then she responds incredulously, "How can this be?" How could God need her? And once she starts asking questions, she probably can't stop. Will I be safe? Will Joseph really stick with me and endure the shame of marrying a woman who will bear a child that is not his? Will I be written off by my family and friends? Her worries must be endless, but it is clear that this is going to happen whether she gets satisfactory answers or not. Still, she will have a choice—whether to say yes to the life she is being handed, give herself over to it, and see what God wants to do with it, or to fight it and rebel against it.

Some scholars have suggested that Mary's response to the Annunciation is actually unhealthy. It's a woman's act of submission and obedience in a male-dominated culture, they say, and it has long been used to encourage passivity in women. But Mary's is a deeper sort of yes. It is for her a profound affirmation of who she is and of her willingness to be an instrument of God, and it calls forth tremendous courage and strength. Our culture is fixated on our expressing ourselves, whatever superficial version of the self we happen to be absorbed with at the moment. Doing your own thing seems to be our creed. But God's annunciations are always calls to a deeper, larger self. They draw out not our passivity but our strength.

Mary stands alone in history as the receiver of this particular Annunciation to be the God-bearer. But we, too, receive annunciations. Isn't it true that many of the most important events in our lives actually choose us? We build elaborate plans, we think about our goals. And then an unexpected job offer comes, or a sudden illness hits, or we fall in love, or we feel called to change our lives and make a difference somewhere else, or aging parents need us, or a troubled child turns our lives upside down. And it seems as if we are being asked to do something, to change something, to endure something, for someone else's sake, maybe even for God's.

None of it we planned. We find ourselves, like Mary in the Lotto painting, anxious and disturbed, wondering what to do next. And when that happens, we have two choices: to say, yes, I will live this life that is being held out to me; or, no, I will resist it.

Psychiatrist and spiritual writer Gerald May says there are two fundamental life-orientations: one of willfulness, an attitude of constantly seeking to force our will on our lives and those around us; and one of willingness, which entails our desire to move with the deepest, truest currents of our lives. The former is about control; the latter is about acknowledging that there is a deeper life moving through us. When our moments of annunciation come, will our response be willfulness or willingness?[2]

The stakes are high. We can, of course, say no. We can ignore this new call, get back to our busy lives, pretend the moment never came. Or we can be willing, we can say yes. We can say, "Here am I; let it be with me according to your word."

A few years ago, there was a week-long front-page series in the *Boston Globe* about a young couple who learned that the child they were about to have would be born with Down Syndrome and would need heart surgery almost immediately after birth. The story described the couple's devastation at learning of their child's condition. It recounted their struggle to decide whether to have the child or terminate the pregnancy. Then it described their ultimately bringing the child they named Naia to birth, caring for her in the dangerous early weeks, helping her through surgery, watching her grow stronger. The final installment showed a radiant one-year-old and a happy couple preparing for a different sort of life with their developmentally challenged child.

It was a beautiful story of ordinary people caught up in an extraordinarily difficult crisis. The most critical decision of all, of course, was whether to proceed with the pregnancy. They received all sorts of advice from friends, family, and doctors. One piece sticks out, the words that Greg, Naia's father, hears from his own father: "Gregory . . . this is not a tragedy. This is not the end of the world. All of us are born with defects. If you and Tierney give this child the love you have for each other, this child will be all right."[3]

The couple was terrified by what they faced—how painful would the surgery be for Naia, how many more medical problems would there be, what would happen if raising Naia proved to be just too much for them? They asked every question they could think of, but when there were no more words they looked at each other and knew they had decided to have this baby.

The depth of the story rested in honoring all the ambiguities, in showing a couple's agonizing struggle with questions only they could answer, in the portrayal of two courageous young people who were in over their heads. They listened deeply, heard what they believed they were being called to do, and said a courageous Yes.

God's annunciations always come in the concrete circumstances of our lives. And they are often hidden in situations that God would never choose to happen—a loss, the end of a job or marriage, hard times for us or for those we care about. They come as doors that open, as new work to be done, new relationships to begin, new burdens to carry. They come in glimpses we get of the need of the world around us. A friend of mine whose home in Mississippi barely survived Hurricane Katrina told me recently that this year her family had seen too much loss to waste money giving a lot of gifts no one really needs. This year, she says, they may give each other a book or a sweater, but otherwise they are sending checks to relief agencies.

Now, let me ask you: What new life is stirring in you this year? With what new life are you pregnant? A yearning for a deeper, more connected life at home with family and friends? A longing for a deeper relationship with God in the new year? A deeper call to a generous life that makes a difference in the world around you?

These annunciations when they come say quietly, "Greetings, O favored one, the Lord is with you!" and they invite us to let our lives be disrupted by this intrusive God. And then God waits with bated breath for our response.

And the hope of this season is that we will have the courage to answer with Mary's own words: "Here am I, a servant of the Lord. Let it be with me according to your word."

Christmas

God Comes In

Some years ago Annie Dillard, in a book called *Teaching a Stone to Talk*, wrote a wonderful reminiscence of a childhood Christmas Eve she has never forgotten. She and her family had come in unusually late that night from dinner and were happy to arrive in their warm living room with stockings hanging from the mantel and beside them, a special table holding a bottle of ginger ale and a plate of cookies.

Soon after she had taken off her coat she heard a lot of commotion at the front door. "Look who's here! Look who's here!" she heard. And there he was. Santa Claus, looming in the doorway, the one person, she says, she had never wanted to meet. Annie instead dashed upstairs.

Like so many, Annie Dillard says, she feared Santa Claus because at some level she thought he was God. You know, the old man you never saw, who nevertheless saw you, who knew when you had been bad or good. "And I had been bad," she said. [1]

Her parents pleaded with her to come down. She refused. She leaned over the stairwell, though, and she looked at Santa Claus standing in the doorway repeating "Merry Christmas, Merry Christmas." Little Annie Dillard never came down that night.

Years later she learned that this Santa Claus was actually Miss White, an elderly friend of the family, who lived across the street. But that night it was Santa Claus she saw there, and that night it was God she saw, too. All in all it was just too much.

Part of the strangeness of Christmas is how things sacred and secular get jumbled together. Here we are on this holy night, when we celebrate God's coming among us in a child born two thousand years ago. But here we are, too, having arrived after weeks of Muzak renditions of "White Christmas" and "Rudolph the Red-Nosed Reindeer" filling the airwaves in shopping malls and endless TV ads for the perfect gift. There have been purists, and I have been one, who complain about the commercialization of Christmas—all the spending and frenzy. My guess is that all of our Christmas celebrations will contain a jumble of secular and sacred traditions. And, at least for tonight, I want to repent of my purist ways and say, "God bless them all." Because Christmas is about the night God came into our very secular world, and that means we can look for God in even the most secular parts of the Christmas story.

Take old Santa Claus, for example. He wasn't much of a player in Christmas until 1823 when an Episcopal Old Testament professor in New York wrote a little poem called "The Night Before Christmas." After that, Santa was off and running, and was all set to go into the big time when Macy's had its first big parade to get people into the buying mood in 1924. But you know, there really is a lot of Christmas in Santa Claus's mysteriousness, his endless ho-ho-ho goodwill, and his unflagging determination to get a present down every chimney on earth, even if the house doesn't have a chimney. The brilliant Christian writer G. K. Chesterton was convinced that there was profound meaning in the Santa Claus story:

> What has happened to me has been the very reverse of what appears to be the experiences of most of my friends. Instead of dwindling to a point, Santa Claus has grown larger and larger in my life. . . . As a child I was faced with a phenomenon requiring explanation. I hung up at the end of my bed an empty stocking, which in the morning became a full stocking. I had done nothing to produce those things that filled it. I had not worked for them, or made them or helped to make them. I had not even been good—far from it. . . . And the explanation was that a certain being people call Santa Claus was favorably disposed toward me. What we believed was that a certain benevolent agency did give us those toys for nothing. And, as I say, I believe it still. I have merely extended the idea. Then I only wondered who put the toys in the stocking. Now I wonder who put the stocking by the bed, and the bed in the room, and the room in the house, and the house on this planet, and the great planet in the void.[2]

Chesterton goes on to say that once he was grateful for a few toys, but later he became grateful for stars and faces on the street and good wine and the vast sea. Once he was grateful for a gift so big only half of it went into the stocking. Now he says he is delighted every morning to find "a present so big it takes two stockings to hold it, and then leaves a great deal outside: it is the large and preposterous present of myself."[3]

So much of the romance and wonder of Christmas is at its heart intended to evoke in us this sense of amazement. Christmas is about a God who gives us life and then comes to live with us, who wants us to know that we are loved and wants the best for us. On this night, God comes in.

Or take Christmas trees, another indispensable part of the season. On top of many trees is an angel or a star. The tree is strung with lights and decorated with ornaments, many of them accumulated with a story attached to each one. Somewhere in the vicinity of the tree might be some gifts or maybe a crib with a few figures gathered around it. The tree is saying that heaven and earth are united on this night. The tree is saying that while Santa Claus, God's agent, is coming down the chimney, the Son of God is climbing down this brightly lit tree to enter the village of the human race. He is God's gift for us, wrapped not in bright Christmassy paper, but in bands of rough cloth to keep him warm against the cold night. On this night, they say, God comes in.

Or take all those gifts we give and receive. Of course the, first gift givers were the Wise Men who came from the East. Since then, the gift giving has gotten out of hand, leaving us with long lists of things to buy for people who already have too much, and leaving us on the receiving end of a lot of things we will never use. But, we shouldn't squelch the impulse to give and to delight another. We're self-absorbed enough as it is. And to have a season that insists that we focus on blessing the lives of those around us—well that can't be all bad.

Gift giving is the language of the tongue-tied, allowing us to say thank you, or I care about you, or I love you. And, of course, the best gifts of all aren't big, expensive purchases, but the gift of time with one another, or words of appreciation, a note, a card, a hug. How far is all this, after all, from the spiritual center of Christmas, expressed as "God so loved the world that he gave his only Son"? God comes in through our gift giving.

Of course, the danger of our cultural Christmas is that it can so dazzle us that we forget where it all began—a young woman and man living in a Palestine as troubled as it is today, struggling just to get by, yet somehow called to be agents of God's coming into the world.

Angels sing their song, shepherds gather near, Wise Men make their way—all the pieces of this beautiful story are orchestrated to make as vivid as possible the unthinkable: that the mysterious Holy One who created the cosmos came to live one life with us. And this birth didn't happen simply to amaze us once, but to say for all time that God comes to us again and again, and that the whole point of our lives is the love and gift giving and joy we celebrate in this season. And that wherever we find ourselves on this cold winter night in December, the Maker of heaven and earth loves us and will never let us go.

Ever since that holy night the spirit of Christmas has been at work wherever people refuse to give up hope, wherever peace is cobbled together out of the broken fragments of relationships, wherever human beings reach out to build better lives for everyone—fighting disease, feeding the hungry, working for a just, fair life for everyone.

My guess is that whatever we think we believe, we know more about Christmas than we can say. Why else would you be here tonight? Why pay any attention to all the trappings of this season, if there were not some un-Scroogelike, un-Grinchlike place in us that believes we are meant for love, for sheer wild gratitude for the gift of being, and that in some inscrutable way we are known and loved from the heart of the universe?

In Annie Dillard's memory of Santa Claus in the doorway, of God in the doorway, she says there were other times, too, when the good and generous Miss White reached out to her, only to end up unintentionally frightening her again. And looking back she realizes how much God's love has been like that—so constant, so often ignored, sometimes so frightening, making her run away. She closes her memory this way:

> Miss White, God, I am sorry I [hid] from you. . . . For you meant only love, and love, and I felt only fear. . . . So once in Israel love came to us incarnate, stood in the doorway between two worlds, and we were all afraid.[4]

Once in Israel a child was born, who came to say, "Open your eyes, don't be afraid, don't run away." God came into our lives two thousand years ago. And mixed up in all the twists and turns of our lives, God comes again and again. The question is, will we run away in fear and confusion, or, will we open the questions, the struggles, the hopes of our lives and our world, and let God come in?

The Birth of the Messiah

What a strange season Christmas is. We begin to prepare for it weeks and months in advance, as if it were a tidal wave we knew was coming and would wash over us ready or not. More than a billion Christians will commemorate the birth of their Lord around the globe this year, and many more will turn up just to enjoy the candlelight and Christmas carols.

People who haven't darkened the door of a church for a year will enter into the mysterious beauty of a Christmas service. Sometimes the minister will use this as an occasion for a little scolding: Where have you been for the last fifty-two Sundays when you didn't have to get a pass to be here? Let me be clear I would never say such a thing!

I'm glad you're here, all of you, whether you are a believer or an unbeliever or a skeptic, whether you came out of curiosity, or cultural tradition, or were dragged here by family members, or whether you're like many of us who couldn't be kept away for anything. There's nothing in the world quite like this night of being here together, hearing the old story of a child born in a manger, and singing those great carols.

Tonight, I want to begin, not with Mary and Joseph and the Child, but with an eighteenth-century rabbinic tale of a worshiper, Ben Ezra, who on the eve of Yom Kippur, the Day of Atonement, prayed long and ardently in the synagogue. Meanwhile, the impatient rabbi wondered what was keeping Ben Ezra there so long, and so finally he asked. "I will tell you what I have been saying," Ben Ezra said. "To the Master of the Universe I say, 'These are my sins and I confess them:'

> I argue with my wife. But you know my wife.
> I lost patience with my children. But what parent doesn't?
> I cheated a little in the shop. But just a little. Among friends.
> How small my sins are, Master of the Universe!

Now consider your sins.
You dry up the sky, and our crops wither.
You let the rains come before the poor man has the roof repaired.
You do not stop war, and young men die.
The marriage bed is empty; there is no child in the womb.
You take away the light from the eyes of a child, and he is blind.
You take away loved ones, and we are left alone until we die.
These are your sins, Master of the Universe, and they are very great.
But I will make you a proposition:
You forgive me my little sins, and I will forgive you your great ones!'
That was my proposal, Rabbi, and I ask you, was that so wrong?"

The Rabbi did not answer for a long time. "No, Ben Ezra," he said at last, "it was not wrong, it was not wrong. But why did you drive so small a bargain? For sins like these you could have asked him to send the Messiah. You could have asked him to redeem the world."[1]

The story of Christmas begins with the sort of world we live in—a world where our lives are marred by struggle and pain, and this year, in particular, by an economic recession that is damaging countless lives across our country and the world. Our huddling here on Christmas Eve, at the time of the winter solstice when the days are at their darkest, is our acknowledgment of our need for hope and joy in lives that often are not easy.

Christmas is God's answer to the darkness we face. "For sins like these," the old rabbi says, "we could have asked for a Messiah." All the carols and beauty of the night are a response to our conviction that the Messiah has come, and comes again and again.

And the heavenly message is always the same: "Fear not." Those are the Angel Gabriel's first words to Mary. They are the angels' words to shepherds. The arrival of the Messiah is the revealing of the deepest truth we know, that the God of the universe is not a remote deity, but has taken on flesh as one of us, to share our lives, to show the world a love that overcomes fear.

In fact, Christmas didn't really begin with wise men, shepherds, and angels. It began with a life of immense freedom and love. It began with a young man walking through the hills and valleys of Palestine, teaching about a kingdom of peace and joy right here at hand, and calling people to live in it. It began with people being given back their sight, their dignity, and hope, by his healing words and touch. And it began with his gathering around him the losers and outcasts of his society and treating them as royalty.

Strangely enough, an instrument of torture, a cross, was part of the beginning of Christmas, because that perfect love was willing to be mocked and put to death. And ultimately Christmas began with an empty tomb, and the conviction that he was alive, and that death and darkness had been conquered for good.

Through all that, people began to believe that the Messiah had come. That the Creator at the core of space and time loved them and had come to live with them to draw them into lives of hope and peace.

All the rest—the angels, the manger, and the shepherds—came later, as people realized they had met and known a man who had set them free, and as they began to look back to tell the story of what his beginning must have been like.

It must have been hard, just the way Luke's gospel describes it in our lesson this evening. The child's parents seem like insignificant pawns as Caesar Augustus and the Governor Quirinius go about their business of keeping control of the empire with a census.

But Luke's story is saying that the secret of the universe won't be found in Rome, or in the American White House for that matter, or in the laboratories of the National Institutes of Health or along the canyons of Wall Street, or among the scholars of Cambridge. No, the mystery of the Incarnation is revealed in the most unexpected of places—in a squalling child born to a young mother and her faithful but troubled husband as they are bandied about by the forces of empire.

And who are the first to receive the news of the Messiah? Not the cultured and educated, so distracted with their important agendas, but the poorest of the poor, the ignorant and troublesome shepherds. It comes to those who are willing to listen to unexpected voices that seem like angelic messengers, and to follow their unexpected lead.

It is a strange, even stunning thing, isn't it—for God to take the risk of coming to us in this tiny child in a lost corner of the Roman Empire? Could it be the Master of the Universe rules this Universe only with the power of love—a love that refuses to coerce or control, but gives the universe and us freedom to grow and to become? Could it be that to serve this Master is to give ourselves to lives of compassion and generosity, and that the deepest call we have is to find our way to care for the hungry, the broken, and the lost?

As our world faces recession, we need this vision. Let me read you a few lines from a letter a priest friend of mine received some years ago:

> The most meaningful Christmas I remember in my family was the Christmas when all we had to give was love. It doesn't pay the bills. It won't pay the rent. But sometimes love is all you have to hang onto. Like the Babe in the manger. All he had was the love of two people. Without that he had nothing.

That is what the birth of that child is about. It is about a God who in the end has only love to give. That is why the world can be so hard. But that is why we are never alone. It is a love so deep that God chose to become vulnerable as a newborn child, to lie in a manger, entirely dependent on two fragile human beings to love him in return.

A memorable moment occurred at a Christmas Eve pageant at Riverside Church in New York a few years ago. The pageant had come to the defining moment when the innkeeper tells Mary and Joseph, "There's no room in the inn."

You imagine then how it must have felt to Mary and Joseph as they turned away. The innkeeper role has only this one line, and it seemed perfect for Tim, a young member of the congregation who was developmentally challenged. Young Tim had practiced his line over and over with his parents and director until he knew it.

The moment arrived. And there he was, standing in the front of the church as Mary and Joseph made their way down the center aisle. They approached, knocked on the door, and said their lines. Then Tim's parents and the whole congregation leaned forward to hear what Tim would say.

"There's no room in the inn," Tim boomed out.

But then, as Mary and Joseph turned to go, Tim suddenly yelled, "Wait!" They stopped and turned, startled and confused.

"You can stay at my house," he called. [2]

That's what this season is about. The Messiah has come. God has taken on flesh in Jesus, and in you and me. And the question is: Will we invite this Christ Child into our home, into our lives?

The words we sang a few moments ago say it best:

> O holy Child of Bethlehem
> Descend to us we pray.
> Cast out our sin and enter in
> Be born in us today. [3]

The Plunge

Luke 2:1–14

Not long ago I was flipping through a year-end gathering of cartoons and came across one from the *New Yorker* showing God sitting grandly on a heavenly throne with stars twinkling around him. You can see the planet earth in the distance. Beside him is God's son looking down at the earth and saying, "Don't make me have to come down there!" Which is, of course, exactly what this night is about—a God who sees the mess we humans have made of things and decides to come down.

"Don't make me have to come down." You may have heard that line at some point in your life. I happened to have been one of six children and sometimes over the years, to put it nicely, we had our issues. We might fight in the basement over a TV channel, or whose turn it was to play Monopoly, and before you knew it voices would rise, a little shoving might begin, and a voice with an edge from upstairs would come floating down, "Don't make me have to come down there!"

That line suggests that there is a powerful presence "up there," and those who are down below feel as if they are left fending for themselves. You can hear that sense of confusion in some wonderful letters to God written by children in a little book called *Children's Letters to God.*

> Dear God,
>   My grandpa says you were around when he was a little boy. How far back do you go?
>   Dennis

Dear God,
   Are you really invisible or is that just a trick?
   Lucy

Dear God,
   Thank you for the baby brother, but what I prayed for was a puppy.
   Joyce

Dear God,
   Are you real? Some people don't believe it. If you are, you better do something quick.
   Love, Harriet[1]

Sometimes it would be good for things to be clearer. Sometimes we just wish God would take the plunge and come down.

That's what Christians believe happened at Christmas. God came down. The Christmas story is a simple account of a young Jewish woman and her husband traveling for days to his ancestral home in Bethlehem, where she gives birth to a child in a manger. And far off in a field angels appear to shepherds to tell them the news and they dash off to see the child.

It's as beautiful a story as you can imagine. And it's the way the gospel writers imagined and remembered Jesus' birth many decades later—after the child had become a teacher, healer, and prophet for a new kingdom of peace, reconciliation, and after he had been killed and gone through death to the other side. They became convinced that the Creator of the universe had actually come into their lives, that the Word had become flesh and dwelt among them.

The focus of Christmas is not on what we humans must do to care for our planet. Just look at the mess we're making of things. A newspaper columnist two days ago wrote saying the first decade of the twenty-first century was not a good beginning, and that things are looking worse as we begin the second. What will happen to the climate of our planet, to the victims of our wars, to troubled economies everywhere, to those caught in the endless tension and bickering both around the world and in our own leadership? Left to our own devices, the prospects are not very good.

But Christmas tells us we can put our hope in God, the great mystery of Love who has called this vast cosmos into being, and who decided to take on flesh to live our lives with us.

In fact, all the players in the Christmas story we heard tonight are more receivers than actors—Mary, Joseph, the shepherds, the angels. They aren't launching a program for turning the world around. There are no strategic plans here, no great personal goals. No, they are responding to a God who comes, a God who is seeking them out in the life of this child, who intends to bless the whole world by calling into being a people who are peacemakers, reconcilers, servants, people with hearts overflowing with generosity.

Years ago, J. B. Phillips wrote a fantasy about a senior and junior angel traveling across space past billions of stars in their galaxies until they came to our star and what they call our "insignificant planet." After all the grandeur they've witnessed flying through space, the younger angel wasn't very impressed with our little earth. But the senior angel told him that he didn't understand, that this was the Visited Planet—the one to which God had come and on which God had walked. "'For strange as it may seem to us,' the senior angel said, 'He loves them. He went down to visit them to lead them to become like Him.' The little angel looked blank. Such a thought was beyond his comprehension."[2]

That is the truth of this night. We are a Visited Planet. God has taken the plunge and come down to us and taken on our flesh. Of course, "coming down" is a metaphor. God isn't up or out. God is the life within our lives, the power that sustains the galaxies, the breath within our breath and heart within our heart. That life took on flesh once. And we Christians believe that Christ wasn't born just once, but comes again and again to be born in our lives.

The essential question is, Will I allow the Christ who is in me to be born and grow? Will I make space and time this year for him to come alive in me?

And this Christ continues to be born in our world, too. Christ is born when communities reach out to families suffering in this recession, when peacemakers struggle to bring peace to the Middle East, so that the wall that cuts Bethlehem off from the rest of Israel can come down forever, when in countless ways children are loved and nurtured with the health and education they need.

Not long ago I heard an account of a remarkable rescue effort that sounds like Christmas itself. There is apparently a very high bridge over the river outside Kansas City. One day there was a traffic tie-up that went on for hours and had all the roads in the city backed up. When people arrived home later in the day, they learned on the news what had been happening.

A man had driven up to the middle of the bridge, stopped, gotten out, and then climbed down on the bracing underneath. He was intent on jumping off and ending his life. Things had gone terribly wrong for him, including the fact that his girlfriend had tossed him aside, and he saw no reason to live.

The rescue team had arrived quickly when they saw the stopped car. And a policeman climbed down on the beam. He and his team had attached a strong rope from the policeman to the bridge to catch him if he were to fall. He inched his way along the beam toward the man, very slowly, talking to him calmly. He said to the man, "I want you to know that not only are there hundreds of people who want to help you, there are hundreds who can help you."

And so he inched closer and closer. But then the man panicked and jumped from the bridge, and when he did, the policeman jumped too. And he caught hold of the man in midair and down they sailed. The policeman wrapped his legs and arms around the man so that when the rope jerked, he wouldn't lose him.

The policeman held on tight and blurted out, "I'm going to hold onto you until hell freezes over." And he held on, and on, until they were able to get the man safely back to the bridge. [3]

The mystery of this night, my friends, is that God has taken the plunge for us. We are a visited planet, and God has come to you and me and all this world, and will not let us go until hell freezes over. I hope you'll think about that as you make your way home tonight.

"Don't make me have to come down."

God has come, and lives in us, and will keep coming again and again.

It's enough to make you want to sing with the angels: "Glory to God in the highest, and peace to all God's people on earth."

Epiphany

The Magi and Us

Matthew 2:1–12

> A cold coming we had of it,
> Just the worst time of the year
> For a journey, and such a long journey:
> The ways deep and the weather sharp,
> The very dead of winter. [1]

With those words T. S. Eliot begins his poem called the "Journey of the Magi," which imagines what one of the Wise Men who traveled from the East might have said about his long journey following a star to find the child king in Bethlehem.

Today is the Feast of the Epiphany, the day the church calendar marks the arrival of these Wise Men. Many countries actually make the Epiphany the peak of their Christmas celebrations, since the twelfth day of Christmas is the day when these Wise Men knelt before the Christ Child bringing their gifts of gold, frankincense, and myrrh.

In fact, if we were keeping our Christmas traditions correctly, we would finally put the Wise Men with their camels in our crêches, and we would be taking our Christmas tree down this afternoon as we open our last Christmas present!

It should be said that it is difficult to pin down much in the way of historical fact in the story of the Magi. Much of what we think is in the story actually came into the tradition much later. Nothing in the text tells us that there were *three* Wise Men, for one thing. That seems to have come from the fact that the Wise Men brought three gifts. And nothing says they were kings; that may have been an elaboration of a reference in the psalms we read today about kings bringing gifts. The names assigned to them—Gaspar, Melchior, and Balthazar—don't appear anywhere before the sixth century.

And they weren't necessarily even wise. "Magi" is the Greek word, but we don't even know exactly what the word would have meant—magicians, astrologers maybe, astronomers, philosophers, perhaps.

You may have come across the old joke that asks the question, What if the wise men had been three wise women? Well, clearly things would have been different. They would have asked for directions, arrived on time, cleaned the stable, helped deliver the baby, brought a casserole, and given practical gifts like gloves or a Target gift certificate, instead of useless presents like gold, frankincense, and myrrh.

Matthew's gospel tells a different story from Luke's familiar account of the birth at a manger in Bethlehem surrounded by shepherds and angels. For Matthew, the story of the Magi is *the* Christmas story, the arrival of Gentiles from the far corners of the earth to worship the next king. In fact, the earliest pictures of Christmas in the catacombs in Rome showed the Magi, not the shepherds. And to this day the story of brilliant, wealthy foreign magicians or philosophers following the leading of the star remains maybe our most beautiful portrayal of the meaning of Christ's birth.

Well, on they traveled mile after dusty mile following that star. In Eliot's poem, one of the Wise Men describes their journey this way:

> A hard time we had of it.
> At the end we preferred to travel all night,
> Sleeping in snatches,
> With the voices singing in our ears, saying
> That this was all folly.[2]

The story of these traveling magi is intended to be about us sophisticated, savvy, educated, secular types, searching for signs of the world's deepest meaning. Through hostile cities and loud distractions the Wise Men traveled as many around them were saying that even the search itself was a folly.

I don't know about you, but I sense a lot of searching going on in our time. The polls tell us that people are longing for a deeper meaning in their lives. Only 28 percent of Americans are happy with where our country and our world are going. Some 90 percent believe in God, but many aren't finding what they are looking for in churches. Many are content to drift, put the question of faith on hold, and stay busy looking after today and tomorrow. Presumably, there were plenty of sophisticated people in the Magi's world that included most of what we call the Middle East. But only a few decided to follow a star and search for the key that would unlock the world's mystery.

But the quest for our time is deeper than only our own inner questions. The real adventure of our era, I believe, isn't going to be simply finding our personal happiness, or sending a spacecraft to Mars, or extending our life spans so that we live to be 125. It will be a quest to find a way for human beings to live together on this earth in peace. The great challenge of the twenty-first century will be the quest to create a more habitable earth for everyone, and will require more imagination, daring, and sacrifice than any of us can imagine.

T. S. Eliot wrote his poem on the Magi in 1927, after he himself had been on a long search. This was the year he had been baptized as a Christian at the age of thirty-nine, and this poem is in many ways about his own conversion. It had been a long, hard journey to the baptismal font for him, too, from his own roots as a Unitarian, through his studies in philosophy and Eastern religions at Harvard, to seeking his spiritual roots in England. And my guess is that for many of us here today, it has been a long journey trying to find a place to rest our hearts.

Matthew says that when the travelers arrived, "They were overwhelmed with joy." Joy is the pervading tone of the story. In a child in a manger they found the answer to their lifetime's longing—a Love, a Purpose, a Calling, for them and the whole human family. So they kneel down before this child-king and open their gifts of gold, frankincense, and myrrh.

But then hovering over this story is King Herod, a Jewish puppet installed on the throne by Rome. He is the embodiment of power, but we see him nervous and worried at the news the Wise Men bring that a child is born who will himself become king of the Jews. Herod is also one of history's worst villains. He murdered his wife, three of his children, and most of his good friends—anyone who made him feel threatened. And not only was he terrified, but Matthew tells us that "all Jerusalem" was terrified with him. They knew how bloody Herod could be, but at least he kept order; better that than someone you don't know at all. Soon, Herod, in an effort to destroy this child-king would order the killing of all the male children in Bethlehem.

Jesus was a threat from the start—especially to the ones who hold the reins of power, who have the world working their way. Of course, it was taken for granted that power comes from palaces and that real power rests in armies, swords, and violence. "Everyone knows" that security is built on overwhelming military might and the willingness to use it brutally when necessary.

And then this child is born and the powers start shaking. It's the Wise Men who know that vulnerable love is the only lasting hope for our world, that reconciliation and justice are the only way, that Christ's love is the key to happiness. The Magi are the first ones there to worship a king who comes to bring a peace and security deeper than any army could provide.

This is how T. S. Eliot describes the moment the Magi arrive:

. . . and so we continued

And arrived at evening, not a moment too soon
Finding the place; it was (you may say) satisfactory.

All this was a long time ago, I remember,
And I would do it again, but set down
This set down
This: were we led all that way for
Birth or Death? . . .
We returned to our palaces, these Kingdoms,
But no longer at ease here, in the old dispensation,
With an alien people clutching their gods.
I should be glad of another death.[3]

Strangely, there is no joy in T. S. Eliot's poem. When these Wise Men arrive, the word for their experience is "satisfactory." And then the speaker wonders, "Were we brought all this way for birth or death?"

Maybe that's the question. Are we looking at a birth this morning—the beginning of God's work through this little child? Or is this also about a death—the end of the world as Herod runs it, the end of the world as we want to run it? Is a Love being born in the world that will want to rearrange everything in our world and our lives? Is this new life going to mean both joy and sorrow?

Well, after the Magi have knelt before the child and given their gifts, it's time to leave. But they don't go back to Jerusalem where they know Herod is waiting for them. They head home "by another road."[4]

What about us? We, too, have traveled to Bethlehem this year. We've had our chance to kneel and worship. We've looked down on this vulnerable love born in a world full of Herods.

What will this ask of us? Are we ready to travel home by a different road? The world around us is the same place it was before this Christmas journey— a world of war and anxiety and inequalities. By now we're soon back to our old jobs and familiar relationships. And yet, to follow this child is to live a different way. It is to be called to serve this vulnerable love—creating a space for peace in our world starting at home, then moving to our workplace, our city, and our world.

Do you want a better world in this year? If you do, you need, as a friend of mine once said, "to defect in place." Live where you are, but place your-self in the service of the child and not Herod. Learn to pray, read scripture, find a cause, take a class. Live with the patience and joy of someone who knows Christ's love.

We who have been to Bethlehem this season now face the question, Are we willing to follow this child? If so, we have quite an adventure ahead, traveling by a different way.

Beloved

Mark 1:4–11

Raymond Carver, one of the finest writers of our time, died before he should have. He had lived a hard life, including a struggle with alcoholism, until near the end when he found the love of his life and pulled things together. And then lung cancer hit. Just before he died he wrote a fragment of a poem that goes like this:

> And did you get what
> you wanted from this life, even so?
> I did.
> And what did you want?
> To call myself beloved, to feel myself
> beloved on the earth. [1]

That's not such an unusual wish, I would guess. Isn't that something we would all like to say when our life comes to an end—that we have been beloved, that our lives have been defined by receiving and giving love?

"Beloved" is the word that Jesus heard in our gospel lesson today as he began his ministry. Stepping down into the Jordan River, Mark says the heavens opened, and a voice came from heaven saying, "You are my son, my beloved; with you I am well pleased."

It's also the implicit message in our first lesson today, the opening words of the great poem that begins the Bible. "Let there be light!" God declares. And immediately God sees the light and declares that it is good. And after each of the days of creation God confirms the same thing, until the last when he affirms, "It is very good."

Belovedness—that, in fact, is the core message of the Christian faith, the simplest, and in many ways wildest assertion of all: That for reasons we can't

251

begin to fathom, every one of us is beloved by the Heart of Reality. Many
Christians grew up hearing that the deepest truth of our lives is our original
sin, our rebellion and rejection of God. But both of our lessons say that the
deepest truth of the world is not original sin, but original blessing, a world
that God creates in gladness and calls beloved.

Mark tells the story vividly. The heavens were torn open, the Spirit descended like a dove, and a voice spoke from heaven. It is all vivid language
to describe a reality beyond words—that Jesus experienced himself as delighted in, believed in, held by the one he called Abba, an informal word for
Father, something like "Daddy." And that awareness was so overwhelming
that Jesus spent the rest of his short life trying to get others to discover it for
themselves.

Belovedness. My guess is that most of us spend a good deal of our lives
searching for a sense of belovedness. Therapists tell us that the search for
belovedness is at the bottom of most of our human struggles. We Christians
believe that God took on a human face in Jesus of Nazareth, and the face we
see in him bears the look of compassion and delight. So how painful it is that
religions themselves have so often failed to communicate this bedrock reality. In fact, you hear more and more these days the notion that religion is one
of the great perpetrators of hate in the world, and is actually a major part of
the world's problem, not part of the answer.

Just think of the conflicts—Israelis and Palestinians, Irish Catholics and
Protestants, Hindus and Muslims in India and Pakistan, Muslims and Christians in Serbia and Croatia. Each side has its own vision of God, and often
that god is a projection of the fears, resentments, and angers that one group
has held against another.

Anger and division have invaded our Episcopal Church, too, where different portions of our denomination are declaring that they have no need of
each other and are perfectly willing to pull away and part company.

A Roman Catholic writer named Roland Rolheiser says that both conservative and liberal Christians these days have been holding up a God whose
primary facial expression is a frown. The God of conservatives, he says, is
looking at the world and seeing moral laxity, sexual promiscuity, and lazi-
ness. This God is often angry at us sinful human beings. The God of liberals
is different, Rolheiser says, but is also mostly frowning. This God is worried,
hypersensitive, politically correct, a workaholic. This God is frowning in
disapproval at the world's selfishness and lack of social conscience.[2]

Now, I am sure there is much about our lives as human beings that
saddens and even angers God—our self-absorption and greed, our lack of
compassion for the suffering of the world. But the God we see in Jesus is
nevertheless not a God of bitterness and rejection, but of relentless compassion and eagerness to forgive and start again.

Well, if belovedness is what Christian faith is all about, how did this faith lose the fire of that original vision? Over the centuries Christianity has often become a matter of believing the right set of things. Agreeing to correct doctrines. It began to emphasize that the whole point of faith is not what we do in this life but what will happen in the next—are we going to be saved or not? And so Christian life often became a set of requirements and rules to get our ticket punched for heaven.

But Christianity was and is about a relationship with God in Jesus Christ, about living in Jesus' way, knowing God in our lives, and about our growing deeper, wiser, and more open-hearted in how we live our days.

Jesus' whole ministry is shaped by the experience recorded in our gospel today: "You are my beloved child in whom I am well-pleased." And he seems to have spent the rest of his ministry after that moment living out of a consciousness, a way of seeing the world, shaped by this moment. Because he knows his own belovedness, everyone and everything he saw was also beloved.

And so when Jesus saw the heartbroken, the deathly ill, the hungry and the poor, he saw them all as beloved. As Roland Rolheiser suggests, it is as if God kept whispering in his ear that same blessing all along—"You are my beloved, you are my child, in you I am well-pleased." And because he felt that so intensely himself, he couldn't keep from seeing everyone else the same way.

There's a contemporary Buddhist parable that opens to us what this is really all about. One day the Buddha, badly overweight, sat under a tree, and a handsome young soldier came along, looked at him and said, "You look like a pig!" The Buddha replied, "Well, you look like God!" "Why would you say to that?" asked the surprised young soldier. "Well," said the Buddha, "we see what's inside us. I think about God all day and when I look out that's what I see. You, obviously, must think about other things."[3]

What we see outside us is profoundly shaped by what is inside us. Because Jesus had lived moment by moment with a deep sense of God's love, when he looked at the world around him, everyone was radiant with God's light. The whole world was beloved.

The essence of Jesus' experience was his belovedness, but there is another dimension to this story. His experience was not one cut off from the world around him. John the Baptist was offering a baptism of repentance. The people of Israel were coming there to be cleansed from their sins and failures. Jesus chose to go into the water of their sin with them. And it was there in the rough and tumble of a dusty, raucous crowd that he experienced God's belovedness, not in a remote mountain, not off by a beautiful lake.

The monk and writer Thomas Merton first entered a Catholic monastery in 1948, and for the first decade or more he devoted himself to leaving behind the world and seeking to know God's belovedness for himself. But

some years later he had his own Jordan River experience on a day he had left
the monastery to run some errands in nearby Louisville, Kentucky. This is
how he describes it in his journal:

> In Louisville, at the corner of Fourth and Walnut, in the center of the shopping
> district, I was suddenly overwhelmed with the realization that I loved all those
> people, that they were mine and I theirs, that we could not be alien to one
> another even though we were total strangers. It was like waking from a dream
> of separateness . . . to take your place as a member of the human race. . . . I
> have the immense joy of being . . . a member of a race in which God Himself
> became incarnate. . . . If only everybody could realize this! . . . There is no way
> of telling people that they are all walking around shining like the sun.[4]

It was belovedness Merton experienced, just as Jesus had at the Jordan
River. Merton, like Jesus, was able to see the holiness of every creature, of
the earth itself, all of it shining like the sun.

The importance of the baptism of Jesus is not that it happened once for
him two thousand years ago, but that it is meant to happen for us, too. This is
a revolutionary insight, this belovedness. If we could know our own belovedness moment by moment and could look at the world through those eyes,
wouldn't that change the angry, conflicted world we're in?

If we really knew our belovedness, what would happen to the ways we
live with each other at work and at home? What might happen if we Episcopalians actually saw the belovedness of those with whom we deeply disagree? What would happen if we really saw the belovedness of a mentally ill
street person babbling away to himself, left to drift from street grates to
shelters?

What would happen if we saw the belovedness of a child orphaned by the
AIDS epidemic in southern Africa? What might we do? Just before Christmas I met a couple here after church, both of them doctors, raising their
children in Kenya as they work to ease the misery of God's beloved ones
there.

Knowing our own belovedness can help us slow down the rat race we live
in, honor the goodness of the day in front of us, love those near to us, and
serve those who need us.

Belovedness is the gift buried in us all that the church is here to help us
uncover. Has belovedness ever broken through to the center of your spirit?
There is no more subversive message to all the powers that would shrink and
control human life. Belovedness has healed broken marriages and unlocked
the prisons of addiction. It has brought down dictators, has spread a faith
around the globe, and has carried people in crisis through the darkest times. It
is the key that can change the life of our city, our world, our church, even this
Cathedral.

And it starts with a handful of people who begin knowing this beloved-ness for themselves—who somehow discover it in the support of a friend, or a gesture of help when they thought it impossible, in the silence of prayer or in the words of a book, in serving those who need us or in a piece of bread and a sip of wine that say, "You are my beloved." And when they glimpse it, they will begin to see everyone shining like the sun.

> And did you get what
> you wanted from this life, even so?
> I did.
> And what did you want?
> To call myself beloved, to feel myself
> beloved on the earth.[5]

Lent

The Truth of Ash Wednesday

Matthew 6:1–6, 16–21

Ash Wednesday is to me the most penetrating service in the entire Christian year. This is a day when we tell ourselves hard truths about who we are and about what we are doing with our lives. They're hard truths, but they're also hopeful truths. In a few moments we'll have ashes rubbed in our foreheads, and someone will say to us, "Remember that you are dust and to dust you will return."

The first liberating truth of Ash Wednesday is that we are going to die. Maybe tonight. Maybe tomorrow. Maybe years from now. All in all, our ground time here will be brief. We tear through our lives doing more and more, setting unrealistic expectations for ourselves, deferring time and again the point when we will really start to live now.

You know, as soon as the start-up gets going, I'm going to get some balance back in my life and things will settle down. As soon as I've proven myself in my new job, or as soon as I have saved enough for retirement, then I'll spend time with my family, or friends. Then, I'll get around to being serious about my faith. And, of course, that moment always recedes before us.

Nobel Prize winner Saul Bellow wrote a short novel near the beginning of his career called *Seize the Day*. In it, a man named Tommy Wilhelm is tearing through the streets of New York City trying to hold his life together, pressing as hard as he can, determined to keep it from falling apart. He's an ex-salesman. He's now unemployed and he's down to his last $700, with his wife demanding that he pay that in support payments. Tommy himself is going to seed. He's neurotically overeating. He's unable to even catch his breath for a minute.

And then his day of reckoning comes. In desperation, he's given his last $700 to someone to invest in the stock market for him. But then he learns that the fellow has run off with the money, and there's nothing left. So Tommy goes tearing up Broadway in hot pursuit trying to find him. He's on the verge of collapse, and he finds himself in the middle of a crowd, being shoved into a room which turns out to be a funeral parlor where there's a service going on. And low and behold there Tommy finds himself staring down, looking at a dead man. And he begins to weep. First a little. Then more, then louder and louder until he's sobbing. Saul Bellow describes it this way: "The source of all tears had suddenly sprung open within him. That great knot of ill and grief in his throat welled upward and he gave it utterly and held his face and wept. He cried with all his heart." [1]

Tommy's been pushing and pushing, but no matter how hard he pushes, he can't pull it off. He can't hold it together. His life is crumbling. But then something shifts. Bellow describes it this way: "The flowers and lights fused ecstatically in Wilhelm's blind, wet eyes. The sea-like music overwhelmed his ears. He heard the music and sank down deeper and deeper. Deeper than even his own sorrow, through torn sobs and cries he sank down into the fulfillment of his heart's deepest need." [2]

In other words, he falls into, of all things, a surprising sense of peace. When he takes his hands off his life, when he gives up struggling so hard, he finds that underneath it all is a well of peace and hope. And he gets up and walks out after a few minutes knowing that he's going to survive this crisis and go on.

The ashes that we are going to receive on our foreheads are intended to be the funeral of our pretenses, our fantasies that we can press on and pull it all off all by ourselves. Our notion that if we keep pushing we'll achieve the peace that we're looking for. Death is the great teacher. Death tells us we are not in control. Death tells us to surrender our fantasies of immortality and being almighty. It tells us all we have is today.

In a book called *Bird by Bird* Anne Lamott writes of how she learned to be a writer. In it, she describes being with a close friend, a single mother who was dying of cancer, and she tells of some advice she received from a mutual friend about what she could learn from this friend who's dying. "Watch her carefully right now," the friend said, "because as she is dying, she's teaching you how to live."

And then Lamott goes on to say, "I remind myself of this when I cannot get any work done. To live as if I'm dying, because the truth is that we're all terminal on this bus. To live as if we're dying gives us a chance to experience some real presence. Time is so full for people who are dying in a conscious way. Full in a way life is full for children. They spend big round hours. So instead of staring miserably at the computer screen trying to will my way into writing something that will be a breakthrough, I say to myself, 'Okay, hmm, let's see, dying tomorrow, What should I say today?' Dying tomorrow or whenever we die, now is the time to live."[3]

That's the first hard hopeful truth that Ash Wednesday has for us.

The second is that if we are really going to live, we've got some work to do. After the ashes are rubbed into our foreheads we will pray the Litany of Penitence which is intended to probe our lives and point out where we're missing it, where we're not living the kind of life we're made for. It's intended to show forth to us our self-absorption, the compromises we strike to look after ourselves, the games we play with ourselves and others.

We'll pray, for example, "We confess to you, Lord, all our past unfaithfulness, the hypocrisy and impatience of our lives, our self-indulgent appetites and ways." These words are intended to be like a scalpel that the Great Physician uses to probe us, to open up the places we're caught, where there's infection in us, so that we can be healed.

Our lessons for tonight speak of our caught-ness as our sin, self-absorption, anxiety looking after ourselves first. And the response the church makes is to give us this season of Lent and a set of practices, ways that can help to set us free.

Both the prophet Isaiah and Jesus focus on specific paths to aid our healing—fasting, sharing our treasure, and praying—all of them ways to grow closer to God. Lent calls us to create space for God in the way we live our busy, often driven days. It invites us to take time to pray, to be quiet, to listen to what's actually going on in our overcharged minds and hearts and to ask God to help us to simplify and deepen our inner and outer lives.

They both call us to fast—that ancient, to most of us strange, practice of denying ourselves some creature comfort, or taking on some additional duty. The tradition of fasting called for giving up something, some food, some activity, and experiencing the sense of not being full and satisfied all the time, as a reminder that there is a place in us that only God's love can fill. So whether we give up chocolate, or wine, or something more serious like anger we've been carrying against someone for a long time, or whether we decide we're going to read a book or join a class to deepen our faith, we are creating some intentional way for God's love to enter into the flow of our days.

But Isaiah doesn't stop there. "Is this not this the fast that I choose also to loose the bonds of wickedness, to break every yoke?" he asks. "Is it not to share your bread with the hungry and bring the homeless poor into your house, and when you see the naked to cover him?" To cleanse ourselves before God is also to open ourselves to the brokenness and pain of the world around us.

Fasting for Isaiah means finding a way to connect to what our fellow human beings are facing in New Orleans, or the Philippines, or Darfur or Iraq. It means writing a check or letter, or joining a group, or finding some way to put ourselves alongside the pain of the world around us.

These are hard truths we face tonight—the fact that we're going to die and the fact that we don't have our lives together. We have healing, changing, and, yes, even conversion ahead of us. All that would be hard to face were it not for God's determination not to let us go. Tonight we are here because God was calling the whole world home in the words and actions of Jesus. And when his listeners refused and turned away from him and the leaders hung him on a cross, God still didn't give up. Through that cross God declared that no evil, no brokenness, no turning away will ever stop God from loving every last one of us to the end.

And because of that, the journey of Lent is in fact a way of hope and joy, as it allows us to name the truth of our lives day by day and to grow in the paths that can shape our healing. Come home to who you truly are in this season, God says. Come home to the love that has always been waiting for you. Come home with all your questions and doubts and all the complexities of your life.

That's the last and deepest truth of Ash Wednesday: this God who will stop at nothing until all of us are home.

The Joy of Ash Wednesday

Matthew 6:1–6; 16–21

I believed in Ash Wednesday before I was sure I believed in God.

I was a graduate student studying modern literature in a rigorously secular Department of English, surrounded by friends, few of whom were believers, and nearly all of whom were unhappy. I was doing a good deal of intellectual wrestling with my faith, and I was also trying to sort through where the rest of my life was headed.

One afternoon I decided to stop by the Ash Wednesday service at the university Episcopal Church, not recalling much about the service except that it had something to do with ashes.

And I remember even now the power of the moment when I walked up to the front and a priest rubbed ashes into my forehead and said, "Remember that you are dust, and to dust you shall return." I was overwhelmed by the sheer raw truthfulness of that act. It came crashing home—"I am finite, fragile, a creature who has been given these few short years to live." My agonizing about exactly what I believed seemed less pressing; my anxieties about where my life was going seemed a waste of time. I have been given this time now, I realized, before I return to dust, to be what I have been given to be. I was amazed by the power of a church service to tell me the truth about my life.

It was not a particularly theological experience, at least in any obvious sense. I wasn't particularly aware of God at the time. But it was profoundly spiritual. I found the church telling me what we usually learn only in crisis times of tragedy or loss—that most of the things we obsess over, exhaust ourselves with, get furious about, and lose sleep over are secondary. They are the chess pieces we anxiously move around, forgetting all the while that the whole board has been given to us.

And I found the church telling me that there was nothing in the world more freeing than giving up my fantasies of immortality—the notion that I have to create my eternal worth, I have to prove myself to myself, to make my mark. "Remember that you are dust." You're a creature—made, limited, free.

The ashes rubbed on our foreheads this evening are our own encounters with death and dust. And to have a close scrape with death can enable us to breathe more deeply, to know you are free.

That is why I think of this as a joyful service. There is a real joy in knowing that the world doesn't rest solely on our shoulders.

But there is joy in this Ash Wednesday for other reasons, too. After the ashes are rubbed on our foreheads we will read together Psalm 51, which is a great prayer about our sin. "Wash me through and through from my wickedness," we will pray, "and cleanse me from my sin." And then we will join in the Litany of Penitence that will probe the places in our lives we would rather not think about.

It is sobering to let these words probe our inner lives:

We confess to you, Lord, all our past unfaithfulness: the pride, hypocrisy, and impatience of our lives.
Our self-indulgent appetites and ways . . .
Our anger at our own frustration, and our envy of those more fortunate than ourselves . . .
Our intemperate love of worldly goods and comforts . . .
Our blindness to human need and suffering [1]

Of course, this can seem like so much pseudo-guilt or unnecessary self-criticism. But something much more mysterious is happening here. These prayers of confession are our acknowledgment that we are made for better lives—deeper, truer, wiser—than we are living. The first thing the doctor asks when we arrive for an appointment is, "Where does it hurt?" The first step to health is naming the pain. These confessions allow us to take off the mask of our coping so well, and to name, here in the silence, before the great loving Mystery of God, where it is our lives are caught, or hurting, or hurting others.

Confession assumes that we are made to be healthy. Confession acknowledges that there is One who cares, who longs for us to be more truly alive.

You see, it is our awareness of being loved that enables us to look at our sin. You may remember the movie *Shadowlands*, about the English writer C. S. Lewis. Lewis fell in love for the first time in his life when he was well into middle age, and soon after he realized that the woman he loved was dying of cancer. That experience of profound love led him to look back and see the truth of his life for the first time. Let me read you a poem he wrote looking back at his life. Remember, these are the words of probably the most famous Christian writer in the world in his time.

> All this is flashy rhetoric about loving you.
> I never had a selfless thought since I was born.
> I am mercenary and self-seeking through and through:
> I want God, you, all friends, merely to serve my turn.
> Peace, reassurance, pleasure, are the goals I seek,
> I cannot crawl one inch outside my proper skin:
> I talk of love—a scholar's parrot may talk Greek—
> But, self-imprisoned, always end where I begin.
> Only that now you have taught me (but how late) my lack.
> I see the chasm. And everything you are was making
> My heart into a bridge by which I might get back
> From exile, and grow man. And now the bridge is breaking. [2]

Only when we know deeply that we are loved and are loving are we fully able to see how self-absorbed our lives have been.

We will confess tonight not to grovel in our sin, but to name how caught we are in our own selfishness—so that the One who loves us can help us to become more free. I have found it true repeatedly that the least profound, most superficial people I know are the ones who find talk of sin either depressing or ridiculous. And the wisest, holiest people I know are the ones who see their sinfulness, the tangled web of their own motivations and desires and actions, with penetrating clarity. In fact, many of the great saints of the church seem to combine an intense sense of their own failures with a joyful sense of God's forgiving love for them.

So there is joy in our sobering confession. Because it implies we are made for more, that there is something wrong that explains why we and our world often feel so burdened, and that we can be healed.

There's a third kind of joy we see this evening. We can call it the joy of being ready for anything. This Ash Wednesday service launches us on a Lenten journey that you can think of as something like spring training for baseball. How do baseball players manage to be the best they can be when they step out on the playing field in April, May, and June? They use these weeks in the spring to work on their game, to do the exercises and drills, to get stronger and clearer about their game and what matters. And it's all that practice and discipline in spring training, and all year long, too, that makes it possible for them to play so well and in a way that seems so spontaneous.

The church gives us Lent to take us back to basics, to pick up the practices and disciplines we've let slide but that are essential if we are to be gracious, patient, wise Christians out on the playing fields of our lives.

How were the Amish in Nickel Mines able to forgive the killer of their children? They had been practicing forgiveness all their lives. How are you or I going to be able to be strong and trusting and hopeful when stress, tension, and even loss hit? By making time to be still and quiet, by reading a gospel and soaking ourselves in Jesus' life, by practicing forgiveness and patience.

Jesus lays out the basics in our gospel lesson this evening. Give alms, he says, be generous. And how can we not in a world of so much need and of the privileged lives that all of us here live?

Pray, as Jesus says. Sit in front of a lighted candle for fifteen minutes a day, and, as you do, feel your mind race and then slowly begin to settle down. Join a prayer group here at the Cathedral. Go to our bookshop and pick one of dozens of books on prayer to guide you.

And then, as he says, fast. Do your life differently for these weeks. Give up something—to remind you that you're making room for God. Or take on one of these good practices. Or take up what the prophet Isaiah says fasting should entail: "To loose the bonds of injustice, . . . to let the oppressor go free, to share your bread with the hungry and bring the homeless poor in to your house." Find your ministry. Everyone needs one.

The demanding joy of this evening comes to its completion as we gather at the altar to receive Christ's Body and Blood. The table will be spread for you and me. And we will come, all of us who have been running from our mortality, wounding ourselves and each other, avoiding our connection to the pain of the world around us. We will come, just as we are.

And there we will be fed by a Love who hung on the cross for us, a Love who holds all of our failures in the wounds of his love. A Love who forgives us and sets us free.

This is all strong medicine. Ashes, sin, discipline, bread and wine—all of these point to the journey of Lent ahead. And all are for our joy.

Going for Broke

John 12:1–8

One night each month a small gathering of soldiers takes place here in the Cathedral. Chaplain Randy Haycock from Walter Reed Army Hospital brings over a group of "wounded warriors," young men who have been seriously injured in Iraq or Afghanistan and are spending months here in recovery. He brings these injured and often emotionally devastated young soldiers for a time of silence, reflection, and even healing.

For a couple of hours they wander this mysterious, holy place. At one point, they sit for awhile in War Memorial Chapel and tell stories of their battle buddies who never made it home. The figure of Christ in Memorial Chapel only shows his torso and his head, which often reminds the soldiers of their paraplegic and quadriplegic friends. After awhile they make it to the high altar where all the carvings of the saints help them to imagine someday being reunited with those they love who are gone. They listen to a rock song, "Tears in Heaven," and then they hear the mournful tones of "Taps" to close the night.

As I have listened to Randy talk about these young men, what strikes me is that they put everything on the line for what they believed in, and the cost has been incalculable. What an immense, extravagant sacrifice they have made.

For centuries, this Fifth Sunday in Lent was known as Passion Sunday, the day when Christians were invited to focus on the meaning of the cross in preparation for Holy Week. A week from today is Palm Sunday, and from that day on the terrible events of Jesus' last week will unfold relentlessly. A young man, probably close to those soldiers' ages, is making his way to Jerusalem. There is tension in the air. Jesus was a disturbing figure. He had challenged everyone and every institution. He was in constant danger of being arrested and assassinated and was called an agent of the devil. His own disciples didn't know what to make of him.

But what was most striking about Jesus was his determination to put everything on the line for God. "My meat and drink is to do the will of the one who sent me," he said. "Lose your life to find it," he kept telling his followers. He called his friends to go for broke with him, to surrender themselves to God's call and God's love.

Now, in today's gospel, it's the day before Jesus will ride into Jerusalem on the back of a donkey and unleash the events that will lead to his death. Jesus comes to dinner with some of his closest friends—Mary, Martha, and their brother Lazarus, and some of his disciples. Word has gotten around that he has raised Lazarus from the dead. Jesus is a wanted man. The meal must have been charged with fear and worry.

All of a sudden, Mary gets up, goes over to Jesus, and without warning pours a jar of very expensive perfume on Jesus' feet, so much that the aroma filled the room. This precious oil, worth a year's wages in those times, was used to anoint dead bodies and very rarely for people to sprinkle on themselves for a special occasion. And then Mary, in an act of startling intimacy, loosens her hair to bathe his feet. All this was a shocking act of extravagance. Was there something romantic in what Mary was doing, as some suggest, or was it overwhelming gratitude that her brother was back from death? It's hard to tell. Judas Iscariot, the moneyman for the disciples, was there, and he was outraged. "What a waste! Shouldn't this be used for the poor?" he cried. "No," Jesus says, "leave her alone. She is anointing me for my burial ahead."

Mary's response to Jesus is excessive, over the top, you might even say irrational. But she can't hold back from giving to him in the best way she knows how. Love is like that, and Mary is caught up in a love she won't restrain.

The twentieth-century theologian Paul Tillich was riveted by this story. "What has she done?" he wrote. "She has given an example of a waste which . . . grows out of the abundance of the heart . . . [and] without the abundance of the heart nothing great can happen. . . . The history of mankind," he goes on to say," is the history of men and women who wasted themselves and were not afraid to do so."[1]

Extravagance, going for broke, putting our hearts and souls on the line— that's something that doesn't come naturally to most of us prudent types. We like to be measured, careful people—moderate, risk-averse. Recently, *New York Times* columnist Ross Douthat wrote an op-ed piece about how user-friendly much of our religion is these days.[2] He says that as society has become more materialistic, churches have given up on the really challenging things, the spiritual disciplines that make real demands, and have emphasized the more worldly expressions of faith—the cultural wars issues for the conservatives and the social justice issues for the liberals. They've left behind the quest to know the depths and heights of a vast and mysterious God, the yearning for closeness to God, the willingness to wrestle with the darkness in their own souls.

More Americans than ever, Douthat says, report having religious or mystical experiences—up from 22 percent having them in 1962 to 50 percent today. Seekers now have a wide array of options to choose from. This has been good in many ways, he says, as ancient practices have been reclaimed. But the danger is that these have simply become a set of options to complement our upwardly mobile lives, rather than provocative alternatives to the success-driven lives we're leading.

And Douthat declares what the great spiritual writers have always said, that real spiritual breakthroughs require us to go deep in a particular tradition. Without that, faith just becomes a form of comfortable therapy, with no capacity to deepen or challenge our lives. We have to give ourselves away, to draw closer to God.

There was never anything cautious about St. Paul's faith. In that wonderful passage from his letter to the Philippians we heard today, he is locked in a Roman prison for refusing to stop spreading Christian faith, and even there all he wants to do is give everything he has for Christ.

> I want to know Christ and the power of his resurrection, [he says] and the sharing of his sufferings by becoming like him in his death, if somehow I may attain the resurrection from the dead.

There is so much more to discover, he says:

> [And] this one thing I do: forgetting what lies behind and straining forward to what lies ahead, I press on toward the goal for the prize of the heavenly call of God in Christ Jesus.

You don't hear that kind of spiritual ambition much these days, that willingness to put our lives on the line, to ask God to take us where God wants us to go, to show us what we need to see.

The reality is, C. S. Lewis says, we'll never fully know what Christ can do with us without going for broke:

> The terrible thing, the almost impossible thing, is to hand over your whole self—all your wishes and precautions—to Christ. But it is far easier than what we are all trying to do instead. For what we are trying to do is to remain what we call "ourselves," to keep personal happiness as our great aim in life, and yet at the same time to be "good." We are all trying to let our mind and heart go their own way—centered on money or pleasure or ambition—and hoping, in spite of this, to behave honestly and chastely and humbly.[3]

You see, Lewis says, Jesus wants to do big things with you: "Make no mistake," Lewis hears Jesus saying, "if you let me, I will make you perfect. The moment you put yourself in my hands, that is what you are in for. . . . You can push me away. But understand that I am going to see this job through."

Kay Warren's recent book, *Dangerous Surrender*, tells the story of how she put everything on the line. It is a moving account of someone with her own share of joys and tragedies who, at a critical moment, was willing to be as extravagant as Mary and Paul and go for broke.

She was sitting on her couch one spring day with a cup of tea and picked up one of the weekly newsmagazines and happened to notice a story about AIDS in Africa. She quickly flipped the pages to see what else was in the magazine that day.

> As I began to read, I quickly realized that the graphic pictures that accompa-
> nied the article were horrific–skeletal men and women, children so weak they
> couldn't brush the flies away from their faces. I couldn't look at them. But for
> some strange reason, I was compelled to continue reading. I partially covered
> my eyes with my hands and tried to peak through the cracks in my fingers at
> the words without looking at the faces of dying men, women, and children. [4]

The phrase twelve million children orphaned due to AIDS in Africa jumped off the magazine page and she threw the magazine on the floor in horror. The images haunted her in bed that night and the next day, and she came to see that God had begun an intense conversation with her.

Ultimately, she realized that she had to make a decision, either to retreat to her comfortable life or, as she put it, "Would I surrender to God's call and let my heart engage with a cause I was pretty sure would include buckets of pain and sorrow?" And the moment she said yes, she says, "I became a seriously disturbed woman." [5]

She has faced many struggles since, entailing countless trips to Africa and involving herself in an array of ministries, and along the way she has endured two bouts of cancer. But she sounds a lot like Mary of Bethany—extrava-gant, excessive, going for broke.

I don't believe that all our breakthroughs, all our extravagant surrenders, will be that vivid. Many of the people I talk with are often more muddled, and take more time, and aren't as clear as Kay Warren. They take smaller steps. They tutor younsters here in Washington, they work in soup kitchens, they work at their marriages, they do their work well, they campaign for universal health care, they look after aging parents. They stay with their faith and keep asking God to show them more, to challenge and lead them more.

"Do not suppress in yourselves or others the abundant heart, the waste of self-surrender," Tillich said. "Without the abundance of heart nothing great can happen." [6]

Jesus is heading to Jerusalem now. He's lived God's love flat out, in ways that will soon have him hanging on a cross. He doesn't have to go. It would be the wise thing to turn around and go back to Galilee and lay low for awhile, which is what some of his disciples have been urging him to do.

But instead, after the dinner with his friends and Mary's anointing, he will get up the next day and ride into Jerusalem and to the fate that awaits him.

He's going for broke. What a wasteful, extravagant thing to do, for us.

Palm Sunday

Love So Amazing

Luke 23:1–49

What a strange day this is. There's almost a whiplash effect to it. Our service opens with a grand procession as we sing an exuberant hymn about a young man's triumphal entry into the holy city of Jerusalem, with crowds cheering and waving their palms. It all seems like a grand spectacle.

Some years ago my family and I were at Salisbury Cathedral in England for Palm Sunday, and the congregation on that chilly spring morning gathered outside for the beginning of the service, long palm fronds in hand. In the front were hordes of children surrounding a somewhat nervous donkey appointed to lead the parade into the church. Slowly and somewhat chaotically we followed the donkey in. It wasn't quite Disney, but it was impressive.

But then as we've just seen, after the parade things quickly turn dark, the cries of "Hosanna" fade, and soon we are hearing a crowd calling out "Crucify him!" In a matter of minutes, the story that began in joy has led us to a twisted figure hanging on a cross. It can seem disorienting and confusing. What's going on here? What are we supposed to be thinking and feeling?

The best window into the meaning of the cross I've come across in a long time is a movie that came out last year—*Gran Torino*. Somehow I never imagined viewing Clint Eastwood as a Christ figure, but that is what he becomes in this riveting film. Clint Eastwood, bear in mind, has made dozens of Westerns, war movies, and cop films, and has seemed always to play the same role—the good guy who goes after the bad guy and manages to win the day by being more violent and better at killing than the bad guys. In his movies the good guys win with guns, testosterone, and bravado. You may remember his movie *Dirty Harry* and the line, "Go ahead. Make my day."

275

In *Gran Torino* Eastwood turns all that on its head. Walt Kowalski is a bitter retired autoworker grieving the death of his wife and despising almost everyone he encounters. His only real love is his beautifully cared for 1972 Ford Gran Torino, a sacred relic from what he sees as a better world that's now disappeared. His neighborhood, for example, is more and more filled with Hmong immigrants from Laos, including the family next door. He is constantly stereotyping them and uttering every racist epithet he can come up with. But over time he slowly gets to know his next-door neighbors, and we watch an especially strong bond grow between him and the teenage girl and her younger brother.

There's a dangerous gang in the neighborhood that is recruiting the boy for their group, and when he resists joining they beat and rape his sister to intimidate him. This would be the moment for the classic Clint Eastwood/ Dirty Harry response. Kowalski drives his pickup to the gang's house, stands out front, and demands that they come out. They've seen him wield his pistol and know he has other weapons and are sure he's there for revenge. They have their guns ready to blaze. He reaches inside his jacket and the gang members open fire with a barrage of bullets. He collapses to the ground, lying with his arms spread like a cross. You see his hand now, which is holding not a gun but a cigarette lighter.

The police, already summoned by the neighbors, arrest the gang. They have murdered an unarmed man and will be sent safely away to prison for a long time. Kowalski had concluded that the only way his young Hmong friends were going to have any chance for peace was to get rid of the terrifying gang, and the only way to do that was to give up his own life.

It's a breathtaking ending, and the viewer is left looking at Kowalski's bullet-riddled body lying in the form of Christ. And what a turn at the end of Eastwood's career. Violence has always been his answer—now it's surprising relationships that reach beyond deep-seated prejudice, it's human love, and it's sacrifice. We Christians believe that something like this powerful event is what happened when Christ died on a cross. A man gave up his life to save others. We can't explain exactly how and why Jesus' death changes everything, but at the core of our faith is the conviction that what happened on that hill outside Jerusalem has made all the difference. On that day he became our savior.

Jesus didn't have to go to Jerusalem. For three years he had traveled around his native Galilee, healing, teaching, and announcing everywhere that a new way of living he called the Kingdom of God was breaking into their world. Before long, though, he was infuriating the religious leaders and becoming a threat to Roman authorities. He was claiming that their power to enforce and coerce, to intimidate and torture, was, in fact, empty and that the ultimate power in this world is God's and its prime character is love.

Now he wanted to take the challenge of God's Kingdom to the heart of Israel. He had decided to confront the whole web of influences and powers that wounded and diminished ordinary people in his world—oppressive political power, economic disparities, class systems and hierarchies, rigid religious control. He was soon arrested and put on trial by Pontius Pilate, the Roman governor, and before long orders were issued for his execution. Romans were skilled at torture and crucifixion to discourage troublemakers.

In South Africa the phrase opponents of apartheid used when police were coming after their fellow countryman was, "the System is coming," which meant the whole set of forces of evil that were imprisoning a people, that were now embodied in the police, was coming.[1] I saw "The System" at work up close in the American South of the 1950s and '60s especially—a way of thinking that maintained a brutal social order. And here's the frightening thing: Nice people, good people, participate in the system and adopt its values. Without ever consciously knowing what they are doing, they buy into a world based on power and domination.

Jesus was going to Jerusalem to confront the whole system—the powers, the attitudes, the ways of thinking and relating in both the religious establishment and the Roman Empire that were undermining people's lives. To Herod and Pilate this looked like the beginning of an insurrection. To the religious leaders this unauthorized rabbi was out of control. He had to go.

Some thirty years ago, the exiled leader of the Philippines, Benigno Aquino, had decided to renounce violence and commit himself to nonviolent struggle against the dictator Ferdinand Marcos. He chose to return from his exile to almost certain death. He was choosing to go to his Jerusalem, confronting the powers of the system, but he was shot by the military before he even descended from the plane. His death at the moment changed nothing. Marcos remained as powerful as ever. But his death also changed everything. Two and a half years later Marcos was nonviolently removed from power. For those who had eyes to see, Marcos fell when Aquino fell to the ground.

We Christians believe that when Jesus hung on that cross he was confronting the powers that dominate and diminish human lives. You could say that on Palm Sunday Jesus went public. This day marks the end of any thought of Christianity as an otherworldly religion, concerned only with private experiences and getting to heaven. The business of the church, as someone has said, is not the church, but the world for which Christ died. The great Scottish churchman George MacLeod, the founder of the Iona Community, put it this way:

> I simply argue that the cross be raised again at the center of the marketplace as well as the steeple of the church. Jesus was not crucified in a cathedral between two candles, but on a cross, between two thieves, on the town garbage heap, at a crossroads so cosmopolitan that they had to write his name in

Hebrew and Latin and Greek . . . at the kind of place where cynics talk smut
and thieves curse and soldiers gamble.[2]

Jesus comes today to confront the fear, anger, and bitterness in our lives,
our country, and our world. He comes to turn us to care for the outsiders—
whether they are Hmong or Nigerian or Hispanic. He comes to turn our
hearts to the people of Haiti and to the children in this city torn by fractured
families, violent streets, and failing schools.

And it is on the cross that we believe that Jesus is winning for us a
freedom and new life we could never receive any other way. I vividly remember watching friends of mine years ago as they coped with their four-
year-old child who had a rare neurological disorder. When the little boy
became upset he would fall into uncontrollable fits of flailing and rage that
no amount of soothing could quiet. There was no treatment for it; no way to
medicate it away. All they could do was firmly but gently hold him to try to
keep him from hurting himself, and to stay with him until his destructive
energy was spent. That's what we see God doing on the cross, Christ's arms
spread wide to embrace us, holding us in our fear and violence, refusing to let
go, loving us until our fury is spent and we're ready to pick up the task of
loving again.

Part of my preparation for Holy Week this year entails visiting an exhibi-
tion at the National Gallery of Art called "The Sacred Made Real." It is a
small show of stunningly powerful religious paintings and wooden sculptures
from seventeenth-century Spain. Many are life-size portrayals of the crucified Christ. Some of the sculptures are painted figures that show every
detail of Jesus' decimated body. You see the hairs on Jesus' legs, the worn
sores on his feet, the lash marks from the whips, his gray face surrendering to
rigor mortis, his knees bloodied from falling down carrying the cross.

The figures you see are meditating, pleading, weeping, and the emotional
impact is intense. For some visitors, it's too much and they don't want to
stick around. Others are riveted by the genius of the artists and the power of
the central figure. This crucifixion isn't just a story, you realize. It was real
and terrible and, in a strange way, awe-inspiring.

I was struck by Francisco Zurbaran's *Christ on the Cross*. All you see is
Jesus' exhausted figure almost glowing in white light as he hangs against a
pitch black background. His body seems exhausted. He has absorbed all the
violence, hatred, and fear that can be thrown his way, and he hangs in calm
dignity, as if somehow victorious. It's an unforgettable image of what Christ
has done.

But there's more. A light seems to shine out from his agonized body. The
soft, glowing light seems to suggest the radiant light of God, and you realize
it's God you're looking at on the cross. The Creator of the Universe has gone

through the worst this world can do to set us free. God has taken a barrage of bullets for us.

It makes you think of the words of the great old hymn:

> When I survey the wondrous cross
> where the young prince of glory died,
> my richest gain I count but loss
> and pour contempt on all my pride. . . .
>
> Was the whole realm of nature mine?
> that was an offering far too small;
> love so amazing, so divine,
> demands my soul, my life, my all.[3]

Strange Fruit

Luke 23:1–49

Some time ago, not long after the war in Iraq began, I remember seeing a photograph from Iraq that appeared on the front page of the *New York Times*. It showed an American GI, dusty, looking tired in his helmet and battle garb, cradling a little Iraqi girl six or seven years old, her face crinkled with weeping. The caption explained that both her parents had just been killed in a battle explosion.

The picture captured the dark ironies of these times. A soldier, sent to fight and kill on a mission to liberate an oppressed people, now holding the innocent young victim of a war she couldn't begin to understand. The picture said more than words ever could about the intermingling of good and evil, love and hate, violence and compassion.

I thought of that picture two weeks ago, when the Cathedral hosted a service of prayer for peace and an end to the war in Iraq. Representatives of peace groups from nearly every Christian denomination across the country gathered here to listen, sing, and pray together. No one who was there that night will forget the simple witness of a woman whose son had been killed in Baghdad. In a quiet, heavy voice, she described answering her door, only to see a man in uniform, who asked if she were the mother of that young man. That was the day, she said, that death came to her door. She spoke to us that night of the tragedy of war, of the terrible losses to Americans, and the even more terrible losses to the people of Iraq.

I remember, as I sat in the nave and listened to her, that it seemed as if there were a great cross standing here, in the crossing of this Cathedral, and on it was hanging Jesus himself. As she spoke, it seemed as if her grief was God's grief, and that it was something we all shared. And, for some reason, the words of a haunting song came to mind, an old Billie Holiday jazz song that goes, "There's a strange fruit hanging from the tree." The song was based on a poem about the lynching of African Americans in the South, and I first heard it in a television documentary showing old photographs of those terrible killings.[1]

It struck me that both these moments—the soldier cradling the child and the mother grieving her son, are strange fruit, the fruit of a human race that has not learned to live without destroying one another, that has turned to violence time and again to solve its problems. We are part of a species that will easily seek vengeance, that will steadily ignore the suffering of others, that seems to know little about forgiveness. Think of the massive toll of the wars of the twentieth century, the devastations of Hitler and Stalin, of the Khmer Rouge in Cambodia, and the warring tribes in Rwanda. Here, in Washington, the murder toll continues to climb. Our own country sees far more people die from gun wounds—more than thirty thousand each year—than the rest of the developed nations combined.

Then there is the "violence" of abject poverty. One billion of the world's people aren't sure they will live until tomorrow. Our world has the capacity to end this, but it doesn't.

There is strange fruit hanging from the tree, the fruit of our selfish, fearful, violent ways. We human beings have a lot to answer for.

Palm Sunday is a complex day. Things shift so fast it makes your head spin. In the last few moments we have hailed Jesus as the triumphant king entering Jerusalem, and then we've heard his anguished cry from the cross. We have waved our palms in praise, and then stood in the presence of a dying man crowned with thorns. We honor a king who becomes a convicted criminal. And we realize that we ourselves began this morning crying out "Hosanna," and have ended up in the last few moments crying out the awful words, "Crucify him!"

Then entering the city from the other side, was Pontius Pilate, the Roman governor, leading a column of imperial cavalry and soldiers. It was the standard practice of Roman governors of this area to come to Jerusalem for the major Jewish festivals, in case there was trouble, and this was Passover, the biggest of them all. Pilate came to keep the peace. There had been riots the year before. Sometimes it took crucifying a few troublemakers to settle things down.

Jesus proclaimed the kingdom of God. Pilate proclaimed the power of empire. These two processions were headed for a collision.

Once in Jerusalem, Jesus would soon be turning over the tables in the Temple whose leaders were now collaborating with the Romans. Soon his support would fall away, and by the end of the week his disciples would be hiding, as the religious leaders condemned their leader and the political leaders sentenced him to death. The story would end with Jesus hanging alone in agony. Perfect love, hung on a cross. Strange fruit hanging from that tree.

Do you remember the stir made several years ago by Daniel Goldhagen's book *Hitler's Willing Executioners*?[2] It is a quietly chilling account of how ordinary German people participated in Hitler's "Final Solution." It took a whole society to keep the death trains running, to round up the Jews, to be careful not to question what was going on. He describes the sheer ordinariness of it all. Plain people slowly, subtly became part of overwhelming evil.

As a Southerner living there in the sixties I can tell you plenty about that—about kind, good, churchgoing Southerners who would turn red-faced with hatred at the thought of an African American setting foot in their church. And it makes me wonder, where have I quietly bought in to the world's evil? What is my part in a nation with an ever-widening gap between rich and poor, a nation that is the world's greatest exporter of weapons, cigarettes, and violent movies, a nation that will unravel its social service net before it will raise taxes or challenge other priorities?

And what can we make of this war in Iraq that has clearly drawn us into the world's violence and destruction? We are implicated in this war. Regardless of how we got here, or of the solution that any of us could propose now, we should pause to reaffirm a few Christian essentials. One is that war always represents a failure. We are made to be people of peace, to pray and work for peace. Christ calls us to use our resources not to kill but to heal. But, secondly, as long as there are dictators and terrorists, a strong military will be necessary, and we must be grateful to our soldiers who risk their lives to defend our country and helpless people around the globe. Third, nations with power run special risks, including that of assuming that military might is the best answer to the problems they face. Force is a clumsy, destructive instrument, better at halting evil than building something good. And, fourth, given our capacity for self-deception, and because the line between good and evil runs through every nation and every human heart, we must be slow to fight and quick to listen to the voices who challenge us. Finally, we must not leave Iraq any worse than we find it now, and must commit ourselves to rebuilding a shattered nation.

It is easy in a world like this to hunker down and think only about me and mine, or what our nation needs and wants. Let the rest of the world with all its problems fend for itself. Like the people of Jerusalem, it's easy to say, "Who needs this troublemaker, or these troubling questions, intruding into our lives?" "Crucify him!" We said it a few minutes ago. In some ways, we've been saying it all our lives.

There's strange fruit hanging from the tree. It's the fruit of my fear and yours, my self-protection, my desire to make the world work my way, and yours.

But that's not the whole story. This fruit reveals something more. It shows us a Love that will stop at nothing to go with us through the evil and lostness of our days. Here on this cross, God takes all of our fear, violence, and anger into his own life, accepting the consequences of what we do to each other.

With war so much on our minds, I want to tell you about a scene from a novel called *The Soldier's Return*, in which British writer Melvyn Bragg recounts the story of a soldier named Sam returning home from the battles of the Second World War. There is a scene in which the soldiers were sitting around in a large clearing, hundreds of them resting after hard days of fighting. They were cleaning their equipment, getting everything organized. Everyone sensed they had a day or two to relax. But then Ian, one of the soldiers sitting there casually cleaning a grenade, for some reason no one could understand, pulled the pin out before removing the fuse. So all of a sudden, he had a count of five before it blew up.

Sam saw the look on his friend's face. Both knew that there was nowhere to throw the grenade without killing some of the others. Then, Sam remembered, Ian smiled gently, sweetly, and he tried to say something before he violently twisted himself over and flattened himself onto the grenade, taking the full blast. He lived for two hours after, and all he could say was that he was sorry.[3]

We are here because we believe that Jesus, hanging on the cross, has twisted his body to take the full cost of our human folly and failure. Why did the pin come out of the grenade? We don't know, just as we cannot explain why we human beings continue to kill each other. What we know is that we humans have unleashed immeasurable damage on ourselves and our world, and today Christ throws himself on the explosive force, taking it all into himself.

The evil of our world will never stop unless somehow the evil can be absorbed. That is what Christ does today. Today he takes the explosive evil into himself, smothering the evil in love, forgiving, embracing the human race. He takes on your sin, betrayal, and fear, and mine.

And the hope of the world is that we human beings will slowly learn to let Jesus' way be ours. Ian used his body to give life. And that is our calling as followers of Jesus—to use our bodies to give life, in how we live with each other, how we serve the world's pain around us, how we forgive, how we shape our nation's life. Christ died so that you and I, one by one, can learn to be people of peace and healing ourselves. It is a hard task in a culture that is violent and self-absorbed, but if we let him, Christ will make us people of peace.

There's a strange fruit hanging from that tree. Today we have seen the fruit of the human race's ways, its violence and arrogance and love of power.

But this is stranger fruit yet. He hangs there now loving us, forgiving us, giving his life for us. He offers us his strange fruit of love, joy, peace, patience, and kindness. And in a few moments he will offer us his life, his Body and Blood, and we will feast on his love.

This is the beginning of Holy Week. In the days ahead, let us feast on this strange, life-giving fruit. He did this for us. Now it is our turn—to spread his healing love.

Good Friday

What a Way to Run a Universe

I heard once of a retreat conductor who began a meditation by pointing to a cross, with that twisted figure of pain and torment hanging on it, and saying, "What a way to run a universe!"[1]

You can say that again. Someone once described the universe as a first-class hotel run by a tenth-rate manager. What a spectacular cosmos we inhabit, and what a gorgeous planet we're given to make our home. But so badly run, it seems. If there is a loving Creator behind all this, then what do we make of cancer cells, terrorist bombs, the daily genocide in Darfur, a senseless murder on the streets of Chapel Hill or Washington, D.C.?

As someone once put it, "It's the only question." How can we see God in a world of so much tragedy? Yes, we know almost unspeakable goodness—the love of parent and child, the beauty of mountains and oceans, the sweep of a Beethoven symphony, and the shimmering aliveness of Renoir's "Boating Party" at the Phillips Gallery here in town.

But we also know a world where conflicts and hatreds among cultures, ethnic groups, and nations continue. Holy Week this year coincides with the fifth anniversary of the launching of a devastating, demoralizing war that seems only to have magnified the bitterness and violence in our world. We see the nations of the world hell-bent on a global climate disaster. And, as we in America have been reminded in recent days, we seem unable to move beyond chasms of racial misunderstanding and social injustice that continue to infect our life.

A mother in Mozambique watches the last shallow breaths slip from her child's lips as malaria takes his life. Another mother in Los Angeles picks up the phone for the call she always dreaded—her son shot down on the street walking home.

What a way to run a universe. Does the creator of the universe care—as children starve, or prisoners are tortured, or a whole generation of African American men are lost to the largest prison system in the world? I once heard Michael Mayne, the former Dean of Westminster Abbey, tell of a letter he had received from a distraught father after his eleven-year-old son had died in the night of an asthma attack:

I have sat in many churches and felt the quiet enter me. The colored glass, the candles, and the man hanging on a cross. Yet I ask: Does my Creator weep?

Maybe that's the question. Does God really care?[2]

You can search the philosophies of the world and the pages of the Bible itself and get no adequate explanation. Some of the most profound poetry ever written, the Book of Job, probes for a way to make sense of it all and fails. There is only one answer to the question, "Does my Creator weep?" And it stands in our midst today—a cross that holds the tormented body of Jesus of Nazareth.

We talk a great deal about "almighty God," God the omnipotent, a God who rules and reigns over heaven and earth. The Christian church has over the centuries been steeped in triumphalism, accumulating more and more trappings of power and glory—from the grandeur of cathedrals such as this one to the massive campuses of Protestant megachurches today. Many church leaders over the centuries have happily signed up with a king or emperor or politician or president in order to wield influence. With God we expect order, we expect things to work out properly, for people "like us" to come out just fine.

But here's the shocking news of Good Friday. The suffering man hanging on the cross is the truest picture of God the world has ever seen. Christians came to believe that this man Jesus was so close to the heart of God that when we look at him it's actually God that we see. It isn't that Jesus is just like God. It's much more radical than that. It's that the God who made the universe is Christlike.

Think of Christ's compassion, his endless forgiveness, his welcome of the lost and the broken, his refusal to control and manipulate, his loving his enemies, his kneeling and washing his disciples' feet. That tells us all we will ever know or need to know about the creator of the universe. God is like that.

We begin to see that God is not an emperor or king controlling every event that happens, but instead has called into being a world of chance and accident, of black holes and exploding galaxies, of atomic particles that go in and out of existence, and of a painstaking process of evolution, of construction towers that fall and flood waters that destroy. But that is the only kind of world in which freedom and responsibility and love could emerge. Parents know that. A child can only grow through freedom, risk, responsibility. Yes,

God's power is infinite, but it is the power we see hanging on the cross, the power of suffering love to hold, to forgive, to heal, and to begin again.

Writer Helen Waddell once offered an image for how this could be. A character in one of her novels comes across a fallen tree in the woods that had been sawed in the middle.

> That dark ring there, [one character says], it goes up and down the whole length of the tree. But you only see the ring where the tree is cut across. That is what Christ's life was—the bit of God that we saw. And we think God is like that, because Christ was like that, kind and forgiving sins and healing people. We think God is like that forever, because it happened once, with Christ. [3]

Over the centuries there have been some troubling understandings of the meaning of the cross, such as the one suggesting that on the cross Jesus is paying the penalty to an angry God who requires his son's suffering. That gets it wrong. God is Christlike. God has climbed up on the cross to forgive us before we even ask, to love us when we are unlovable, to say that nothing in all creation can separate us from that love.

"It is finished," Jesus says as he is about to die. The Greek word means "accomplished, fulfilled," not simply that it's over. It's a word an artist and composer might use—the work is now completed. The Gospel of John tells the story of the cross through the lens of Easter. For John, the cross is a story of a victory taking place through Christ's suffering. God is winning a cosmic battle against suffering and evil and injustice and death—by showing forth in this one life of perfect love how endless and unstoppable is God's own love. God goes through everything with us—absorbing evil, enduring the worst, and that means that we can never fall out of the arms of the one who made and loves us.

Can we not see at least a glimmer of God's saving way in the legacy of Martin Luther King Jr.? A man of no power but the power of love and truth, willing to endure all the evil forces that came at him and his movement, and determined to bring healing and hope to a suffering people and tormented nation. He was killed for it, we know. But his life released a healing force still at work.

In a few moments, we will sing one of the most ancient Good Friday hymns. It looks at the cross and sees unfolding an immense battle and a great victory, not of armies and soldiers but of love and forgiveness:

> Sing, my tongue, the glorious battle, of the mighty conflict sing;
> Tell the triumph of the victim, to his cross thy tribute bring.
> Jesus Christ, the world's Redeemer, from that cross now reigns as King. [4]

Christ on the cross reveals God's love and passion for justice that will not stop until every child's death from hunger, every tyranny, every genocide, every act of cruelty large and small, has been halted by the power of forgiveness and new life. God has no strategy but the cross of Christ to win us and convince us—the power of the cross to move you and me to live Christ's love in the struggle of hope and healing here and now.

"What a way to run a universe!" With a Christlike God, who rules by love, there can be no other way. God has entered into it all with us, and won a victory of love. Now it is up to us to live it.

May Christ, the crucified victor, reign in our hearts, and heal our world.

Staring Into the Dark

John 18:1–19:42

What a strange thing we are doing here for these three hours. If people needed any proof of how peculiar Christians are, this would be a good place to begin. We might have thought that Christian faith was a good way to live happier, more productive, more positive lives. But then comes Good Friday, when our only job is to stare at the twisted figure of a dying man on a cross.

Surely if we were interested in doing something "spiritual" there are more pleasant ways to do it. Go for a walk in Dumbarton Oaks or Rock Creek Park. Look at the glories of spring blossoms and flowers; listen to the birds that are back and singing in fine form. Contemplate the beauty of the planet. But no, the church compels us to sit here for a long time, with a lot of silence, contemplating a terrible story and forcing us to talk about matters we would rather not discuss. "It is finished," we just heard that man say, and now he bows his head, gives up his spirit and dies. What are we to make of this?

And strangest of all, we Christians believe that when we look at this man on a cross we are seeing far more than one agonizing death. We are seeing as much of God as we can ever hope to see. It's all there in front of us now—all of our human lostness and everything God is doing to heal us and bring us home. This is not just the tragedy of a death, but the great unveiling of how God is saving our world.

In case you haven't noticed this world does in fact need saving—from tragedy and suffering and from the sin and evil that so damage our lives. I would bet that everyone here could make a list of the wounds and tragedies that make us wonder about this loving God. You can start with cancer cells and terrorist bombs, with a tsunami in Japan and a vicious dictator killing his people in Libya, with a child struggling with autism and a family where parents are losing their jobs and their home.

You can imagine the questions parents in Darfur and Sierra Leone, in Afghanistan and Mozambique would want to ask of a loving God. It is a natural and deeply human impulse to hold God responsible for the terrible things that happen. The Quaker hymn writer Sydney Carter captured that powerful sentiment in a hymn about the crucifixion sung from the perspective of one of the two thieves who are dying beside Jesus:

> It's God they ought to crucify, instead of you and me,
> I said to the carpenter a-hanging on the tree. [1]

Many of our prayers in church speak of an "Almighty God"—God the omnipotent, who rules and reigns over heaven and earth. We like to associate God with grandeur—in cathedrals such as this, in vast evangelical megachurches, in seeing God as being on the side of success and wealth for ourselves, our businesses, our churches, our country. If we Christians believe we meet God in a man on a cross this must be a strange god.

Just after the Second World War a German Lutheran pastor named Guenter Rutenborn wrote a play called *The Sign of Jonas*, in which he tried to come to terms with the horrors his nation had been through. [2] The setting was a trial to find out who was to blame for the terrible Nazi years—the Holocaust, the bombing of civilians, the devastation of Europe.

Some charged that it was all Hitler's fault. Others said it was the arms manufacturers. Others had the nerve to blame the Jews. And some blamed the average German citizens who stood by and did nothing. But none of that seemed quite satisfactory, and finally one man stood and declared that there was only one person to blame, and that was God. Isn't God the one who created this awful world? Didn't he have the power to stop all this? And so they decided to put God on trial for the crime of creation. Prosecutors laid out the full case, and after heated debates found God guilty.

The judge then said that because of the enormity of the crime God had committed, the punishment would have to be the worst conceivable. And so she sentences the Creator God to have to live in this world under the same anguish as everyone else. Then voices in the courtroom chime in. This God will have to be born in a cave in the middle of nowhere, a wanderer with no rights, no home, always hungry and thirsty. He will be surrounded by the sick, the feeble, the corpses of the forgotten. He will suffer the agony of losing a son. He will die humiliated and ridiculed.

Then finally three Archangels are charged to deliver the verdict to God. One will go into a lost, defeated country ruled by a brutal foreign power, and there tell a young woman named Mary that she, a Jew of all things, will bring God into the world. Another will make sure that this man is a failure, that his plans won't be fulfilled, that no one will understand him. And the third says he wants to be there standing by his grave when they bury God so he that he can witness for himself that God is dead.

Then, as the Archangels finish, the lights go out and the stage is utterly dark and quiet. Slowly the realization dawns. God has gone through it all. God has served the sentence.

Staring at the cross today we begin to see that God is not an emperor controlling the world, but instead has called into being a cosmos of chance and accident, of black holes and exploding galaxies, of dazzling sunsets and deadly viruses, of the beauty of human love and the ugliness of human hatred. But that is the only kind of world in which freedom, responsibility, and love could emerge. Parents know that children can only grow if we give them space and ultimately set them free.

Yes, God is all-powerful, we Christians believe, but this power is the power of love. It's the power of vulnerable love to nurture and to sustain, to confront and to challenge, to heal and forgive, and to bring new life out of the worst tragedies. Staring into the dark we see this God of suffering and love.

But there's more that we see sitting and staring at the cross. And that more is the evil and sin that so wound our world. When we look at Christ's endless love, we have to face all our selfishness, all our self-absorbed ways of worrying about our own little happiness. We have to face the wounds we have inflicted on others, the ways we have hurt and used others, the ways we have chased only after our own concerns. We have to face the fact that we are part of a human race that is destroying our planet and part of a world of far too much violence and poverty, and part of a nation with far too many left out of a decent life.

Today we watch Jesus on the cross absorbing the evil being so brutally done to him. And as we hear him say, "Father, forgive them, for they do not know what they are doing," we are gazing directly into the heart of God. For all time and everywhere that is what God is doing—absorbing the evil we do, taking it into the depths of God's life, smothering it with love, and releasing new life to begin again.

"It is finished." "It is accomplished." In those words there is a sense of victory, even in this dark hour. Jesus, the victim of the world's evil, has remained steadfast to the end, loving God, loving us, all the way into death. In the end, his life wasn't taken from him. He gave it away, laying it down for his friends and for the whole world.

Our staring is nearly over now. Now we will sing of this victor hanging from a cross, and we will come to be fed by the bread and wine of his love. Christ on the cross has revealed God's love, a love that will never stop. God has no strategy but the cross of Christ to win us and convince us—the power of the cross to move you and me to live Christ's love in the struggle of hope and healing here and now.

Today we see it all—all the darkness of our world, and all that God has done to turn our hearts and heal our world. It is finished. It is accomplished. Thanks be to God.

Easter

Death Be Not Proud

John 20:1–18

This is the high point of the Christian year, the one day every year when just about everything seems over the top—trumpets, tympani, and flowers everywhere, long lines for services. I have to admit we clergy have been known to say to ourselves, "Why can't it be like this every Sunday?"

I remember once hearing of a man who complained to the priest one Easter morning, "You know, I'm getting tired of this. Every time I come to church here you sing the same hymn, 'Jesus Christ Is Risen Today.'" Well, I want you to know that we're actually here doing this fifty-two Sundays a year. And I hope you'll come back again. I promise you, the crowds won't be nearly so bad!

But if you are going to choose one day a year to come to church, this is the one. This is the day when we explore the central claim at the heart of Christian faith—that God raised Jesus of Nazareth from the dead. Because of that nothing in this world—not evil, not cruelty, not illness, not loss, not even death—can ever be the last word for us.

Do you find that a lot to believe? I think all Christians struggle with it along the way. For one thing, the world often looks more like Good Friday than Easter Day. I know it does for the people of Red Lake, Minnesota, after a teenager shot to death ten of their friends and loved ones. I know it does in Iraq, in Israel and Palestine, among the tsunami victims in southern Asia. Every front page brings ample reason to grieve. And on a much more mundane level, pain and loss continue to make their way through our lives. Day by day our world often looks very much like Good Friday.

But for many, Easter is hard to believe for more fundamental reasons, too. It goes directly against our materialistic mind-set. It challenges head-on our

299

deepest belief that birth and death are the only certainties, that the only things we can know and trust are what physics, chemistry, biology, Madison Avenue, and television tell us, that "nothing but" is the real truth of our lives. Love is nothing but a feeling, or a survival mechanism. Life is nothing but a few years to enjoy before we die.

From the beginning Easter has been confrontational. There is nothing subtle, for example, about the Easter story we just heard. It's a string of startled discoveries. First, Mary Magdalene, coming to visit the tomb of her Lord, is stunned to see that the stone at the entrance has been rolled away. So she runs to tell two of the disciples, and then they run to the tomb, and this time they see that it is empty, that Jesus' body is no longer there. And then we see Mary again outside, talking to a man she thinks is a gardener, and in a moment of stunning recognition she realizes that she is seeing her risen Lord, back from the dead.

Now, what do you make of that? There are no efforts to win you over, no gentle bridges to understanding. Those followers of Jesus came to his tomb with their minds sealed tight in grief. The world had done its same old brutal business—killing off their Lord, reminding them, as if they needed it, that death and defeat are where everything is headed.

For all the differences in their reports of the first Easter morning, the four gospel accounts agree on this—that Jesus' followers visiting his tomb heard news of earthshaking proportions: "Do not be afraid. He is not here; he is risen as he said; he has gone before you to Galilee. Go back to your homes and he will meet you there."

That is the shocking Easter message. We shouldn't assume somehow that it was more believable then than it is now, as if we are so much more sophisticated. Those disciples had invested their whole lives in their Lord. They knew how dead he was.

There is no way to my mind to conceive that these frightened, defeated disciples would make up a story of seeing their master again and galvanize themselves into a force capable of spreading their faith across the Mediterranean world. No, they saw something, encountered Someone, and that simply broke open the closed worldview in which they were living.

Easter says something immense—that the Source of all life, the Power behind the universe, is capable not just of creation, but of new creation. Those early disciples experienced something vast and nearly incomprehensible—that the God who brought the universe out of nothing into existence brought Jesus out of the nothingness of death into eternal life. Of course, it's almost impossible to imagine. And so we naturally keep the tombs of our minds firmly shut, the stone rolled securely in place.

But what if we let this Easter news begin to roll the stone away? What if we began to imagine a world where death is not the end, where God always has more life to give every last one of us? What if we saw that this world of loss and injustice and violence is not the last, dreadful word?

Of course, it's hard to imagine. Remember it wasn't easy for the first disciples either. Their first experience of the risen Lord was of an absence, not a presence. "He is not here," they were told. Now go back home and look for him. Trusting that God brings life out of death can take years, even a lifetime.

In fact, I don't know anyone who started out being a Christian by accepting the notion of resurrection first. It's too outrageous, too much an assault on our shrunken worldviews. For most of us, trusting Easter comes slowly, as we spend time learning about Christ, following him, coming to meals like this, slowly getting a sense of a dimension of love and holiness embracing all of life, including death.

Recently, I had a chance to watch a movie made from the Broadway play called *Wit*.[1] It tells the story of Vivian Bearing, a brilliant, crusty, demanding English professor, whose specialty is the poetry of John Donne, the seventeenth-century poet and Anglican priest. Vivian is dying of cancer, and she seems to be going through it alone, having kept virtually everyone in her life at a safe distance. We watch her deal with doctors, nurses, hospital administrators, and see her go through grueling chemotherapy. She is miserably sick from it, losing her hair and a lot of weight, and what's more, the therapy doesn't work. It's a dark tomb of a world she's in, and she uses her ferocious mind and wit to cope.

Strangely enough, though, the poem she keeps thinking and talking about is a John Donne poem about death that goes like this:

Death be not proud, though some have called thee Mighty and dreadful, for thou art not soe, For those, whom thou think'st, thou dost overthrow Die not, poore death, nor yet canst thou kill me . . .[2]

It's a poem mocking death. It belongs to the Easter world that Vivian seems to have missed. And yet it comes back, awash in the memories of her revered mentor, a distinguished professor who managed to etch it permanently in her mind. It ends in more proud defiance:

One short sleep past, we wake eternally, And death shall be no more; Death, thou shalt die.[3]

In so many ways, the great driving force in our lives is fear. Nations live in fear, our professional lives are haunted by fears of losing our jobs or not getting promoted. Our politics are often driven by fear of the polls. We fear illness and getting older. We fear violence and terror.

And to all these fears the risen Lord this morning says, "Do not be afraid." He doesn't say it, though, because hard things won't happen to you. He says it because God has raised him from the dead, and that means no loss, no illness, no terrible mistake, can ever be the end for you. Death, be not proud.

On Easter Day a few years ago, an English newspaper published an interview with Archbishop Desmond Tutu, one of the great Christians of our time, and in it the interviewer asked him his thoughts on Easter. Tutu smiled.

> You have traveled to the Dark Continent [of Africa] for an Easter message for your readers. God has a great sense of humor. Who in their right mind would have imagined South Africa to be an example of anything but awfulness? We were destined for perdition and were plucked out of total annihilation. God intends that others might look at us and take courage. At the end of their conflicts, the warring groups around the world—in the Balkans and the Middle East, in Angola and the Congo—will sit down and work out how they will be able to live together amicably. They will, I know it. There will be peace on Earth. The death and resurrection of Jesus Christ puts the issue beyond doubt: ultimately goodness and laughter and peace and compassion and gentleness and forgiveness will have the last word. [4]

That is a mind and spirit living in a bigger, brighter world than the one we usually inhabit. It is a spirit filled with hope that God isn't finished with us yet. And it is that big-hearted, Easter hope that has made it possible for Desmond Tutu never to give up on his work for peace.

Any way you look at it, this Easter vision is an immense mystery. It says that the risen Lord is alive and here, speaking through the magnificent music and the beauty of this Cathedral, speaking through my words this morning, and through the bread and wine we will share. The risen Lord is at work in these troubling times, calling a divided world, a divided nation, a divided city, and yes, even a divided church, to new possibilities of reconciliation and working together. And this Lord is at work in you and me, opening our own tombs, calling us forward.

The play *Wit* takes a surprising turn near the end. Vivian's mentor, now an old woman, comes to visit her, as Vivian seems near death. This sophisticated scholar brings with her as a gift not another great literary work but, of all things, a children's book, a book about a love that will not let us go. And when she sees her gaunt former student near death, she lies down on her bed beside her, and reads this:

> Once there was a little bunny, who wanted to run away.
> So he said to his mother, "I am running away."
> "If you run away," said his mother, "I will run after you. For you are my little bunny."
> "If you run after me," said the little bunny, "I will become a fish in a trout stream and I will swim away from you."
> "If you become a fish in a trout stream," said his mother, "I will become a fisherman and I will fish for you."

"Look at that," Vivian says. "A little allegory of the soul. No matter where it hides, God will find it."

"I will become a bird and fly away from you," said the bunny.

"If you become a bird and fly away from me," said his mother, "I will be a tree that you come home to."[5]

No matter where life takes us, God will find us.

"I have seen the Lord," Mary Magdalene said. "He is not here, he is risen," the disciples heard.

"And death shall be no more; Death, thou shalt die."

What a vast world this day opens to us, because Christ the Lord is risen.

Nevertheless

John 20:1–18

There's nothing quite like an Easter morning. The air is filled with the sounds of trumpets and tympani and with the aroma of Easter lilies. Flowers are everywhere.

In this service this morning we're trying to capture some of what e. e. cummings must have felt when he wrote his ecstatic poem that begins,

i thank you God for most this amazing day: for the leaping greenly spirits of trees and a blue true dream of sky; and for everything which is natural which is infinite which is yes [1]

Everything this morning is Yes. Yes to the tulips and azaleas bursting in crimson and fuchsia, Yes to the love and joy that are woven into our lives, Yes to God.

But for some of us it is just this exuberant Yes here on Easter that rings a little hollow. Many of us consider ourselves Christians, but a lot of us have cut some deals with the faith in order to be here—I can believe this and this, but not that.

And when it comes to the resurrection I know some just aren't so sure. It isn't that they write it off, it's just that they don't really know what to make of it. Not long ago I talked to a newspaper reporter doing an article on what people actually believe about Easter, and he said his sense is that for many, including many Christians, Easter seems more like a fairy tale or wishful thinking. A wise theologian once said to me that he believed that many people in church would actually be more comfortable with Holy Saturday than Easter Sunday. They can believe in a good man now lying in a tomb, but they can't really trust that a dead man is now alive and making a difference in the world around them.

After all, life doesn't really look like an exuberant Yes a lot of the time. Love often withers, wrinkles deepen, we're saying good-bye all our years. People we care for get sick and die. Children struggle, marriages come apart. We are locked inside material lives that will all eventually run down.

And we only have to gaze at the morning papers to wonder if Yes is the right word for us—at the heartbreaking events in Iraq, or the tens of thousands of refugees fleeing for their lives in Sudan, or the victims of a hurricane on the Gulf Coast or an earthquake in Kashmir still trying to put their lives together. In many places, today seems more like Good Friday than Easter. If Easter is real, we need to be able to proclaim its Yes, even in the midst of a fractured world.

With all the trumpets of Easter morning, it's easy to forget that the first Easter didn't begin with a resounding Yes. The four gospels, Matthew, Mark, Luke, and John, give different accounts of what happened, but they all capture a sense of darkness, confusion, and uncertainty on Easter morning, and even when it dawns on the disciples that their Lord may be alive again, we don't hear great cheers of joy, but rather fear and disorientation. Everything is happening in half-light, and the disciples have no better mental categories to put resurrection into than we do with our scientific, materialistic mind-set.

In the version we just heard from John's gospel, Jesus' close friend Mary Magdalene is making her way to the tomb to say good-bye to her leader one more time. He had been crucified on Friday, and now it was before dawn on Sunday morning as she came for her final farewells. But then to her shock she discovered that the stone covering the opening had been rolled away. And she just ran back to tell the others that someone had stolen their Lord's body. The notion of resurrection never occurred to her. Then Peter and John came running next. They stepped into the tomb and looked, but saw no body. Still, something dawned on John. "He saw and believed," the gospel says.

Meanwhile Mary had come back to the empty tomb, and things started shifting fast. Two men, angels John calls them, ask her why she's weeping, and then another man shows up, and she looks right at him and concludes that he's the gardener and asks him what he's done with the body. And then the man says her name, "Mary," and with that she knows. She recognizes the Risen Lord. "Rabbouni!" she cries. "Teacher!" It's a riveting moment of recognition and reunion, filled with dawning awareness, and incomprehension, and stunned joy.

What exactly the disciples saw we don't know, but we do know that people who had seen the worst that life could bring were utterly convinced that God was doing something new, that death was no longer the finale to their story, that new, unimaginable life still lay before them—for Jesus himself and for them too. They were as confused by these encounters at first as many of us still are. But slowly they began to trust that the One who had sent Jesus to show them what life can be had raised him. And that changed them—from frightened, timid followers into bold, risk-taking witnesses to what life can be.

We should be clear as we hear this story what this resurrection event is not. Some would say that it simply means that the teachings of Jesus are immortal, like the plays of Shakespeare, or that the spirit of Jesus is undying and that he lives among us the way Socrates does or Gandhi or Martin Luther King Jr. Some say it means the cause of Jesus goes on in spite of his death. Some enjoy it as the rebirth of spring, with the return of robins and daffodils and with all those fertility symbols such as eggs and quick-breeding rabbits.

Some would say that all this Easter talk is the language of poetry and shouldn't be taken literally. That's true of important parts of the Bible, but here we're dealing with the lynchpin of the whole story—God's power over death itself. "If Christ be not raised from the dead," St. Paul wrote a few years later, "then we are of all people most to be pitied." Easter demands that we reframe how we see the world. It tells us that the prison house of our material lives has been blown open, and that God intends to do for the whole world what was done for Jesus that first Easter morning.

Of course, this resurrection is hard to believe. It belongs to a world beyond the materialistic space-time box of Good Friday. But as theologian Walter Wink has put it, "We are just suckers if we let the reigning intellectual fashion decree that resurrection is unbelievable. What is believable changes from generation to generation."[2]

Take a time machine back a hundred years and tell those good people that passengers in our day now travel around the world in long narrow tubes with wings called airplanes, defying the law of gravity. Tell them about this little gadget people hold in their hands that connects them instantaneously to people around the world and to unlimited stores of information. See if they believe you. Tell them about black holes in the universe that have the capacity to suck whole galaxies inside them. The universe is a stranger place than we modern types have yet conceived.

Still, a bright, exuberant Yes is maybe too grand an affirmation for a world as ambiguous as ours. It runs the danger of not facing up to the full reality around us. But the great Swiss theologian Karl Barth gave us another way. He said that the Good News of God in Christ has written on every page the word, "Nevertheless." In a world of human freedom, terrible things can happen. But they are never the last word. There is always God's "Nevertheless."[3]

The people of Israel were imprisoned in bondage to the evil Pharaoh. *Nevertheless*, God brought them out of slavery into freedom. Later Israel was captured and its leaders taken into exile. *Nevertheless*, God called them again and led them home. A lame man had lain thirty years by the pool of Siloam. *Nevertheless*, Jesus healed him and gave him new life. Jesus came calling people to trust God and love each other with a welcoming, all-embracing love. And he was executed for threatening the safe systems of political and religious authorities. *Nevertheless*, God brought new life to him. And Peter and John and Mary Magdalene and all the others were plunged into despair by their leaders' death. *Nevertheless*, the Risen Christ appeared to them. And they went on to spread a new faith across the globe and down the centuries.

And haven't we experienced something of God's Nevertheless? A priest I know has written of the deep depression he endured some years ago. It was so deep that he even contemplated suicide. He was lost and saw no way out. But he says that a miraculous combination of things—intensive psychotherapy, the gift of a hope-filled community of faith, and loving, patient family and friends—ultimately rolled the stone away from his despair and gave him a new life. Nevertheless, life could begin again. Resurrection.

One of my closest friends from high school fought alcoholism and drug problems for decades. I never thought he would break free of the tomb he was in. But after a lot of tries, and a lot of patience and support, he finally did. He gives the credit to what he calls his Higher Power. We Easter people call that the Risen Christ. Nevertheless.

My guess is that you've known God's Nevertheless. When you were sinking under the weight of worry, or grief, or the struggles of a child; when your own health, or that of someone you loved, was under assault; when you saw that you were losing what you thought you had to have to live, somehow life came again. God wrote Nevertheless across that page of your life, and you began again, limping maybe, but strong and alive.

History is filled with dead ends, sealed tombs, that miraculously were broken open. Almost no one imagined that the grip Communism had on Eastern Europe would loosen in our lifetimes. But in 1989, thanks to the Christian Polish leaders Lech Walesa and Pope John Paul II, it happened. One journalist writing about what happened in that year put it succinctly: "Couldn't happen. Did." God's Nevertheless was written across their lives.

You see, if Christ is raised from the dead then all bets are off. Easter declares that the God who created heaven and earth is capable of a new creation, taking the broken pieces and closed tombs of our world and making of them something new.

And if Christ is raised from the dead, if Nevertheless is God's answer to all that would defeat and diminish our days, then you and I are called to watch for where the Risen Christ is at work and to join in. There are families to be strengthened, relationships to be healed, children to be tutored; there are AIDS and malaria, killing God's children by the millions each year, to be fought; there is this city, black and white, rich and poor, to be brought together; there is a fair and hopeful response to the needs of the immigrants in our country to be found.

The fine minister of the last generation, William Sloane Coffin, for many years chaplain at Yale and then at Riverside Church in New York, died this week. He summed up the difference Easter should make this way: "Christ is risen to convert us, not from life to something more than life, but from something less than life to the possibility of full life itself." "Christ's resurrection," he says, "[promises] to put love in our hearts, decent thoughts in our heads, and a little more iron in our spines."[4]

This Easter morning says that Christ is among us, my friends. He's here feeding us with the bread and wine of his risen life. He will be in our homes this afternoon and our work tomorrow opening doors, inviting us to risk and to love.

Watch, my friends, for the stirring of our Risen Christ Lord, here, and everywhere, writing Nevertheless over every dead end in our lives and world. You see, he is not dead; he is risen. Alleluia.

Ascension

Christ Has Gone Up

Acts 1:6–14; John 17:1–11

If you were listening to our lessons today, and especially the first one from the Book of Acts, you heard some pretty strange things. The Risen Lord gives his followers a last few words of encouragement, and then Acts says, "He was lifted up, and a cloud took him out of their sight." It's the moment the church calls the Ascension, which we affirm every week when we say in the Nicene Creed, "He ascended into heaven and is seated at the right hand of the Father." I remember once years ago explaining the story to a group of teenagers, and hearing one youngster blurt out, "Sounds like you're talking about Jesus the Rocket Man!"

There have been many paintings of the Ascension down through the years. They usually picture Jesus rising before the eyes of his dumbfounded followers, or at least, in one case, simply portraying the clouds in the sky with only the soles of Jesus' feet in view.

Preaching about the Ascension has always been a complicated assignment. Are we supposed to think that Jesus rose like a divine rocket into the sky? Is the Ascension one more proof of how primitive Christianity is, or could it be that the problem is really our narrow worldview, and that there is something here essential for us to attend to?

You may have heard of the story published by an English headmaster named Edwin Abbott in 1884 called *Flatland: A Romance of Many Dimensions*. The main character, whose name is A^2, lives in a place called Flatland, where everything has just two dimensions, height and width, but no depth. If people turned sideways, they would disappear. They lived in flat houses, eating flat food, raising flat children, and having only flat thoughts.

But one day A²'s son, named Pentagon, has a dream that no one had ever dreamed before—that there was another dimension of reality called depth. In his dream, trees and buildings, other children and adults all looked deeper, more alive, more complex, somehow more real. Everything seemed different.

Needless to say, the vision disturbed his parents and their friends, and eventually they put him in a home for the mentally ill. But some of them, and especially A², continued to be haunted by what his son saw. At one point he cried, "Either this is madness or it is hell." But a voice responded, "It is neither; it is knowledge; it is three Dimensions; open your eye once again and try to look steadily." And eventually A² began to see this new reality.[1]

Well, one thing for sure is that the story of the Ascension is never going to make any sense if our worldview is as flat as that one. Of course, we see everyday things in three dimensions, but most of us think in a flat world way, a world where the only things that really count are the things we can measure and see and touch—money, houses, career achievements, SAT scores, batting averages, sales figures, voting results, poll numbers, Dow Jones numbers. And we are often urged to think of Jesus in flat world ways—as a noble teacher, or as a fighter for the poor, as a moralist who wants us to behave ourselves, or as a budding capitalist urging us to pray for success. We make him understandable and manageable by removing all the depth.

And yet we come here week by week to hear stories of a deeper world. And today we hear the story of how Christ made his way home directly into the heart of reality itself. The Ascension is concerned less with historical fact than with ultimate truth. For nearly two thousand years, the church never worried about what really happened, only whether it told us things we needed to know about God and our lives.

The Ascension story tells us that after forty days of resurrection appearances, Jesus had gone away, not to abandon his followers, but to surrender the limitation of one life in order to become part of the healing of the entire cosmos. And in going away he did two things.

First, he took our human life into the heart of God. It's an enormous assertion—that one human being representing all of us has entered into God's own life. Those paintings of the Ascension always portray Christ rising into heaven still bearing the wounds of the cross, the marks of his own life in the world. Christ takes his whole human life into God, and our whole life, too, including the suffering and confusion and wounds of our days.

And because of that we have something to say to people who know what it means to be wounded and broken. Several years ago a man stopped me after church one Sunday and asked me a tough question: "What would you do if you were God?" he said. That's enough to give one pause. Playing for time, I bounced the question back. "What would you do?" Then, as if out of the blue the answer came, "I would end all this—all this world with the mess and pain of it."

I never came to understand what lay behind that man's statement. But I imagine it was a feeling not alien to most of us—of being overwhelmed by what's happening around us, by the amount of change and uncertainty, by the talk of terrorists and nuclear arms, by a sense of a world and a society gone badly awry.

I remember in the aftermath of the Oklahoma City bombing years ago a member of one of the militias was asked why he was stockpiling weapons. "Things are out of control," he said. "The only answer is to be armed and ready for anything." We heard a lot of talk like that after 9/11.

But Ascension Day means that we have something to say to people haunted by worry and uncertainty. And our response is, Christ has gone up into God taking the burden of our life with him. That means that finally Christ's love will reign over all that exists, and our own struggles and pain are now being held in the heart of God.

And so to the victims of 9/11 and the war in Iraq and the terrible bombings across the Middle East, we can say, "Christ has gone up, taking your struggle into God's heart."

To people who can't find homes or jobs, to people with terminal illness, we can say, "Christ has gone up, taking your pain into God's heart."

To the hungry, the sick, the desperate we can say, "Christ's love rules in heaven, and so we who follow him, will not rest until there is food and health and hope for everyone."

And to the lonely, the lost, the confused, to those locked in thin, two-dimensional lives, we can say, "Christ has opened the way into a deeper dimension, where you are safe and loved forever." The healing of the world has already begun in heaven and will gather us up in the end.

But there's a second part to this story. In the account in the Book of Acts, the disciples aren't left with their heads craned upward, staring into the sky. Two mysterious figures appear and say to them, "Men of Galilee, why do you stand looking upward into heaven?" And with that prodding the disciples turn to go back to their lives in Jerusalem, where they have been promised more power is coming to them through the Holy Spirit. Jesus stops being one teacher, leader, and friend, and will become the life and energy within them that will change the course of history.

In Jesus' farewell words in the gospel reading for today he speaks of how the disciples and he have become one. "As you, Father, are in me and I am in you, may they also be in us, so that the world may believe that you have sent me." Jesus now becomes the life inside his followers. "I in them," he says, "and you in me," as if there is no distance between them at all.

Ernest Hemingway's novel *For Whom the Bell Tolls* describes a human moment much like this. In it, Robert Jordan, the hero, has been fatally wounded in a war, and the girl he loves, Maria, wants to stay behind to die

with him. But he tells her she must go on ahead and leave him behind, and
this is how he tells her:

> "Now you will go for us both," he said . . . "Now you are going well and
> fast and far and we both go in thee . . . Not me, but us both. The me in thee.
> Now you go for us both, truly . . ."
> But Maria starts to turn around. "Don't look around," Robert Jordan said.
> "Go!"
> "Roberto!" Maria turned and shouted. "Let me stay! Let me stay!"
> "I am with thee," Robert Jordan shouted. "I am with thee now. We are
> both there. Go!"[2]

Jesus is sending his disciples. "Go!" he says to them. "I am going with
you. Now it's your turn, and you must go for both of us. I will be in you and
you in me."

Even though Jesus has gone away, he is now living inside us, leading us,
teaching us, stretching us, opening our eyes to see, sending us out to do his
work.

And so Jesus is saying to us, Go! Be my hands and heart and feet. Go,
with the me in thee. Go to your work tomorrow and I will be with you as you
serve me there. Go into the public realm and stand with me for a just and fair
life for everyone, for housing in a city where the poor are having to move
out, for schools that can give their students hope of a good life.

For those who have had enough of life in Flatland, Jesus says, come with
me. Yes, I have gone to the heart of God, and have taken you with me. But
here and now I am with you too. The me in thee. Trust in me, and we will do
holy, life-giving, surprising things.

"He ascended into heaven." What strange, consoling, challenging words
those are. Christ has gone up. And Christ has come in.

Pentecost

The Spirit of Life

Acts 2:1–21

One of the things people love about a cathedral is the way it embodies permanence, order, and stability. Drive up toward this Cathedral and it looks as if it has been here forever. Walk through the West End doors and you're overwhelmed by the sheer, glorious order of one arch after another, arrayed perfectly, reminding you of the harmony of God's creation.

And when you worship here, especially if you're an Episcopalian, you seem to like the stately, dignified order of things. Everything in its rightful place. Everything tasteful. Nothing too sentimental, emotional, or extravagant.

There is an inscription on the eighteenth-century tomb of the Countess of Huntington just outside Winchester, England, that captures what has often been the Anglican approach to worship. It says, "She was a just, godly, righteous and sober lady, a firm believer in the Gospel of our Lord and Savior Jesus Christ, and devoid of the taint of enthusiasm."[1] Order is in the Episcopal DNA.

You may have heard the story of a Sunday morning in a proper New England downtown church, when a woman who clearly had come from a different part of town slipped into one of the pews and stayed restrained and quiet, until the sermon. But then as the preacher launched into his sermon she called out, "Amen! Yes, Lord, preach it!" And then a few minutes later she yelled, "Praise Jesus! Praise Jesus!" Well, by this point an usher had made his way over to her pew and leaned down and said to her, "Madam, is there something wrong?" "No" she said, "I've just got the Spirit!" To which the usher sternly replied, "Well, Madam, you certainly didn't get it here!"

I couldn't help but think about that lady's rowdiness as I heard the story of the first Pentecost. Do you remember the scene? A cluster of disciples were gathered in an upper room some fifty days after their Lord's death and resurrection, when suddenly they heard a sound like a mighty wind, and they saw tongues of fire, and all of them were filled with the Holy Spirit and began to speak in tongues. They were shaken by an experience that had touched every part of them, body and soul. And when they went out into the streets speaking in many different languages, people thought they were drunk.

Now, does that experience sound like Sunday morning at Washington National Cathedral or your home church? You know, Pentecostal churches, with their energy and excitement and hands-in-the-air abandon are the fastest growing churches in the U.S. and across the globe. When was the last time you felt shaken in church from the top of your head to your toes? When was the last time you knew for sure that you were in touch with a Power from on high that had come upon you?

I'll bet that *has* happened for a lot of you, though maybe not quite that way. My guess is that something here or at some other church has touched you—a glimpse, a stirring, an insight—and that is what brings you back week after week. But it is easy for the word "God," especially in traditional churches, to be only an idea word for us, a set of principles, of oughts and obligations. When a religion starts getting old and creaky, it becomes a set of dry, formal words people recite, and a set of rules and obligations to obey. But in every vital religion the word God is a power word. To talk about God is to talk about a Power at the heart of life that moves and shakes and draws and acts and leads.

The word the Scriptures use for talking about a God of power is Spirit. The Spirit of God is the power of God at work in the world. At the beginning of creation, Genesis says, the Spirit of God brooded over the waters of chaos and stirred it into life. When the people of Israel were slaves in Egypt, it was the Spirit of God who led them through the desert to the Promised Land. When Israel and its leaders lost their way and turned away from God, it was the prophets, filled with the Spirit of God, who called Israel back to lives of justice and faithfulness to God.

And Jesus was himself the completely Spirit-filled person. "The Spirit of the Lord is upon me," he said, quoting Isaiah, "because he has called me to preach good news to the poor, release to the captives, recovery of sight to the blind." He became the channel of the Spirit for all the world.

We call the Feast of Pentecost the birthday of the church because in this event the Spirit filled one group of people with an overwhelming sense of power and new life in Christ. His power became their power. Now *they* were to be channels of the Spirit of God in the world, vanguards of the new world God is building.

But what is this Holy Spirit? I once asked a youth group to draw their own pictures of the Spirit, and many of their sketches looked vaguely like the cartoon character Casper the friendly ghost or a big, amorphous blob.

But the Holy Spirit is a reality we have been experiencing all our lives. It is as real as the air we breathe. Like the air, we can't see it, but like the air our life depends on it. You aren't aware of the air until it starts moving, and when it really starts blowing, it's hard to miss. Just for today let's try a new word for the Spirit, a word I learned from the Czech psychologist Mihaly Csikszentmihalyi in his book *Flow: The Psychology of Optimal Experience*. Experiencing the Spirit is like experiencing Flow.[2]

Do you know what it is like to experience moments when you have really come alive, when whatever you are doing is clicking, when everything seems to be working just the way it should? When that happens, you're in the flow.

You know those days when the tennis balls are landing inside the lines for a change. Or when you're out in a sailboat, dead in the water, and all of a sudden a strong, steady breeze picks up, and you're off. In the flow. Or in families and other close relationships that are filled with day-to-day dealings and tensions and worries, every once in a while an easy intimacy just happens, and for awhile nothing needs to be explained. Flow. It can happen at work, too—when you're firing on all cylinders, giving your best, and your best seems to be just what is needed.

Flow isn't something you make happen. You don't do it. It does you. You don't find it. It finds you and carries you.

And when you find yourself in the flow it feels as if it has always been there, always available to you, but now it is finally happening. Now you are in it. And you know then and there that this is the way things were meant to be, though there are a thousand and one reasons why it often doesn't happen that way.

In the same way there is a flow to the universe. We are part of a great, emerging life, the vast movement of the universe as it flows on, developing new forms of life, and moving our spirits, drawing us toward love and connection.

The Spirit, the inner power of the whole creation, is at work everywhere, drawing us into communion with God, the world, and each other. That's what happened at the time of the first Pentecost. All of a sudden people from every corner of the world of that time found an unimaginable sense of connectedness. They experienced a oneness with each other across every barrier of race and nation. That Spirit is always at work, creating connection, communion, belonging.

Ours is a time that urgently needs the work of the Spirit. We are caught between powerful forces driving us closer together, such as the Internet and globalization, and at the same time, equally powerful forces driving us farther apart into tribalisms of every kind. Gazing now into the twenty-first century, we see great questions facing us: Can we humans learn to deal with our conflicts and differences without resorting to violence and destruction? Can we change the way we relate to our fragile Earth before we destroy the nest that bears our life? Can the Christian churches that have lost so much of their stability in Europe and North America be renewed by the work of the Holy Spirit to again be powerful agents of hope and health?

You can sense the Spirit everywhere. Whenever we have been stunned by the beauty of a late spring day in Washington, so that we can't believe how good it is to be alive, we have been caught up in the flow of the Spirit. Whenever we are grasped by the suffering we see on television, on the street, in a news magazine, we are being moved by the flow of the Spirit. Whenever a nation finds itself swept up in long-delayed social change, as happened in the civil rights movement or the movement to care for our endangered planet, it is being caught up in the flow of the universe toward care for the whole creation, and that is the work of the Spirit of God.

The church is meant to be the Spirit's cutting edge, its vanguard, moving with the flow of the Spirit, helping to advance its work.

You see, it's power we come here for—a strangely self-emptying power for healing, for living, for being at one with the world. This power comes as we allow ourselves to be caught up in the flow of God's Spirit and find ourselves becoming more alive, more free, more loving.

The catch is that we have to be willing to surrender control. We can't go with the flow while we're holding on tight. That is what the Pentecostal churches seem to know. You won't tap into the loving, giving, self-emptying power of the universe if you're still trying to generate all the power and control yourself.

I don't know whether any of you will find yourselves clapping or speaking in tongues or falling out in the aisle this morning. But who knows, you might! That's God's business. But I do know that it was the Spirit of God that drew you here today.

Pentecost says that the Spirit of life is loose among us. So pay attention. You might even feel a breeze blowing through here, blowing within you. Get ready—to get caught up in the flow of the Spirit of God.

Ordinary Time

The Trinity and the Nearness of God

Matthew 28:16–20

If there is one comment I've heard more than any other in talking to people about their faith, it's something like this: "You see, I believe in God, but I'm not sure how to connect with him. God seems so far away." I've heard the same thing in church groups, from bright young college students, a tough-minded social worker, a venture capitalist, a custodian, and a mother.

In fact, I've come to think that this lack of connection is the unspoken thought carried in the heart of a great many who sit in the pews, as well as those who never darken our doors. God is the great Mystery and Purpose beyond us, the thinking goes, and Jesus came to teach us how to live God's way. That means that our job is to do the best we can to follow Christ and hope we get a glimpse of God sometime.

In the life of the church, today is called Trinity Sunday, the only major feast devoted explicitly to a doctrine of the church. It's not a simple one. Rectors have been known to hand the sermon for this day off to a young associate and sit and watch him or her drown in theological concepts. Even St. Augustine, who wrote a whole book on the Trinity, once said, "If you don't believe in the Trinity you will lose your soul. But if you try to understand it you will lose your mind." The whole notion of the Trinity sounds pretty abstract: God is three "persons" in one divine life, and we call this God "Father, Son, and Holy Spirit" or "Creator, Redeemer, Sustainer."

But why all the complexity of three in one, you might ask? How can it be that $1 + 1 + 1 = 1$? It is hard enough to believe in one God, you might say, now you're telling us we have to believe in three? And there have been important movements, especially in the past two centuries, attempting to throw all this complexity overboard. Those great American writers, Ralph

Waldo Emerson and Henry David Thoreau, found it all unnecessary, as do our Unitarian friends to this day. Thomas Jefferson thought the doctrine of the Trinity was primitive:

> When we shall have done away with the incomprehensible jargon of the Trinitarian arithmetic, that three are one, and one is three; when we shall have knocked down the artificial scaffolding reared to mask from view the very simple structure of Jesus . . . and get back to the pure and simple doctrines he inculcated, we shall then be truly and worthily his disciples. [1]

Jefferson was a Deist, and, in fact, I've always sensed that many Christians and Episcopalians are closet Deists, who might say God is something like a moral law, or a watchmaker, or a warm feeling, a power who creates the world and sets it going. A distant God. And Jesus was a great teacher.

But the Trinity is about the closeness, the involvement of God. It's about our being able to look behind the curtain and see what is actually going on in God's life. And, of course, what we discover is filled with paradox and mystery that overwhelm the limits of words. But this morning let us attempt to pull back the veil just a little and peer into God's life.

Our first step is to understand why all this talk of God as three in one arose. Christianity began, of course, as a movement within Judaism, a faith that had come to the radical insight that in back of all reality is a single, coherent mystery; that we live in a cosmos not of many competing gods but of one holy God. Every Jewish service contains the *Shema*, the central statement at the heart of their faith, "Hear, O Israel, the Lord our God is one."

But Christians had discovered in their experience that this holy mystery had also come to them in a person. God had entered history in Jesus of Nazareth, and then, after the resurrection, he continued to be with his followers in the form of a tremendous energy and power they called the Holy Spirit.

Belief in the Trinity grew out of the struggle of those early Christians to make sense of the experience that they had met the one God behind the universe in three different ways. They needed a new language.

Think of a child discovering different dimensions of a parent's love. In the early years of a daughter's relationship with her mother, the daughter experiences her as an immense and powerful figure who rules and orders her world. From the mother the child learns what she must or must not do. It is a relationship of superior to inferior. But then when the child gets older the mother invites the daughter to go with her on a trip, just the two of them alone, and along the way the daughter begins to see a different person, someone who is a contemporary, a companion. She and her mother laugh together and talk openly about their lives. The relationship has become different, more of equals. And then, much later, after the mother dies the daughter one day hears someone say to her, "You sound just like your mother."

And the daughter realizes that she now carries inside her much of her mother's own spirit.

One love has been experienced in three ways, as parent, as friend, and as inner spirit. The Trinity is believing in one God who comes to us in three ways.

That is where our notion of the Trinity begins. But now let us go a step deeper. The doctrine of the Trinity says that the God Christians know is the one we see in Christ. That means God isn't an inscrutable, all-controlling deity. God isn't sitting out there somewhere running everything, or simply watching everything, or having some single plan for our lives that we keep trying to guess.

No, Christians believe in a *Christlike* God. Yes, God is all-powerful, but Christ has redefined the meaning of power. Power is not the emperor's power to control, but rather the power we see revealed in Christ and on the cross—the power of love, of forgiveness, of invitation, of opening up possibilities. We see Christ-like power in a love that refuses to control, but goes with us even through the worst that life can bring.

No one saw that any clearer than a remarkable English chaplain in the First World War, G. A. Studdert-Kennedy, who prepared for going out to the front lines by visiting casualties in hospitals. In a base hospital in France, he met a bright young British officer suffering from severe wounds. He heard the anger and despair that had come from seeing the carnage of trench warfare. God seemed to be either inaccessibly remote or completely uncaring. The officer pressed the chaplain by asking, "What I want to know, Padre, is what is God like?"

Studdert-Kennedy didn't know what to say, but as he groped for an answer his eyes fell on a crucifix nailed to the wall beside the officer's bed. Pointing toward it Studdert-Kennedy said, "God is like that." For awhile there was only silence. Then the broken man said:

> What do you mean? . . . God can't be like that. God is Almighty. That is a battered, wounded, bleeding figure. . . . I admire Jesus of Nazareth. But I asked you not what Jesus was like, but what God was like.[2]

That officer knew only a God above and beyond everything. But Studdert-Kennedy's response was, "No, that is God on the cross." God is Christ-like, God suffers with us, God's compassion is poured out for us, God enters into our suffering, our trenches, and there we find our hope and our strength. That is the God of the Trinity.

But now let us go one final step further into the mystery of God. At the heart of the universe, in God's inner life, is a dynamic flow of love. God's life has eternally been one of giving and receiving love, pouring out life, and also of receiving life and love. From long before the Big Bang launched the universe into being, God's own life has been one of constantly flowing love.

One implication of that is that we will discover the fullness of our life as we allow ourselves to be caught up in God's life of giving and receiving. The gesture of care you offer a friend, the effort parents expend raising their children well, the time a teenager takes to build a house in Haiti, the check you write in support of a cause, the struggle you go through to forgive, the little acts of help you offer at home or at work—all of these are not simply good moral actions, but are ways of participating in the life of God. When we do those things we are actually allowing ourselves to be part of the ongoing eternal flow of God's love.

One of the most helpful ways I've found of imagining what this means comes from C. S. Lewis's description of what is actually happening when you or I pray. Imagine, Lewis says, that you are in your own home and you have decided to take a few moments to pray. You are seated in a chair, or kneeling, or even lying in bed, and you begin with thoughts and words to try to get in touch with God. God is the One to whom you reach to pour out your concerns. And God is also the one whom you have caught glimpses of in Christ. Still, God can seem far away.[3]

But, and here's the real surprise, your simple desire to pray, your yearning to be connected to the heart of life itself is the presence of God in you. "When we cry Abba, Father," St. Paul wrote, "it is that very Spirit bearing witness with our spirit that we are children of God." The simple, naked desire for life, the holy longing for a mysterious more, seemingly ineffectual calling out to God into the darkness, is itself the movement of God in us. It is God moving in us who draws us toward God. "The Spirit prays within us with sighs too deep for words," St. Paul says.

Do you see the closeness of God? The whole threefold life of God is actually going on in the little room where you are praying. Right there you are being pulled into God by God. God is more in you than you are yourself, whether you even believe in God or not. God places that yearning in us, and through it keeps seeking to draw us closer.

So maybe it's not so surprising that it often seems as if no one is listening when we pray. Because the One we are praying to is already within us, and prayer becomes less a matter of our trying to carry on a dialogue with someone out there beyond us than it is our allowing ourselves to be drawn into in the life of God.

Do you see how near God is? At the end of the great poem the *Divine Comedy*, Dante, having traveled through Hell and Purgatory, comes to Paradise and looks directly into the light of God. He catches a glimpse of the three circles of the Trinity, but can see little because of the dazzling brightness. The poem ends as he describes how his vision failed him so that he couldn't take it in, but instead his desire and will were caught up in what he called "the Love that moves the sun and other stars."[4]

To believe in or to know the Trinity is finally not to see it or understand it. It is to have our desire and will caught up in this endless flow of God's love, which is this "Love that moves the sun and other stars."

Who Do You Say That I Am?

Mark 8:27–38

The account we just heard comes at the mid-point in Jesus' three-year ministry as he was traveling through Galilee teaching, healing, and calling people to follow him. In those early months he has been working closely with his twelve disciples, preparing them to be his messengers. Now he is about to make the fateful turn to go to Jerusalem, the capital city and spiritual center of his Jewish faith, and he knows well that conflict and crisis lie ahead.

And so as he's walking along the road, he decides to give his disciples a midterm exam. Out of the blue he poses a question, "Who do people say that I am?"

That's a safe way to begin. What are people saying about me? What's the word on the street? And their answer is a little like what you'd get from a Gallup poll. "Well, 38 percent say you're John the Baptist; 23 percent say you're Elijah; 39 percent are undecided." These are guesses people are making, efforts to understand this enigmatic leader. In fact, Christians for two thousand years have been trying to answer this same question about this strange fellow Jesus and their answers have been all over the place.

The Yale historian Jaroslav Pelikan, in a book called *Jesus Through the Centuries*, describes many of the different images of Jesus that have seized the Christian imagination. At first Jesus was seen as a teacher and rabbi. Soon after his death, though, people were beginning to call him Lord and Savior. A century or two late, he was being seen as the cosmic Christ, ruler of all creation. And still later Christians focused on him almost exclusively as the crucified one suffering for the sins of the world. [1]

Thomas Jefferson, our Enlightenment president, saw him as a noble teacher and sat up in the White House at night using a razor to cut out of his

Bible all the passages that had supernatural and miraculous accounts so he could get down to the real Jesus for him—the philosopher and moralist. Then later, in the nineteenth century, wandering preachers taking the gospel across the American continent began to emphasize Jesus as a personal savior who rescues individual souls one by one.

According to Boston University professor Stephen Prothero, Americans at different times viewed Jesus as a socialist and a capitalist, a pacifist and a warrior, a civil rights activist and a Ku Klux Klansman. Prothero suggests that our favorite image for our Lord these days is, "Mr. Rogers Jesus: a neighborly fellow one can know and imitate."[2] And if you check the business shelves in the bookstore you can even find a title such as *Jesus the CEO* filled with such solid advice as: hire the right staff (Jesus seemed to fail miserably in this with a group of followers who often seemed clueless and unreliable); have a clear plan (that didn't go so well either and it all came to an end in less than three years); and stay in close touch with the boss (that he clearly did!).

"Who do people say that I am?" While Christians through the years have continually found fresh ways of knowing Jesus, they have often ended up shrinking him into their own categories, turning him into what they seem to need most.

Writer Bill McKibben, in an essay called "The Christian Paradox," thinks Americans in recent years have been doing just that. Our country, he says, is perhaps the most spiritually homogeneous wealthy nation on earth, with about 85 percent calling themselves Christian. "But is it Christian?" he asks. Jesus was specific about what he had in mind for his followers, McKibben says. It's there in his teachings—blessed are the poor, blessed are the peace- makers, love your enemy, welcome the outcast, if someone is in need and you have two cloaks, give one away.[3]

And yet McKibben notes that we are among the least generous nations on earth. We rank second to last among developed countries in amount of foreign aid we give compared to our size and wealth. In every measure of caring for the poorest—childhood nutrition, infant mortality, access to pre- school—we come in nearly last among the rich nations. And we are by a large measure the most violent developed nation, with a murder rate four or five times that of other developed nations.

How can this be? Well, it seems that our culture has turned Jesus into an expression of its own private, selfish individualism. Our public preachers focus on personal salvation, growth, and success. The Jesus we hear about is all about us.

Still, his power to attract has continued unabated down through the centu- ries. In recent decades, he has been almost universally admired—including by atheists and humanists--even when they disdain Christian churches and the Christian faith itself. Many college students these days seem interested in

Jesus and even drawn to him, but have little interest in Christianity itself, which they often see as prejudiced, mean-spirited, anti-science, and homophobic. There's a new book out about young adult Christians called *They Like Jesus But Not the Church.*

I was struck a few years ago when a former Forum guest here at the Cathedral, ABC television's medical expert Dr. Timothy Johnson, wrote in his memoir called *Finding God in the Questions* that he prefers to call himself a "follower of Jesus" rather than to use the label "Christian," even though he's been a lifelong churchgoer. It keeps him focused on Jesus' life and teachings, he says, and puts some distance between him and the flaws of so many churches. And he says he likes the personal commitment in that phrase "follower of Jesus" and feels as if it makes him more accountable to trying to live the kind of life Jesus led.

All of this makes the second question, the real question Jesus is asking, all the more important. He focuses his gaze on his disciples and says, "But you—who do *you* say that I am?" Not what are people saying or what's your opinion? Jesus is asking, "Where are *you* with God, with me, with this life into which I'm trying to draw you?"

Did you notice that only one disciple, Simon Peter, had an answer for him? "You are the Messiah," he says. "You are the Christ, the son of the living God," he blurts out in Matthew's version. No one else says a word, but Peter just lets loose with far more than he can understand. He will only learn all that that brash declaration implies over time as he follows his master. That's why the last part of our lesson is so crucial: "If any want to become my followers, let them deny themselves and take up their cross and follow me. For those who want to save their live will lose it, and those who lose their life for my sake will save it."

To be a Christian is to follow Jesus, to be a disciple, to know him, to have a relationship with him. It isn't first a matter of intellect or accepting a set of beliefs. In the gospels, people are attracted to Jesus first and then they start to follow. And along the way they come to love and trust him long before they work out exactly what they believe. They become followers first.

If this story were just about figuring out who Jesus was, then it might seem that Christianity is primarily about having a correct set of beliefs. But what if you don't really know what you believe? Can you be part of the church? I've heard many people in Inquirers' classes through the years ask that question.

Jesus not only thinks that it's okay not to know what we believe, he thinks it's the natural way to grow into this faith. Come on along, he says. You can figure this thing out as you go. If you want to be a disciple, just follow me. Do what I do. Pick up a cross, take on a mission, learn to read the Bible and to pray, live your life wide open and responsive to the world around you.

Give yourself away—your energy, your passion, your time and resources. Just stick with me. Do that and you'll learn who Jesus is.

Following Jesus is a deeply personal answer to a deeply personal question. "Who do *you* say that I am?" And since we're talking this morning about a response that we can only make for ourselves, I think I owe you a sense of how I would answer the question myself.

First, Jesus is the one teacher I couldn't live without. I wouldn't know what a real life could be without Jesus' teaching about loving our neighbors, turning the other cheek, letting go of our anxiety and trusting God like the lilies of the field. Without his sayings and stories I wouldn't have the guideposts I need, such as those hard words saying you have to lose your life in order to find it. Without his radical demands—to forgive those who hurt me, to love my enemies, to welcome the stranger and the outcast—I would stay locked in the bubble of my self-absorbed little life.

But there have been many wise teachers through the centuries. Jesus offers me something more. When I look at him I see what it means to be genuinely free, free to be fully himself, to speak the truth, to live in the moment. He lived without anxiety or fear—of death or failure or loss—willing to suffer and lay down his life every day. He welcomed everyone, especially the untouchables. He gave his love with abandon. He risked everything for love's sake. He lived out of a peaceful center that I yearn for, and at the same time he was passionately involved in the lives of the people around him.

But I have to say, if that were all Jesus were for me, I would have thrown in the towel on being a Christian long ago, because it would just be too hard. I'm not that good; my thoughts almost always turn first to what I want. I often can't get outside my own skin. I like to play it safe and hedge my bets. I easily close my eyes to the world's pain.

I need more than a teacher, however wise, or even a model, however inspiring. I need a savior. I need someone who loves me even when I can't live his way, when I don't even want to live that way. I need someone who cares for me and this whole lost world enough to hang on a cross to open a way beyond my selfishness, fear, and drivenness. I need a presence, a living Lord, someone who will go through times of confusing and suffering with me and lead me through to the other side, someone who will keep working on me through the people and events of my days to lead me home.

But what about you? Jesus is after big game here. He wants you and me to be part of the healing of the world. He wants us to be his friends and companions. He wants to fill us with his life. And all we have to do is to follow, learn from him, and let him live in us.

As far as I'm concerned, the wisest understanding of who Jesus is came from the great Albert Schweitzer, who was first an organist, then a New Testament scholar, and eventually became a doctor and founded a leper colony in Africa. He ultimately gave up the scholarly life and all the analysis of the historical Jesus and went on to find out who Jesus was the only way he decided he could. His book, *The Quest for the Historical Jesus,* ends this way:

> He comes to us as one unknown, as of old by the lakeside he came to those who knew him not. And he speaks to us the same word, "Follow thou me," and he sets us to the tasks which he has to fulfill in his time. He commands, and to those who follow, whether they be wise or simple, he will reveal himself in the suffering, the conflicts, the toils which they will go through in his name. And as an ineffable mystery they will learn in their own experience who he is. [4]

Do you want to know who he is? "Come on along," he says, "and join up with your mind and your heart wide open." Follow him into classes and soup kitchens and the breaking of the bread. Ask your questions. Immerse yourself in his life, and you will learn in *your* own experience who he is.

"You," he is saying, "yes, you, who do *you* say that I am?"

All Saints

The Real Thing

Matthew 5:1–12

I remember a few years ago talking to a friend who said she was thinking about giving up on religion. Her discomfort had been building for a long time—the violence committed in the name of faith through the centuries, the ways Christians have treated the Jews down through history, how often one religious faith has forced its beliefs on another. And 9/11 became for her the last straw.

Thousands of people lost their lives in the name of a perverted form of religion. Andrew Sullivan writing in the *New York Times Magazine* soon after 9/11 said that what we are seeing is a religious war—not one, of course, between Islam and Christianity, but a clash between fanatic fundamentalists in all religions and the true voices of open-minded, compassionate religious faith.[1] Fundamentalists use authoritarian power, they often wield religious texts like clubs, they frequently threaten eternal suffering to those who don't obey and eternal bliss to those who do. They can sometimes be the antithesis of true religion, whether we're talking about Osama bin Laden or the thirteenth-century Christian crusaders heading off to slay the infidels. When the new atheists who have written so many books lately want to argue that religion is bad for the world, they can find plenty of evidence.

Any religious faith, though, is ultimately to be judged by one thing—does it or does it not produce holy people, people of wisdom and generosity, whose lives in some way mirror the Love at the heart of the universe? We can see the hatred and violence of fundamentalists and fanatics for the corruptions of religion that they are—if we can point to religious people who actually have been channels of God's love.

339

Today we celebrate All Saints' Day, the feast of what we could call the real thing, true religion—lives so filled with God's love that they are willing to do remarkable things for God. Today we remember the famous ones, and the not so famous, the whole goodly company of those whose lives have shone with Christ's light.

Maybe the most famous is a fellow named Francis Bernardone. Born into a well-to-do family, he had a fine education and loved his wine, parties, and a good fight now and then. But after months of battle and a brutal time in prison, he came home with a growing awareness of the poverty around him and began giving away the clothes from his father's shop. One day he rode by a leper, and when he saw an especially ragged-looking man he nudged his horse to hurry on, tossing a few coins as he went to ease his conscience. But then, as if from nowhere, he was overcome with an intense wave of pity, and so he turned around, went back to the leper, got off his horse, took all the money he had, and shoved it in the man's hands. And then he did the unthinkable, embracing the man, open sores and all. After that, Francis tossed away everything for God and became known, of course, as St. Francis of Assisi.

On the other hand, you may not have heard of Saint Maximilian, who became the first conscientious objector when he refused to serve in the Roman army. He said his only loyalty was to the army of God. This broke his father's heart because he knew it would mean his son's death. And as Maximilian prepared to be put to death he noticed the shabby clothes of his executioner and asked that his own clothes be given to the man, and they were.

Or there is Constance and a group of New England nuns serving in Memphis, Tennessee, in the late 1870s when a yellow fever epidemic swept through the city. More than half the city packed up and left when the plague began, but Constance and her companions stayed there, easing the discomfort of the dying, emptying their bedpans, and all of it for God. The marker with all their names on it is still there in a Memphis cemetery.

And then there is one of my heroes, Dietrich Bonhoeffer, one of the great theologians of the century, who was a pastor in Germany as Hitler came to power. Bonhoeffer joined the tiny Confessing Church made up of the handful of pastors who refused to give in to Hitler's demands of absolute loyalty. He wrote books, created a new seminary to train faithful ministers, and eventually became involved in a plot to overthrow Hitler. When he was found out, he was taken to the Buchenwald concentration camp, and, on a Sunday in 1945, just as he was concluding a prison church service, he was hanged.

Dorothy Day, working among the poorest in New York City in 1950s and '60s; Janani Luwum, the Anglican archbishop of Uganda killed for defending his people who were being slaughtered by Idi Amin . . . We honor these saints because they show us so clearly what living Christ's love can mean.

Novelist Frederick Buechner describes in his novel, *The Storm*, a writer who became so enchanted by the heroic stories of these saints that he began getting himself to church to learn what made them tick. Buechner says that watching these saints became for this man like looking out the window at a swarm of crazy people running around the street below in a frenzy of excitement over something they were all pointing to in the sky but that, because of the overhang of the roof, he himself was unable to see. He realized eventually what he had to do was come down into the street to find out for himself what all the excitement was about. And so he began to make his way to church where, little by little, over time, he thought he was catching at least a glimpse of what all the shouting was about.[2]

We come here to church week by week to see what the shouting is all about, to spend some time in the company of the saints who have gone before us. In the New Testament understanding, of course, all of us are saints. Sainthood isn't something you achieve, it's given. It's what we become when we're baptized. We're marked as Christ's own forever. Saints in the New Testament are not religious superathletes. Most of them are like us, ordinary people called by Christ to live an extraordinary way. Listen to how Jesus himself describes saints:

> Blessed are the poor in spirit. . . . Blessed are the meek. . . . Blessed are the pure in heart. . . . Blessed are the peacemakers. . . . Blessed are you who are persecuted for righteousness sake. . . . Blessed are you when people revile you and persecute you and utter all kinds of evil against you. . . . (Matthew 5:3–11)

The saints are the ones who don't have their lives together. They seem to have to struggle to get by. They aren't rich or famous or particularly brilliant. They are people like you and me, who have been broken open enough to know God's love and to trust it, and open enough to trying to live Christ's way right where they are.

Every Sunday when we gather here the air is thick with the saints who have lived this way. They are everywhere around us. Every window and carving points to another one—St. Paul and St. Teresa of Avila, St. Chrsysostom, the silver-tongued preacher, and Florence Nightingale, the nineteenth-century nurse, Martin Luther King Jr., and Rosa Parks, the courageous civil rights leader who launched a movement when she refused one day to stand in the back of the bus in Montgomery, Alabama. And so when we step into this Cathedral we are caught up in the communion of saints, the company of all who have lived their lives in God through the centuries. We believe they are with us here, as are our own personal saints, our parents and grandparents and coaches and teachers who showed us Christ—all part of God's eternity, still encouraging us, inspiring us, pulling for us.

As the Letter to the Hebrews puts it, "Because we are surrounded by so great a cloud of witnesses, let us run with perseverance the race that is set before us" (Hebrews 12:1–2).

I have to say, I know plenty of ordinary, everyday saints here in this Cathedral, and I admire them enough not to embarrass them by naming them today. But they are the ones who show me Christ's light day in, day out. They are the great cloud of witnesses that keep showing me what it means to live Christ's way.

This is the real thing. This is what Christianity is for. The church is meant to be a factory for saints. If it isn't making saints it isn't worth bothering with. And if it is, then it is something the world can't get along without.

And so, my fellow saints, our lives are intended to be the only real answer to the age-old saga of religion gone bad. Of course, we could try the excuse that it's hard to be a saint when you work in an office or classroom or lab, or don't have a job at all. Saints are made of more heroic stuff, we may tell ourselves. But we can work out our sainthood anywhere. We can ask God to fill us, to help us keep our heads straight and our hearts open in a pinched and frightened world. We can pray and read scripture and keep our promises and serve the poor. It's not that hard.

Sainthood is mostly about the little things, about what you do for God this afternoon, or tomorrow. There's a moment in the play *A Man for All Seasons* when Sir Thomas More is encouraging his son-in-law to become a teacher. The young man protests, "Who would notice me except God and my students?" And More responds, "Not a bad audience, that."[3]

Not a bad audience for those of us called to be ordinary saints doing God's will day in, day out—getting kids to school, insisting that business is more than the bottom line, hanging in there in a public school classroom, looking out for a neighbor, trying to be helpful and generous with those hit by our sinking economy.

I have a friend who is a Lutheran pastor. Five or six years ago he and his wife took in four Sudanese young men, the ones that have been called "the lost boys of the Sudan," orphans abandoned in the terrible wars there. When the boys moved into their new home, they insisted on sleeping in the same small room, because they could remember no other life than being jammed in a tiny space. But over the next few years they found their bearings, went to American schools and colleges, and are making their way into new lives. My friend talks about it all matter-of-factly. It's just what he and his wife felt called to do.

It has been hard, but they've never regretted it. That's the real thing. It's sainthood. It's your call and mine. It's the only real justification for the church.

The Communion of Saints

John 11:32–44

Years ago I read a novel called *Ironweed* by William Kennedy, which won the Pulitzer Prize when it came out.[1] Now every year I think about it as the leaves fall, the days darken, and the church talks about end times. It's set in Albany, New York, in the 1930s, at just this time of year, Halloween night and All Saints' Day, and is about the life of what we would call today a homeless man, but in those days was just called a bum. Francis Phelan made some terrible mistakes early in his life, had ended up leaving his family to drift from city to city, living in alleys and under bridges, but now twenty years later he was coming home.

From the first page of the novel, I realized something strange was going on. As he rides back into town in the rear of an old truck, he notices the town cemeteries, where, he thinks, even the dead seem to live in different neighborhoods. The story describes Francis' long dead mother stirring in her grave as Francis goes by, and Francis' father in his grave lighting his pipe and smiling at his wife.

Are these people dead or alive? As you're reading, it's hard to tell. What is clear was that in some way they are living on. And as the story goes on, I kept noticing that Francis' struggle to come to terms with his past and to let go of his guilt is taking place in the presence of the people he had loved who were now dead.

Then in the climactic scene of the story, when Francis returns to his old home to see his wife for the first time in all those years, we discover that the dead have set up bleachers in the backyard to watch the reunion. And everyone is there—the man who had run for sheriff years before and got beat and

343

then turned Republican, another man who inherited a fortune from his mother and drank it up, and countless others, good and bad, successful or not.

Reading *Ironweed* I had a sense I often get in cemeteries and churches, especially, of how thick the air is with the lives of those who have gone before us. "The past isn't over," William Faulkner wrote, "it's not even past." And in that story I found a powerful awareness of how connected we all are, the living and the dead.

This All Saints' Day is intended to encourage and give us heart. It is a day when we celebrate the heroes and heroines of the Christian faith, and especially the unsung, ordinary saints—the ones who are in our bleachers as we make our way.

One of the treasured lessons for All Saints' Day is from the Book of Revelation, where it describes "that great multitude that no one could count, from every nation, from all tribes and peoples and languages" gathered around the throne of the Lamb, representing Christ. We call this the "Communion of Saints," and every time we say the Creed we affirm our faith in it. We sang about it in that great hymn "For All the Saints."

> O blest communion, fellowship divine!
> We feebly struggle, they in glory shine;
> Yet all are one in thee for all are thine. Alleluia.

Saints are part of the One Life, God's life, holding all of God's children, the living and the dead.

The Communion of Saints says that we are not alone in our struggle to live faithful, loving, and truthful lives, that we still have with us the company of those who have gone before. In them we have models of what it means to live Christlike lives. But even more than that, the Communion of Saints affirms that they are with us still. Those who have died into God's eternal life surround us now with their prayer, love, and encouragement.

In fact, the Letter to the Hebrews describes it best. The writer is addressing a drifting, compromised, demoralized church, and the best thing he knows to do is to remind them of the great saints of their past—Abraham and Sarah, Isaac and Jacob, and of course Moses, who led them to freedom. So after lifting them up, and reminding his hearers of their stories, he says this: "Since we are surrounded by so great a cloud of witnesses . . . let us run with endurance the race that is set before us, looking to Jesus, the pioneer and perfecter of our faith" (Hebrews 12:1–2).

I remember learning in my youth a way of talking about the church that stems from the Middle Ages. The church throughout time and history, I was told, consists of three divisions—armies you could almost call them: the infants and children in our midst, who are called the Church Expectant; the whole company of Christians living now, who are called the Church Militant; and the company of those who have died, the Church Triumphant. How do you like that? We are the Church Militant, all of us on the march of spreading Christ's kingdom of love!

Those are old-fashioned phrases. But they picture us as one company, some of us alive now, doing the best we can to be channels of Christ's peace, some of us now dead, but alive with God. The saintly Archbishop Oscar Romero, who was martyred in El Salvador some years ago, always read at the Eucharist the names of those members of the community who had been killed or kidnapped, or as he said, been called to the Church Triumphant. As the names would be called out in the service, the congregation would respond to each name by boldly proclaiming, *"Presente!"* ("Present!") They were dead, but they weren't gone.

We need the saints to keep reminding us who we are. We need St. Francis, climbing down from his horse to embrace a leper and give away all his coins to show us that we can't turn our backs on AIDS victims, or Darfur, or on health care for everyone. We need Thomas Cranmer and Hugh Latimer, both burned at the stake for their beliefs during the Protestant Reformation, we need Ugandan archbishop Janani Luwum, shot and killed by the dictator Idi Amin as he knelt in prayer. We need Monica, the mother of the wild young St. Augustine, to show us what long-suffering parenting is all about, and we need Dorothy Day of the Catholic Workers Movement working with the poorest on the streets of New York City. We need saints in every generation to make explicit what it means to live Christ's life in our time.

In fact, one of the realities of being here in the Cathedral is that we can't escape the presence of the saints. Any time you step in here the air is thick with their presence. To come in by the main doors this morning you had to make your way past St. Peter, the impetuous, unstoppable disciple, and St. Paul, who died in a Roman prison after almost single-handedly spreading Christian faith across the Roman Empire. And every window and carving points to another one—to Florence Nightingale, the nineteenth-century tireless nurse, and Howard Thurman, the African American preacher and mystic. They are here to challenge and encourage us, to cheer us on and to push us further in living Christ's life.

Sometimes the saints can seem palpably close. One of the greatest preachers of the nineteenth century was a man named Phillips Brooks of Trinity Church in Boston. Some seventy years after his death another great preacher at Trinity Church, Theodore Parker Ferris, wrote this:

> I have lived and worked in the rectory that was built for Brooks for almost 22 years. There are times when I am so busy with my work that I seldom think of him. There are other times when he is unbelievably close to me. When I read [his words] . . . I [was] proud to be in his company, honored to be one of his followers. It was as though I stood upon his shoulders and therefore could reach higher than I could ever hope to reach if I were standing on my own feet.[2]

Saints give us shoulders to stand on.

The truth is we are accountable here to the saints. My sermons and our prayers are going on while the saints are listening. It can be hard to know that the prophet Isaiah and Martin Luther King Jr. are listening to everything that gets said from here! And so the question I have to ask myself is not whether you find my sermon sufficiently interesting, moving, and short, but will it hold water in the presence of the saints?

But today is a time to remember especially the everyday saints in our lives. If you were to name your saints today, who would you name? Who are the ones in your bleachers, watching you, cheering you on? A parent or grandparent, teachers or coaches, doctors or therapists, old friends, or relative strangers, for that matter—a nurse, say, who saw you through a hospital stay? I remember an uncle, an Episcopal priest, who showed me what Christian courage looks like as he stood against racism in Mississippi, a professor who showed me what it meant to be a Christian scholar, an ancient friend who became like a grandfather to my wife Marguerite and me when we were struggling graduate students.

None of these saints was perfect. But they are saints because somehow God's love came through them. One of the gifts of this day is that it gives us a chance to remember the ones who shaped us, and not just that but to sense how close they still are. During Communion today, why not hold up their names quietly, as if to say, "Present!" because they are here. They are here, because in God time and space fall away.

I was struck reading recently that writer Madeleine L'Engle, who died not long ago, said that she had come to understand her father much better now, years after his death, than she had ever been able to during his life. I imagine that's true of many of us. My hunch is that we have some thanking to do for the imperfect saints in our lives, maybe especially the parents and grandparents, aunts and uncles, as well as the mentors and supporters. If they are still alive, this is a good time to do it. But if they are now gone, they are still in our bleachers, our cloud of witnesses. And some of us have work to do yet—apologizing, forgiving, saying, "I love you." In the communion of saints, it's never too late.

There's an old story that when we arrive at the pearly gates of heaven St. Peter will be there, just to check our name and resumé and be sure we're ready to come in. And as we stand outside the gate, he will ask who our friends are, our bleacher people, who helped us along the way. And we will think back and name all the great and not so great people through whom somehow enough light and love came to brighten our way. And St. Peter will say, "You know, I just saw that very crowd of people you just named, and a few others too! Come on in." And as you walk over the next hill you see them, all standing together, holding up a sign that says, "Welcome home! We've been pulling for you!"

For all are one in thee, for all are thine.

Notes

INTRODUCTION

1. Philip Larkin, "Church Going," *Collected Poems* (London: The Marvell Press, 1989), 97.
2. C. S. Lewis, *God in the Dock: Essays on Theology and Ethics* (Grand Rapids: William B. Eerdmans, 1970), 240.

A GOD WE CAN TRUST

1. Peter Berger, *A Rumor of Angels* (New York: Anchor Books, 1970), 1.
2. Erik Erikson, *The Life Cycle Completed* (New York: W. W. Norton, 1998).
3. T. S. Eliot, "The Dry Salvages," *Collected Poems 1909–1962* (new York: Harcourt, Brace & World, 1970), 199.
4. Anonymous, from Sir Alister Hardy in *The Spiritual Nature of Man* (Oxford: Oxford University Press, 1979); reprinted 1984, then quoted in John V. Taylor, *The Christlike God* (London: SCM Press, 1992), 27.
5. C. S. Lewis, "The Weight of Glory," *The Weight of Glory and Other Essays* (London: Macmillan, 1965), 6–7.
6. C. S. Lewis, *Mere Christianity* (London: Macmillan, 1952), 17–212.
7. Sharon Begley, "Science Finds God," *Newsweek*, July 20, 1998.
8. Ruth Pitter, BBC broadcast, quoted in John V. Taylor, *The Christlike God* (London: SCM Press, 1992), 33–34.

FOLLOW ME

1. Malcolm Gladwell, *Blink* (Boston: Back Bay Books, 2007).
2. William Butler Yeats, Letter to Lady Elizabeth Pelham, January 22, 1939, in Richard Ellmann, *Yeats: The Man and His Masks* (New York: Macmillan, 1948), 289.

3. Fyodor Dostoyevsky, *The Brothers Karamazov*, trans. Richard Pevlar and Larissa Valokonsky (New York: Vintage Books, 1990), 56.

4. William Willimon, *Pulpit Resource* (East Inver Heights, MN: Logos Publications), 28, no. 3 (July–Sept.): 50.

THE CALLING OF HOLINESS

1. Christian Smith and Melissa Lundquist Denton, *Soul-Searching: The Religious and Spiritual Lives of American Teenagers*, cited in Kenda Creasy Dean, *Almost Christian* (New York: Oxford University Press, 2010), 14.

2. D. Brent Laytham, *God Is Not . . . Religious, Nice, "One of Us," an American, a Capitalist* (Grand Rapids: Brazos Press, 2004).

3. Annie Dillard, *Teaching a Stone to Talk* (New York: Harper & Row, 1982). 40.

4. Andrew Harvey and Mark Matousek, *Dialogues with a Modern Mystic* (Wheaton: Theosophical Publishing House, 1994), 226–27.

COSTLY DISCIPLESHIP

1. This ad suggested in William Willimon, *Pulpit Resource* 32, no. 3 (July–September 2004): 42–43.

2. Richard Stengel, *Time*, August 30, 2007.

3. Paul Farmer, *Mountains Beyond Mountains* (New York: Random House, 2003), 191.

WILL YOU DANCE?

1. Cited in Philip Yancey, *What's So Amazing about Grace?* (Grand Rapids: Zondervan Publishing, 1997), 48–49.

2. Lt. General William Boykin quoted in James Carroll, "Warring with God," *Boston Globe*, October 21, 2003.

3. Jonathan Sacks, *The Dignity of Difference* (London: Continuum, 2002), 45.

4. Sacks, *Dignity of Difference*, 201.

5. Alan Jones, personal conversation, May 2005.

COMMANDED TO LOVE

1. Erich Fromm, *The Art of Loving* (New York: Harper and Row Publishers, 1956).

2. Walter Brueggemann, "Neighborliness and the Limits of Power in God's Realm: On the Second Great Commandment," *The Covenanted Self* (Minneapolis: Forress Press, 1999), 79.

3. Thomas Geoghegan, *The New Republic*, unable to trace the citation.

4. John L'Heureux, "The Expert on God," in J. P. Maney and Tom Hazuka, *Celestial Omnibus* (Boston: Beacon Press, 1997).

WHEN GOD THROWS A BRICK

1. Ward Brehm, *White Man Walking* (Minneapolis: Kirk House Publishers, 2003).
2. Brehm, *White Man Walking*, 86
3. The Honorable Tony Hall, "The Sunday Forum," Washington National Cathedral, January 20, 2008.
4. Rick Warren, "The Sunday Forum," Washington National Cathedral, January 27, 2008.

FOLLOWING AN ELUSIVE LORD

1. Philip Yancey, *Reaching for the Invisible God* (Grand Rapids: Zondervan Publishing House, 2000), 15.
2. Yancey, *Reaching for the Invisible God*, 15.
3. Karl Rahner, *Encounters with Silence* (New York: Newman Press, 1960), 19.
4. Emily Dickinson, from a letter to Otis Lord, April 30, 1882; Thomas H. Johnson, ed., *The Letters of Emily Dickinson* (Cambridge: Belknap, 1958), 728.
5. Ron Hansen, *Mariette in Ecstasy* (New York: HarperPerennial, 1991), 174.
6. Peter Matthiessen, *The Snow Leopard* (New York: Penguin Books, 1978).

HAGGLING PRAYER

1. Neely Tucker, "Taking a Whack against Comcast," *Washington Post*, October 18, 2007.
2. Somerset Maugham, *Of Human Bondage*, cited in Philip Yancey, *Prayer: Does It Make a Difference?* (London: Hodder & Stoughton, 2006), 210–11.
3. C. S. Lewis, *Letters to Malcolm: Chiefly on Prayer* (New York: Harcourt, Brace, & World, 1964), 28.
4. Yancey, *Prayer*, 236.

DOES GOD CARE?

1. Reynolds Price, *Letter to a Young Man in the Fire* (New York: Scribner, 1999) 25.
2. Unable to trace source.
3. Elie Wiesel, *Night*, trans. Marion Wiesel (New York: Hill and Wang, 2006), 64–65.
4. Archibald MacLeish, *J.B.: A Play in Verse* (Boston: Houghton Mifflin Company, 1958), 11.
5. Nicholas Wolsterstorff, *Lament for a Son* (Grand Rapids: William B. Eerdmans Publishing Company, 1987), 67–68.
6. Wiesel, *Night*.
7. Wolsterstorff, *Lament for a Son*.
8. William Sloane Coffin, *The Collect Sermons of William Sloane Coffin: The Riverside Years*, vol. 2 (Louisville: Westminster John Knox Press, 2008), 3–6.

THE SILENCE OF GOD

1. Mother Teresa, *Mother Teresa: Come Be My Light*, ed. Brian Kolodiejchuk, M.C. (New York: Doubleday, 2007), 186–87.
2. Mother Teresa, *Mother Teresa*, 214.
3. James Martin, S.J., in David Van Biema, "Mother Teresa's Crisis of Faith," *Time*, August 23, 2007.
4. John Wesley, letter of June 27, 1766, quoted in Rowan Williams, *Open to Judgment: Sermons and Addresses* (London: Darton, Longman & Todd, 1994), 202.
5. Augustine of Hippo, Sermons 117.5, cited in Garry Wills, *Saint Augustine* (New York: Viking, 1999), xii.
6. Frederick Buechner, *The Alphabet of Grace* (New York: Seabury Press, 1970), 47.
7. Karen Armstrong, *The Case for God* (New York: Alfred A. Knopf, 2009).

GOD, SCIENCE, AND THE LIFE OF FAITH

1. Stephen Jay Gould, *Rock of Ages: Science and Religion in the Fullness of Life* (New York: Ballantine Books, 2002), 1–25.
2. Carl Sagan, *Cosmos* (New York: Ballantine Books, 1985), 1.
3. Francis Collins, "Can You Believe in God and Evolution?" *Time*, August 7, 2005.
4. Albert Einstein in Francis S. Collins, *The Language of God* (New York: Free Press, 2006), 228.
5. John Claypool, "Strength Not to Faint," *Tracks of a Fellow Struggler* (Harrisburg: Morehouse Publishing, 1974), 23.

THE NIGHT VISITOR

1. C. S. Lewis, *Mere Christianity* (New York: Macmillan, 1952), 168.
2. Howard Mumma, "Conversation with Camus," *Christian Century* 17, no. 18 (June 7, 2000).
3. Anne LaMott, *Traveling Mercies* (New York: Pantheon Books, 1999), 264–65.

THE MIRACLE OF FORGIVENESS

1. Anne Lamott, *Plan B* (New York: Riverhead Books, 2005), 45–46.
2. Lamott, *Plan B*, 45–46.
3. David Herbert Donald, *Lincoln* (New York: Simon & Schuster, 1995), 580.

HOLY LAUGHTER

1. William Willimon, *And the Laugh Shall Be First* (Nashville: Abingdon Press, 1986), 9.
2. Humour: Funny Church Bulletin Board notices,www.jnweb.com/funny/notices.
3. Frederick Buechner, *Telling the Truth* (New York: Harper and Row, 1977), 63.
4. Amazing Elevator, www.humorsphere.com.

TRUSTING AGAINST THE EVIDENCE

1. Peter Berger, *A Rumor of Angels* (New York: Doubleday, 1969), 67–68.
2. James Hillman, "Betrayal," *Loose Ends* (New York: Spring Publications, 1975).
3. Etty Hillesum, LTR, November 25, 1941, *An Interrupted Life: The Diaries of Etty Hillesum*, trans. Arno Pomerans, Eng. trans. (New York: Washington Square Press, 1983).

GRACE

1. John Newton, "Amazing Grace," *The Hymnal 1982* (New York: The Church Hymnal Corporation, 1982), #671.

INSTALLATION SERMON

1. Susan Howatch, quoted in Hugh Dickinson, "Cathedrals and Christian Imagination," *Cathedrals Now: Their Use and Place in Society* (Norwich: Canterbury Press, 1996), 60.
2. Archbishop Rowan Williams, Enthronement Sermon, February 27, 2003,www. arcbishopofcanterbury.org.
3. Harry Emerson Fosdick in T. A. Prickett, *The Story of Preaching* (Bloomington: AuthorHouse, 2011), 74–75.

AN UNFINISHED CATHEDRAL

1. Reinhold Niebuhr, *The Irony of American History* (Chicago: University of Chicago Press, 1952), 63.
2. Henry Yates Satterlee, private journal, in Richard Hewlett, *The Foundation Stone: Henry Yates Satterlee and the Creation of Washington National Cathedral* (Rockville, MD: Montrose Press, 2007), 98.
3. Satterlee in Hewlett, *The Foundation Stone*, 134.
4. Henry Yates Satterlee, *The Building of a Cathedral* (New York: Edwin S. Gorham, 1901), 64.

A NEW COMMUNITY

1. Cartoonist, *Washington Post*, November 5, 2008.
2. Child's letter, *New York Times*, January 18, 2008.
3. Martin Luther King Jr., *A Testament of Hope: The Essential Writings and Speeches of Martin Luther King, Jr.* (New York: HarperCollins, 1986), 269.
4. Tavis Smiley, conversation in Sunday Forum, Washington National Cathedral, December 14, 2008.
5. John Lewis, conversation in Sunday Forum, Washington National Cathedral, March 30, 2008.

DOUBTS AND LOVES

1. Reinhold Niebuhr, *The Irony of American History* (Chicago: University of Chicago Press, 1952), 173.
2. Elisabeth Kübler-Ross, *On Death and Dying* (New York: Scribner, 1969).
3. From *Spirituality and Health* 2, no. 1 (New York: Trinity Church: Spirituality and Health Publishing), quoted in Desmond Tutu, *No Future Without Forgiveness* (New York: Doubleday, 1999), 272.
4. Yehuda Amichai, "The Place Where We Are Right," trans. Chana Block and Stephen Mitchell, *The Selected Poetry of Yehuda Amichai* (Berkeley: University of California Press, 1996), 34.
5. Amichai, "The Place Where We Are Right."

ON THE FAR SIDE OF REVENGE

1. Martha Horne, "A Challenge for Seminarians: Preparing Leaders for a Ministry of Reconciliation," *I Have Called You Friends: Reflections on Reconciliation* (Cambridge, MA: Cowley Publications, 2006), 65.
2. Hannah Arendt, *The Human Condition* (Chicago: University of Chicago Press, 1958), 236–37.
3. Arendt, *Human Condition*, 238
4. Desmond Tutu, *No Future Without Forgiveness* (New York: Doubleday, 1999), 265.
5. Tutu, *No Future Without Forgiveness*, 146–47.
6. Seamus Heaney, "Voices from Lemnos," *Opened Ground: Selected Poems 1966–1998* (New York: Farrar, Straus and Giroux, 1998), 305–6.
7. Tutu, *No Future Without Forgiveness*.

THE SPIRIT OF UNDERSTANDING

1. William Willimon, *Pulpit Resources*, May 18, 1997, 29.
2. Deborah Tannen, *You Just Don't Understand Me* (New York: Ballantine Books, 1990), 13–23.
3. Don S. Browning, *Pluralism and Personality* (Cranbury, NJ: Associated University Presses, 1980) 134.
4. Desmond Tutu, *No Future Without Forgiveness* (New York: Doubleday, 1999).
5. Steve Roberts and Cookie Roberts, interview, Sunday Forum, Washington National Cathedral, May 22, 2011.

A BIG ENOUGH HOUSE

1. Diana Eck, *A New Religious America* (San Francisco: HarperSan Francisco, 2001), 125.
2. A paraphrase of Augustine by Karl Rahner, *Encounters with Silence* (New York: Newman Press, 1960), 19.

IN THANKSGIVING FOR THE LIFE OF DOROTHY HEIGHT

1. James Weldon Johnson, *God's Trombones* (New York: Penguin Books, 1927), 27–30.

AN EXTREMIST FOR LOVE

1. Martin Luther King Jr., "Some Things We Must Do," delivered in Montgomery, Alabama, December 5, 1957. Quoted in 9marks.org.
2. Martin Luther King Jr., "Letter from a Birmingham Jail," *I Have a Dream* (San Francisco: HarperCollins, 1992), 94.
3. King, "Letter from a Birmingham Jail," 87–88.
4. Cornel West, *Race Matters* (New York: Random House, 1994), 93.
5. West, *Race Matters*, 29.
6. Barry Goldwater, acceptance speech, 1964 Republican Convention, www.wikiquote.com.

BLACK AND WHITE ON THE ROAD TO EMMAUS

1. Condoleezza Rice, "Rice Hits U.S. 'Birth Defect'" *Washington Times*, March 28, 2001.
2. Colbert King, *Washington Post*, April 6, 2008.
3. Cornel West, *Race Matters* (Boston: Beacon Press, 1993), 14.
4. Eugene Sutton, Sermon at Washington National Cathedral, March 30, 2008.
5. Chris Rice, *Grace Matters: A Memoir of Faith, Friendship, and Hope in the Heart of the South* (San Francisco: Jossey-Bass, 2002), 53–54.
6. Martin Luther King Jr., "Remaining Awake through a Great Revolution," *A Testament of Hope: The Essential Writings and Speeches of Martin Luther King, Jr.* (New York: HarperCollins, 1986), 271.
7. Chris Rice, *Grace Matters*, 178.

MIND THE GAP

1. Thanks to Jim Wallis for the image of "a tale of two cities." See Jim Wallis, "The Second Reformation Has Begun," *Envisioning the City: A Reader on Urban Ministry*, ed. Eleanor Scott Myers (Louisville: Westminster/John Knox, 1992), 44–63.
2. Barbara Brown Taylor, "A Fixed Chasm," *Bread of Angels* (Cambridge, MA: Cowley Publications, 1997), 109–14.

TO SAVE THIS FRAGILE EARTH

1. Gerard Manley Hopkins, "God's Grandeur," *Gerard Manley Hopkins: The Major Work* (Oxford: Oxford University Press, 2009), 128.
2. James Hansen, quoted in Bill McKibben, "Warning on Warming," *New York Review of Books*, March 15, 2007.

3. General Anthony Zinni in "Climate Change Seen as Threat to Security," *New York Times*, August 9, 2009.
4. Bill McKibben, "Meltdown," *Christian Century*, February 20, 2007.
5. James Irwin, "Global Warming May Cost 20 Trillion Dollars," *Global Warming*, http://globalwarmingupdates.blogspot.com, January 1, 2008.
6. Wendell Berry, *Home Economics* (San Francisco: North Point Press, 1987), 56.
7. Christine Williams, ed., *The Eleventh Commandment: Caring for Creation: Words of Wisdom from the Great Faith Traditions* (Create Space Independent Publishing Platform, 2011).
8. Hopkins, "God's Grandeur," 128.

A HUMBLE PATRIOTISM

1. William Sloane Coffin, *Credo* (Louisville: Westminster John Knox Press, 2004), 84.
2. Coffin, *Credo*, 83.
3. Charles Marsh, *Wayward Christian Soldiers* (Oxford: Oxford University Press, 2007), 43.
4. Gregory Boyd, *The Myth of a Christian Nation* (Grand Rapids: Zondervan, 2005).
5. Pablo Casals, *Reflections by Pablo Casals*, as told to Albert Kahn, new edition (Richmond, UK: Eel Pie Publishing, 1981).

A THANKFUL HEART

1. Nathaniel Philbrick, *Mayflower: A Story of Courage, Community, and War* (New York: Viking), 117.
2. Harold Kushner, *The Lord Is My Shepherd* (New York: Alfred A. Knopf, 2003), 148.
3. C. S. Lewis, *Reflections on the Psalms* (New York: Harcourt, Brace and Co., 1958), 94.
4. Joan Beck, "In Praise of the Real Bounty," *Chicago Tribune*, November 24, 2010.
5. Raymond Carver, "Gravy," *All of Us: Raymond Carver: The Collected Poems* (New York: Alfred A. Knopf, 1998), 292.

GIVING THANKS IN ALL THINGS

1. William Blake, "Auguries of Innocence," *The Poetry and Prose of William Blake*, ed. David V. Erdman (Garden City, NY: Doubleday, 1994), 484–87.
2. Richard Rohr, Lecture at Kanuga Conference Center, 1997.
3. Harold Kushner, *The Lord Is My Shepherd* (New York: Alfred A. Knopf, 2003).
4. Dorothy Berkley Phillips, Elizabeth Boyden Howes, and Lucille M. Nixon, eds., *The Choice Is Always Ours* (New York: Harper & Brothers Publishers, 1948), xv–xviii.
5. Johnson Oatman Jr., "When Upon Life's Billows," *Baptist Hymnal 1975* (Nashville, TN: Convention Press, 1975), #231.

WAITING

1. Paula Gooder, *The Meaning Is in the Waiting* (Brewster, MA: Paraclete Press, 2008), 4.

2. Abraham Heschel, "Israel: An Echo of Eternity," in *Disputation and Dialogue: Readings in the Jewish-Christian Encounter*, ed. Frank Ephraim Talmage (Jersey City: KATV Publishing House, Inc., 1975), 194.

3. Carl Honoré, *In Praise of Slowness* (New York: HarperCollins Publishers, 2004), 2.

4. Honoré, *In Praise of Slowness*, 3.

5. Honoré, *In Praise of Slowness*, 4.

6. T. S. Eliot, "East Coker," *Collected Poems 1909–1962* (New York: Harcourt, Brace & World, 1970), 186.

MAKING ROOM FOR GOD

1. William Willimon, *Pulpit Resource* 31, no. 4 (October–December 2003): 42.

2. Sister Maria McCoy, S.S.J., Jesuit Spirituality Center, Wernersville, PA, August 2007.

MARY SAID YES

1. Peter Gomes, "Hail Mary, Full of Grace," *Sermons: Biblical Wisdom for Daily Living* (New York: William Morrow, 1998), 10.

2. Gerald May, *Will and Spirit: A Contemplative Psychology* (San Francisco: Harper & Row, 1982), 1–21.

3. Mitchell Zuckoff, "Choosing Naia: A Family's Journey," *Boston Globe*, December 1999, 7.

GOD COMES IN

1. Annie Dillard, "God in the Doorway," *Teaching a Stone to Talk* (New York: Harper & Row, 1982), 140.

2. G. K. Chesterton, quoted in *Starlight: Beholding the Christmas Miracle All Year Long* (New York: Crossroad, 1992), 71–72.

3. Chesterton quoted in *Starlight*, 72.

4. Dillard, "God in the Doorway," 141.

THE BIRTH OF THE MESSIAH

1. Quoted in M. Nadine Foley, O.P., "A Homily for Midnight Mass," *Women and the Word* (Philadelphia: Fortress Press, 1978).

2. Marion Wright Edelman, "Two Christmas Eve Lessons,"www.huffingtonpost.com, December 20, 2011.

3. Phillips Brooks, "O Little Town of Bethlehem," *The Hymnal 1982* (New York: The Church Hymnal Corporation, 1982), #78.

THE PLUNGE

1. Stuart Hample and Eric Marshall, eds., *Children's Letters to God: The New Collection* (New York: Workman, 1991).
2. Stuart Hample and Eric Marshall, eds., *Children's Letters to God* (New York: Workman, 1966).
3. Tex Sample in conference address.

THE MAGI AND US

1. T. S. Eliot, "Journey of the Magi," *Collected Poems 1909–1962* (New York: Harcourt, Brace & World, 1970), 99–100.
2. Eliot, *Collected Poems 1909–1962*, 99.
3. Eliot, *Collected Poems 1909–1962*, 100.
4. Eliot, *Collected Poems 1909–1962*, 100.

BELOVED

1. Raymond Carver, "Late Fragment," *All of Us: The Collected Poems* (New York: Alfred A. Knopf, 1998), 294.
2. Roland Rolheiser, *The Holy Longing* (New York: Doubleday, 1999), 238–39.
3. Rolheiser, *Holy Longing*, 239–40.
4. Thomas Merton, *Conjectures of a Guilty Bystander* (New York: Image Books/Doubleday, 1968), 156–57.
5. Merton, *Conjectures of a Guilty Bystander*, 156–57.

THE TRUTH OF ASH WEDNESDAY

1. Saul Bellow, *Seize the Day* (New York: Penguin Books, 1984), 113.
2. Bellow, *Seize the Day*, 114.
3. Anne Lamott, *Bird by Bird* (New York: Anchor Books/Doubleday, 1994), 179.

THE JOY OF ASH WEDNESDAY

1. "Ash Wednesday," *The Book of Common Prayer* (New York: Oxford University Press, 1979), 268.
2. C. S. Lewis, "As the Rain Falls," *Poems* (New York: Harcourt Brace Jovanovich, 1964), 109–10.

GOING FOR BROKE

1. Paul Tillich, "Holy Waste," *The New Being* (New York: Charles Scribner's Sons, 1955), 46–49.
2. Ross Douthat, "Mass-Market Epiphany," *New York Times*, March 8, 2010.
3. C. S. Lewis, *Mere Christianity* (New York: Macmillan, 1952), 168.
4. Kay Warren, *Dangerous Surrender* (Grand Rapids: Zondervan, 2007), 17–18.
5. Warren, *Dangerous Surrender*, 18.
6. Warren, *Dangerous Surrender*, 18; Tillich, *Holy Waste*, 48.

LOVE SO AMAZING

1. Walter Wink, *The Powers That Be* (New York: Doubleday, 1998), 39.
2. George MacLeod, *Only One Way Left* (Glasgow: Iona Community, 1956), 38, cited in Ronald Ferguson, *George MacLeod: Founder of the Iona Community* (London: Collins, 1990), 261.
3. Isaac Watts, "When I Survey the Wondrous Cross," *The Hymnal 1982* (New York: The Church Hymnal Corporation, 1982), #474.

STRANGE FRUIT

1. Billie Holiday, song "Strange Fruit" from poem by Abel Meeropol, in David Margolick and Hilton Als, *Strange Fruit: Billie Holiday, Café Society, and an Early Cry for Civil Rights* (Philadelphia: Running Press, 2000), 15.
2. Daniel Goldhagen, *Hitler's Willing Executioners* (New York: Alfred A. Knopf, 2002), 23–24.
3. Melvyn Bragg, *The Soldier's Return* (New York: Arcade Publishing, 1999), 116.

WHAT A WAY TO RUN A UNIVERSE

1. Michael Mayne, "Does My Creator Weep?" Meditation preached at Trinity Church, Boston, April 1999.
2. Mayne, "Does My Creator Weep?"
3. Helen Waddell, *Peter Abelard* (New York: Henry Holt and Company, 1933), 288–90.
4. Venantius Honorius Fortunatus, "Sing, My Tongue, the Glorious Battle," *The Hymnal 1982* (New York: The Church Hymnal Corporation, 1982), #166.

STARING INTO THE DARK

1. Sydney Carter, "The Good Friday Song," *God's Advocates* (Grand Rapids: William B. Eerdmans, 2005), 10.
2. Guenter Rutenborn, *The Sign of Jonas*, trans. George White (New York: Thomas Nelson and Sons, 1960), 79–82.

DEATH BE NOT PROUD

1. Margaret Edson, *Wit* (New York: Faber and Faber, 1999).
2. John Donne, "Death Be Not Proud," *John Donne: Selections from Divine Poems, Sermons Devotions, and Prayers*, ed. John Booty (New York: Paulist Press, 1990), 80.
3. Donne, "Death Be Not Proud," 80.
4. Gyles Brandreth interview of Desmond Tutu, "My Idea of Heaven," *Telegraph*, April 27, 2001.
5. Edson quoting Margaret Wise, *The Runaway Bunny* (First: Harper Trophy Edition, 1972).

NEVERTHELESS

1. e. e. cummings, "i thank you god," *100 Selected Poems* (New York: Grove Press, 1954), 114.
2. Walter Wink, "Resonating with God's Song," *Christian Century*, March 1994.
3. Insight recalled from seminary days.
4. William Sloane Coffin, "Like Him We Rise," *The Collected Sermons of William Sloane Coffin: The Riverside Years*, vol. 2 (Louisville: Westminster John Knox, 2008), 29.

CHRIST HAS GONE UP

1. Edwin Abbott, *Flatland: A Romance of Many Dimensions* (Cambridge: Cambridge University Press, 2010), orig. published 1884.
2. Ernest Hemingway, *For Whom the Bell Tolls* (New York: Charles Scribner's Sons, 1940), 500.

THE SPIRIT OF LIFE

1. Source unknown.
2. Mihaly Csikszentmihalyi, *Flow: The Psychology of Optimal Experience* (New York: HarperPerennial, 1990).

THE TRINITY AND THE NEARNESS OF GOD

1. Thomas Jefferson, Letter of 1821 to Thomas Pickering, in Dickinson W. Adams and Ruth W. Lister, eds., *Jefferson's Extracts from the Gospels: "The Philosophy of Jesus" and "The Life and Morals of Jesus"* (Princeton: Princeton University Press, 1983), 403.
2. G. A. Studdert-Kennedy, *The Hardest Part* (Miami: Hardpress, orig. published in 1918), xi–xii.
3. C. S. Lewis, *Mere Christianity* (New York: Macmillan, 1952), 142–43.
4. Dante Alighieri, *The Paradiso*, trans. John Ciardi (New York: Mentor Book from New American Library, 1975), 365.

WHO DO YOU SAY THAT I AM?

1. Jaroslav Pelikan, *The Illustrated Jesus Through the Centuries* (New Haven: Yale University Press, 1997).
2. Stephen Prothero, *American Jesus: How the Son of God Became a Cultural Icon* (New York: Farrar, Straus and Giroux, 2003).
3. Bill McKibben, "The Christian Paradox: How a Faithful Nation Gets Jesus Wrong," *Harper's Magazine*, August 2005.
4. Albert Schweitzer, *The Quest for the Historical Jesus*. (Baltimore: Johns Hopkins University Press, 1998, orig. published 1910), 403.

THE REAL THING

1. Andrew Sullivan, "This Is a Religious War," *New York Times Magazine*, October 7, 2001.
2. Frederick Buechner, *The Storm* (New York: HarperSan Francisco, 1998), 7–8.
3. Robert Bolt, *A Man for All Seasons* (New York: Vintage Books, 1990), 8–9.

THE COMMUNION OF SAINTS

1. William Kennedy, *Ironweed* (New York: Penguin Books, 1983), 1–20.
2. Theodore Parker Ferris, introduction to *Phillips Brooks on Preaching* (New York: Seabury Press, 1960), vi.

About the Author

Samuel T. Lloyd III was dean of Washington National Cathedral from 2005 to 2011. Although a native Mississippian, he has lived much of his life outside the Deep South. Having earned a PhD in English at the University of Virginia and a divinity degree from Virginia Seminary, Lloyd has held positions in both academic life and the church. He has been an assistant professor of religion and literature at the University of Virginia and university chaplain at the University of the South. He served as rector of St. Paul and the Redeemer Episcopal Church in Chicago's Hyde Park, and for nearly twelve years was rector of Trinity Church, Copley Square in downtown Boston. A recipient of various honorary degrees, Lloyd is also an honorary canon of Salisbury Cathedral in the United Kingdom. He has recently returned to service at Trinity, Copley Square.